STAR WARS
EMPIRE

VOLUME SIX: IN THE SHADOWS OF THEIR FATHERS

D1132022

THESE STORIES TAKE PLACE
APPROXIMATELY EIGHT MONTHS AFTER
THE EVENTS IN STAR WARS: A NEW HOPE.

STAR WARS: EMPIRE VOLUME 6

THIS VOLUME COLLECTS ISSUES #31, 29-30,
32-34 OF THE DARK HORSE COMIC-BOOK SERIES
STAR WARS: EMPIRE.

PUBLISHED BY
DARK HORSE BOOKS
A DIVISION OF DARK HORSE COMICS, INC.
10956 SE MAIN STREET
MILWAUKIE, OR 97222

DARKHORSE.COM
STARWARS.COM

TO FIND A COMICS SHOP IN YOUR
AREA, CALL THE COMIC SHOP
LOCATOR SERVICE TOLL-FREE
AT 1-888-266-4226

FIRST EDITION: OCTOBER 2006
ISBN-10: 1-59307-627-4
ISBN-13: 978-1-59307-627-6

1 3 5 7 9 10 8 6 4 2

PRINTED IN CHINA

VOLUME SIX:
IN THE SHADOWS
OF THEIR FATHERS

WRITERS THOMAS ANDREWS
SCOTT ALLIE

ARTISTS ADRIANA MELO
JOE CORRONEY
MICHEL LACOMBE

COLORIST MICHAEL ATIYEH

LETTERER MICHAEL DAVID THOMAS

COVER ART BY TOMÁS GIORELLO

PUBLISHER
MIKE RICHARDSON

COLLECTION DESIGNER
SCOTT COOK

ART DIRECTOR
LIA RIBACCHI

ASSISTANT EDITOR
DAVE MARSHALL

ASSOCIATE EDITOR
JEREMY BARLOW

EDITOR
RANDY STRADLEY

SPECIAL THANKS TO
LELAND CHEE, SUE ROSTONI,
AND AMY GARY AT LUCAS LICENSING

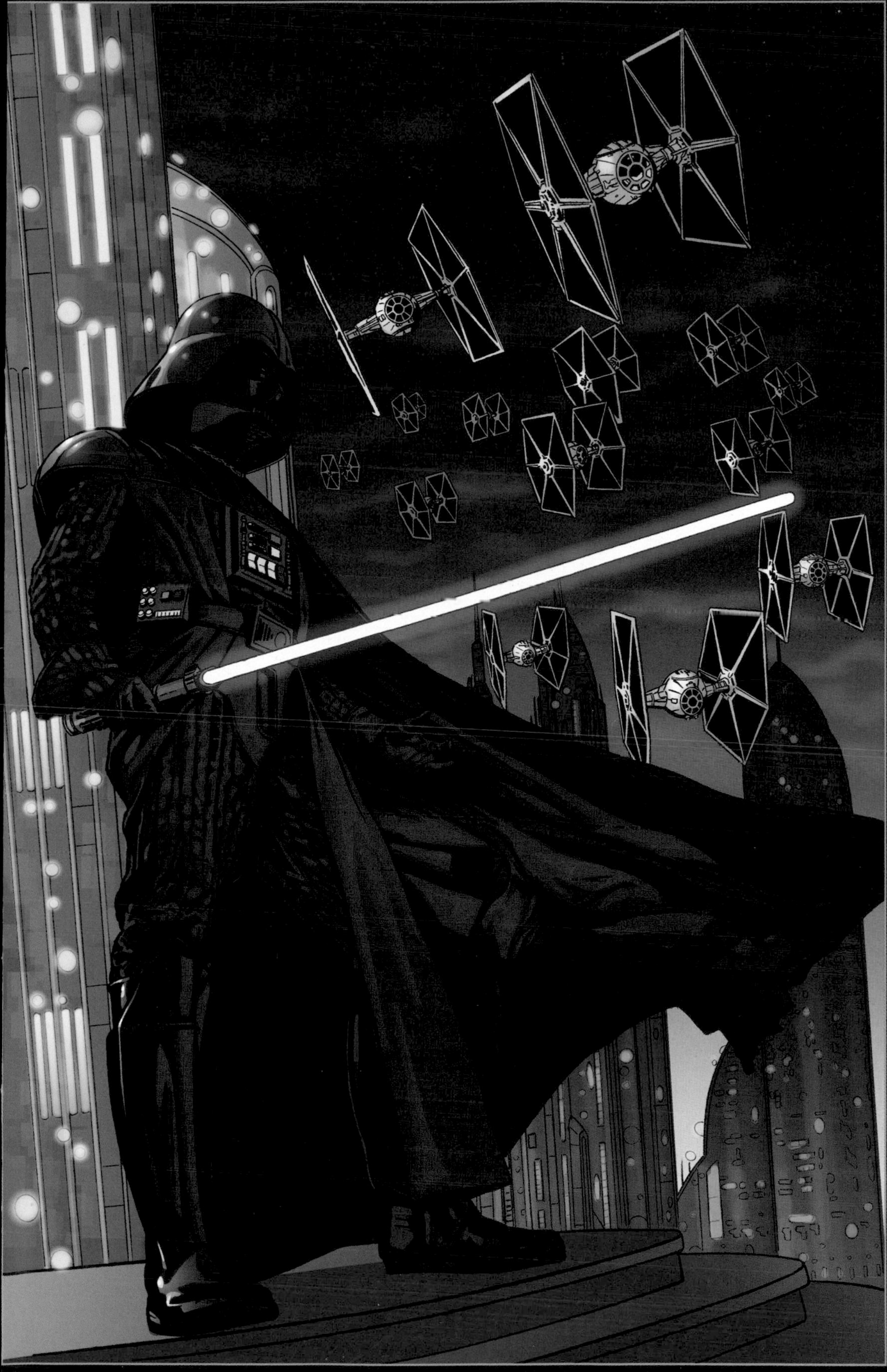

ART: JOE CORRONEY
COLORS: DAN JACKSON

THE PRICE OF POWER

Script SCOTT ALLIE
Art JOE CORRONEY

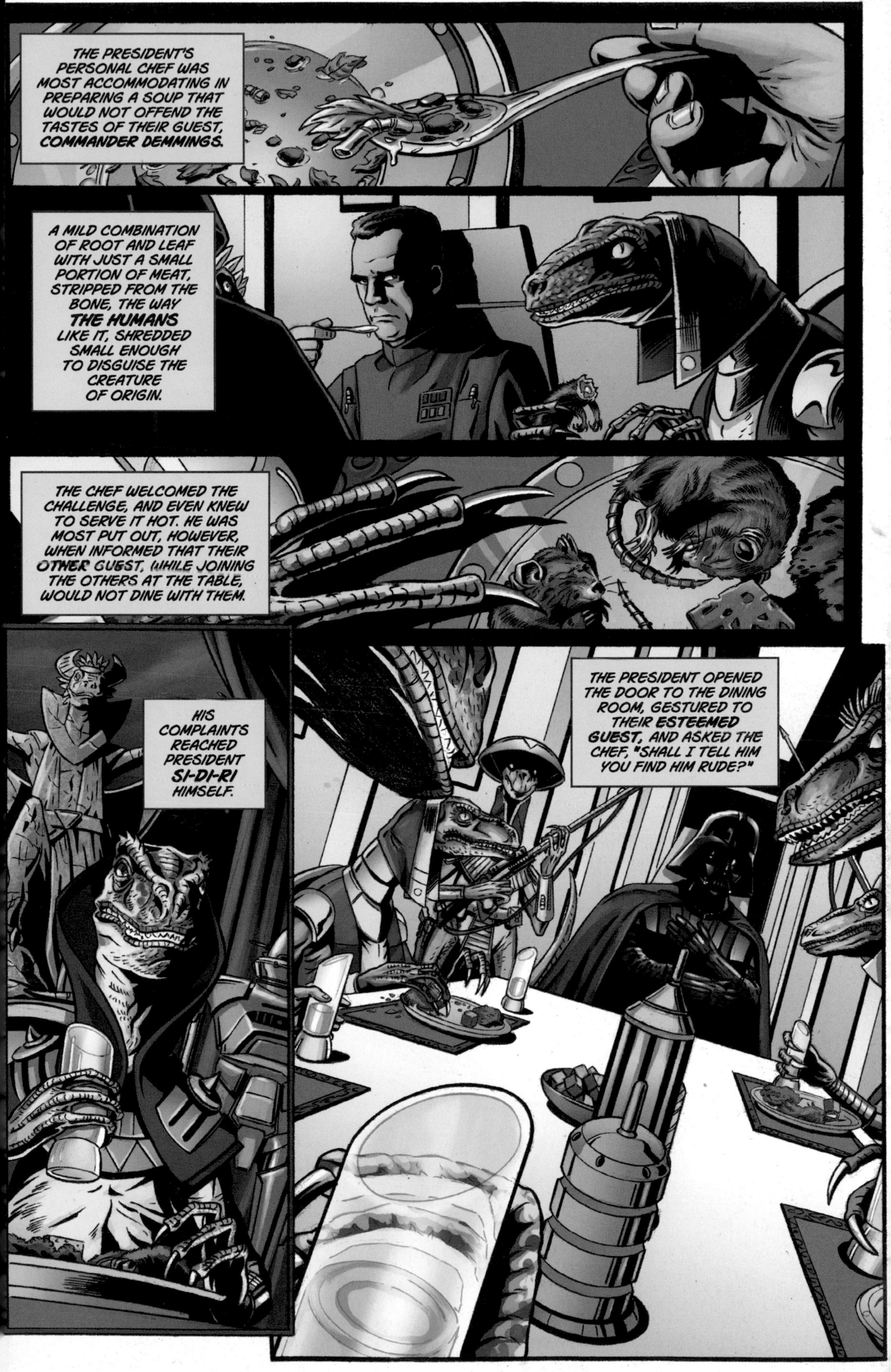
THE PRESIDENT'S PERSONAL CHEF WAS MOST ACCOMMODATING IN PREPARING A SOUP THAT WOULD NOT OFFEND THE TASTES OF THEIR GUEST, COMMANDER DEMMINGS.
A MILD COMBINATION OF ROOT AND LEAF WITH JUST A SMALL PORTION OF MEAT, STRIPPED FROM THE BONE, THE WAY THE HUMANS LIKE IT, SHREDDED SMALL ENOUGH TO DISGUISE THE CREATURE OF ORIGIN.
THE CHEF WELCOMED THE CHALLENGE, AND EVEN KNEW TO SERVE IT HOT. HE WAS MOST PUT OUT, HOWEVER, WHEN INFORMED THAT THEIR OTHER GUEST, WHILE JOINING THE OTHERS AT THE TABLE, WOULD NOT DINE WITH THEM.
HIS COMPLAINTS REACHED PRESIDENT SI-DI-RI HIMSELF.
THE PRESIDENT OPENED THE DOOR TO THE DINING ROOM, GESTURED TO THEIR ESTEEMED GUEST, AND ASKED THE CHEF, "SHALL I TELL HIM YOU FIND HIM RUDE?"

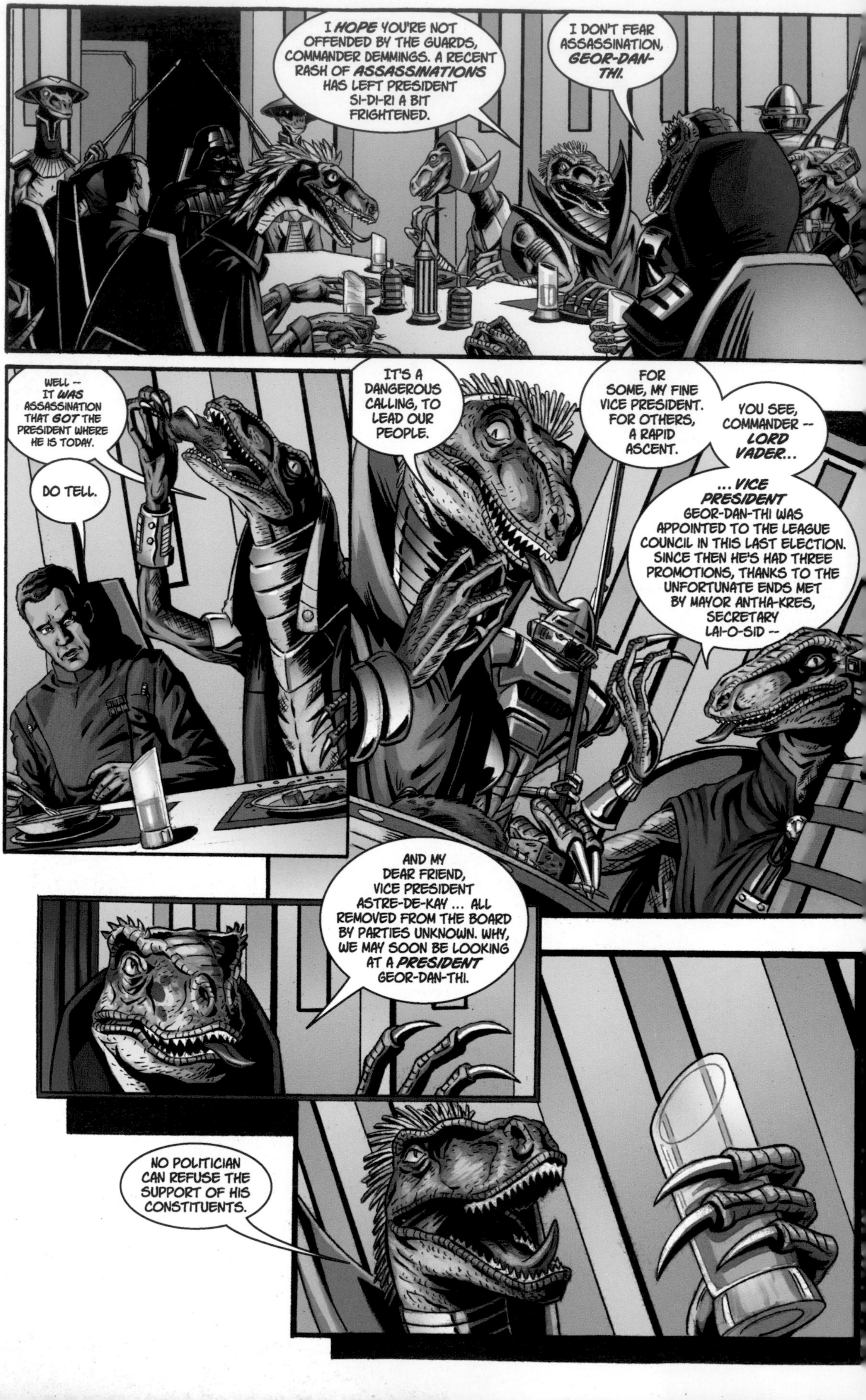
I *HOPE* YOU'RE NOT OFFENDED BY THE GUARDS, COMMANDER DEMMINGS. A RECENT RASH OF *ASSASSINATIONS* HAS LEFT PRESIDENT SI-DI-RI A BIT FRIGHTENED.
I DON'T FEAR ASSASSINATION, *GEOR-DAN-THI.*
WELL -- IT *WAS* ASSASSINATION THAT *GOT* THE PRESIDENT WHERE HE IS TODAY.
DO TELL.
IT'S A DANGEROUS CALLING, TO LEAD OUR PEOPLE.
FOR SOME, MY FINE VICE PRESIDENT. FOR OTHERS, A RAPID ASCENT.
YOU SEE, COMMANDER -- *LORD VADER...*
...VICE PRESIDENT GEOR-DAN-THI WAS APPOINTED TO THE LEAGUE COUNCIL IN THIS LAST ELECTION. SINCE THEN HE'S HAD THREE PROMOTIONS, THANKS TO THE UNFORTUNATE ENDS MET BY MAYOR ANTHA-KRES, SECRETARY LAI-O-SID --
AND MY DEAR FRIEND, VICE PRESIDENT ASTRE-DE-KAY ... ALL REMOVED FROM THE BOARD BY PARTIES UNKNOWN. WHY, WE MAY SOON BE LOOKING AT A *PRESIDENT* GEOR-DAN-THI.
NO POLITICIAN CAN REFUSE THE SUPPORT OF HIS CONSTITUENTS.

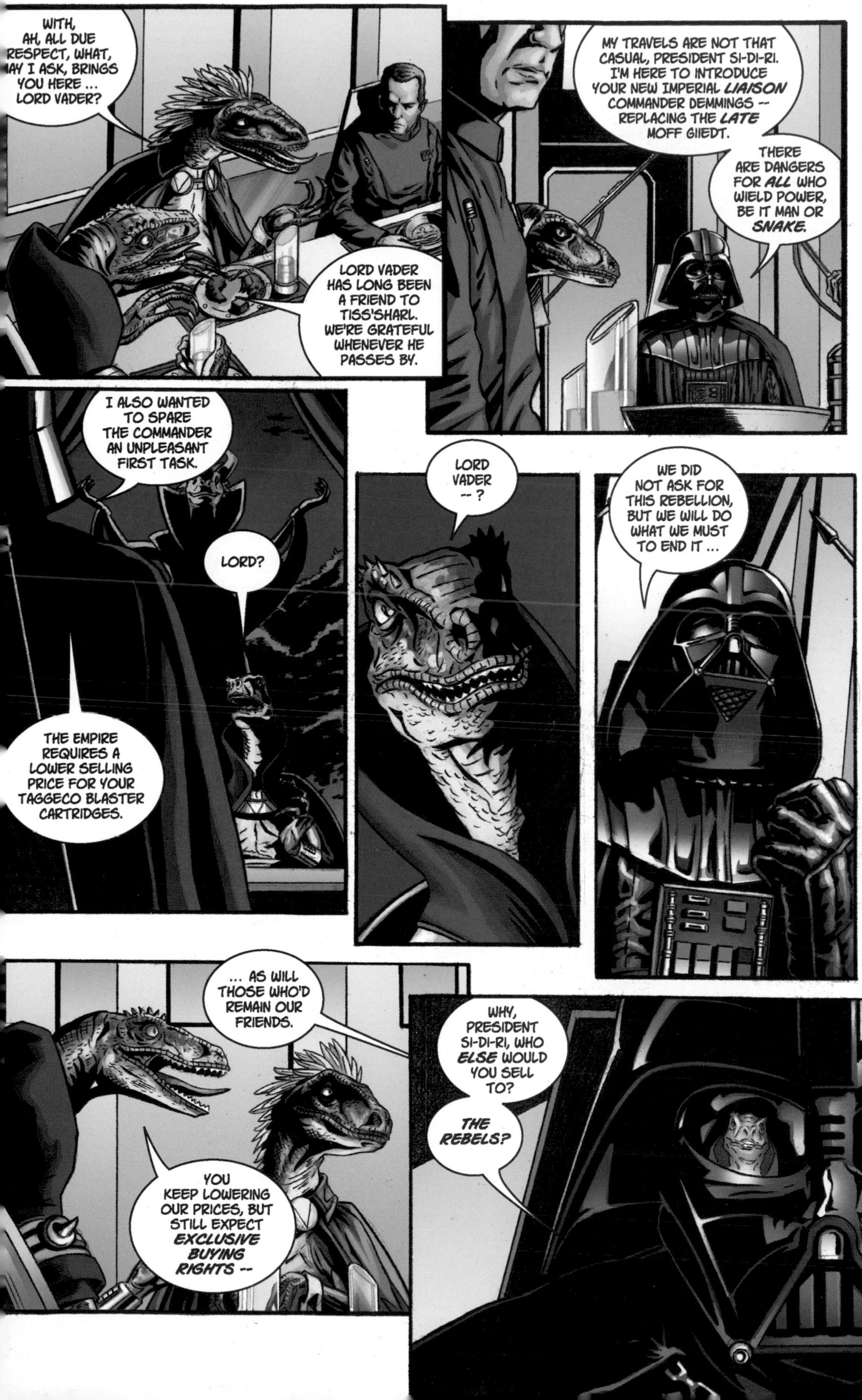
WITH, AH, ALL DUE RESPECT, WHAT, MAY I ASK, BRINGS YOU HERE ... LORD VADER?
LORD VADER HAS LONG BEEN A FRIEND TO TISS'SHARL. WE'RE GRATEFUL WHENEVER HE PASSES BY.
MY TRAVELS ARE NOT THAT CASUAL, PRESIDENT SI-DI-RI. I'M HERE TO INTRODUCE YOUR NEW IMPERIAL LIAISON COMMANDER DEMMINGS -- REPLACING THE LATE MOFF GIIEDT.
THERE ARE DANGERS FOR ALL WHO WIELD POWER, BE IT MAN OR SNAKE.
I ALSO WANTED TO SPARE THE COMMANDER AN UNPLEASANT FIRST TASK.
LORD?
THE EMPIRE REQUIRES A LOWER SELLING PRICE FOR YOUR TAGGECO BLASTER CARTRIDGES.
LORD VADER -- ?
WE DID NOT ASK FOR THIS REBELLION, BUT WE WILL DO WHAT WE MUST TO END IT ...
... AS WILL THOSE WHO'D REMAIN OUR FRIENDS.
YOU KEEP LOWERING OUR PRICES, BUT STILL EXPECT EXCLUSIVE BUYING RIGHTS --
WHY, PRESIDENT SI-DI-RI, WHO ELSE WOULD YOU SELL TO?
THE REBELS?

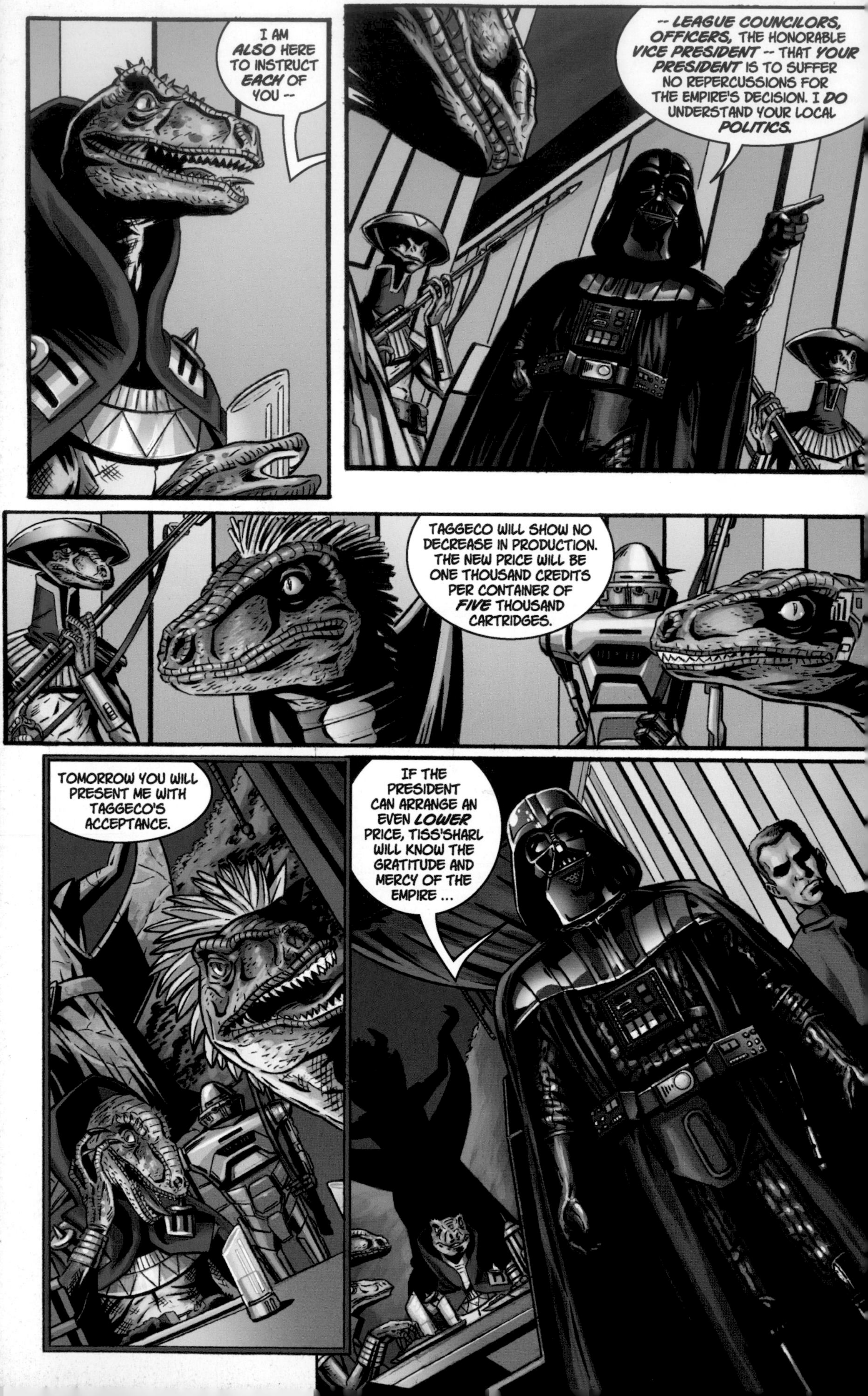
I AM ALSO HERE TO INSTRUCT EACH OF YOU --
-- LEAGUE COUNCILORS, OFFICERS, THE HONORABLE VICE PRESIDENT -- THAT YOUR PRESIDENT IS TO SUFFER NO REPERCUSSIONS FOR THE EMPIRE'S DECISION. I DO UNDERSTAND YOUR LOCAL POLITICS.
TAGGECO WILL SHOW NO DECREASE IN PRODUCTION. THE NEW PRICE WILL BE ONE THOUSAND CREDITS PER CONTAINER OF FIVE THOUSAND CARTRIDGES.
TOMORROW YOU WILL PRESENT ME WITH TAGGECO'S ACCEPTANCE.
IF THE PRESIDENT CAN ARRANGE AN EVEN LOWER PRICE, TISS'SHARL WILL KNOW THE GRATITUDE AND MERCY OF THE EMPIRE ...

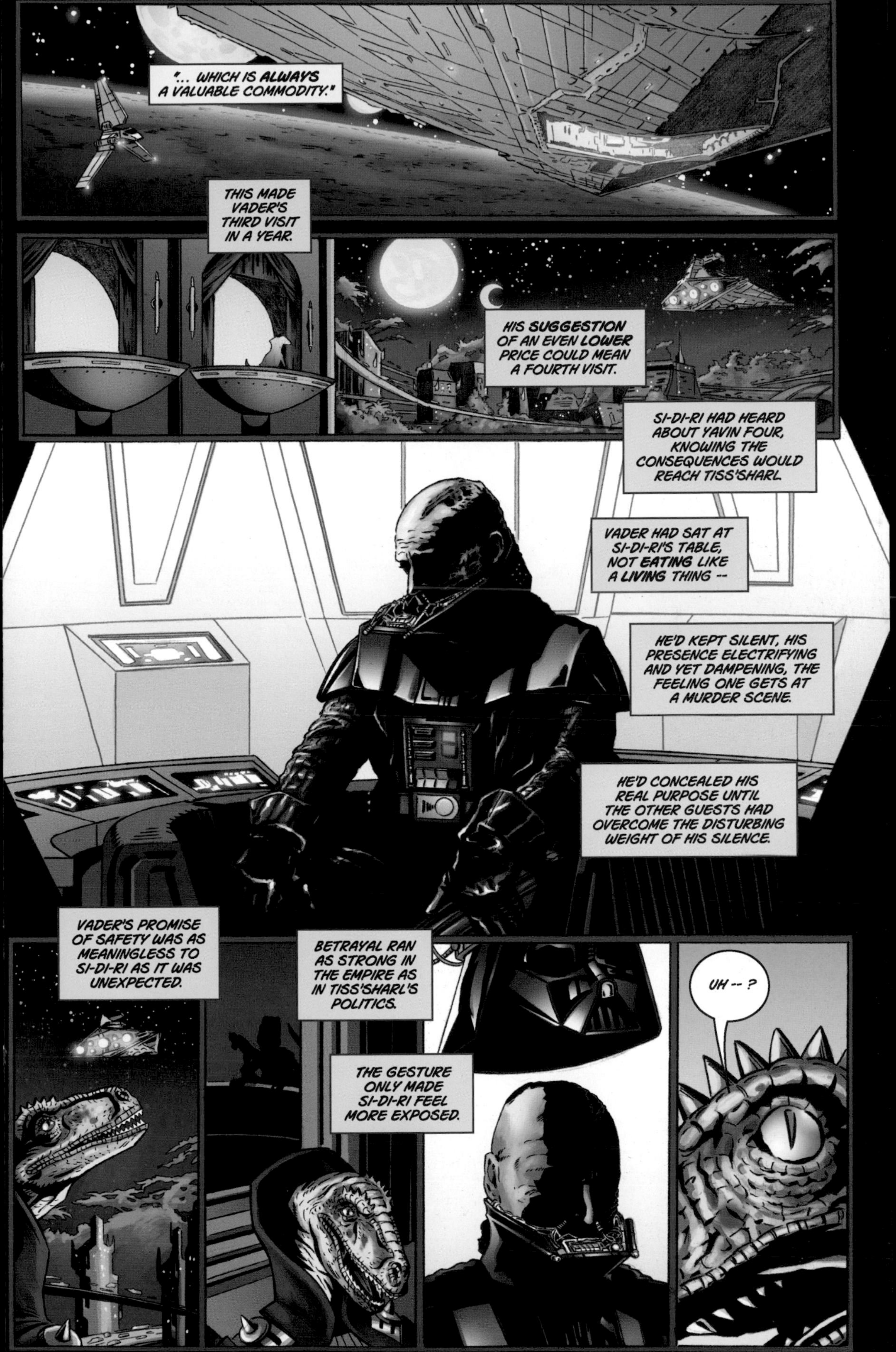
"... WHICH IS ALWAYS A VALUABLE COMMODITY."
THIS MADE VADER'S THIRD VISIT IN A YEAR.
HIS SUGGESTION OF AN EVEN LOWER PRICE COULD MEAN A FOURTH VISIT.
SI-DI-RI HAD HEARD ABOUT YAVIN FOUR, KNOWING THE CONSEQUENCES WOULD REACH TISS'SHARL.
VADER HAD SAT AT SI-DI-RI'S TABLE, NOT EATING LIKE A LIVING THING --
HE'D KEPT SILENT, HIS PRESENCE ELECTRIFYING AND YET DAMPENING, THE FEELING ONE GETS AT A MURDER SCENE.
HE'D CONCEALED HIS REAL PURPOSE UNTIL THE OTHER GUESTS HAD OVERCOME THE DISTURBING WEIGHT OF HIS SILENCE.
VADER'S PROMISE OF SAFETY WAS AS MEANINGLESS TO SI-DI-RI AS IT WAS UNEXPECTED.
BETRAYAL RAN AS STRONG IN THE EMPIRE AS IN TISS'SHARL'S POLITICS.
THE GESTURE ONLY MADE SI-DI-RI FEEL MORE EXPOSED.
UH -- ?

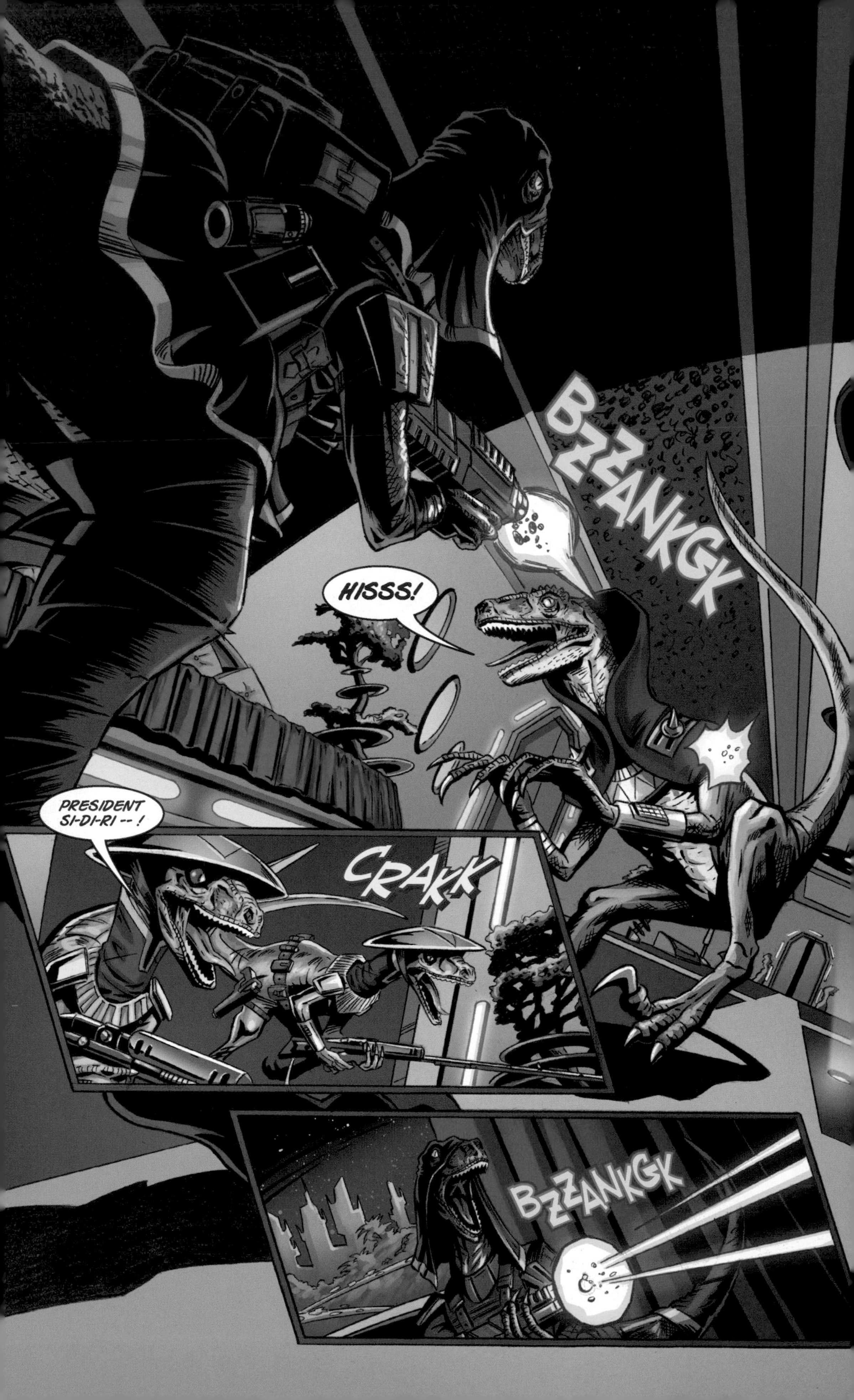
BZZANKGK
HISSS!
PRESIDENT SI-DI-RI -- !
CRAKK
BZZANKGK

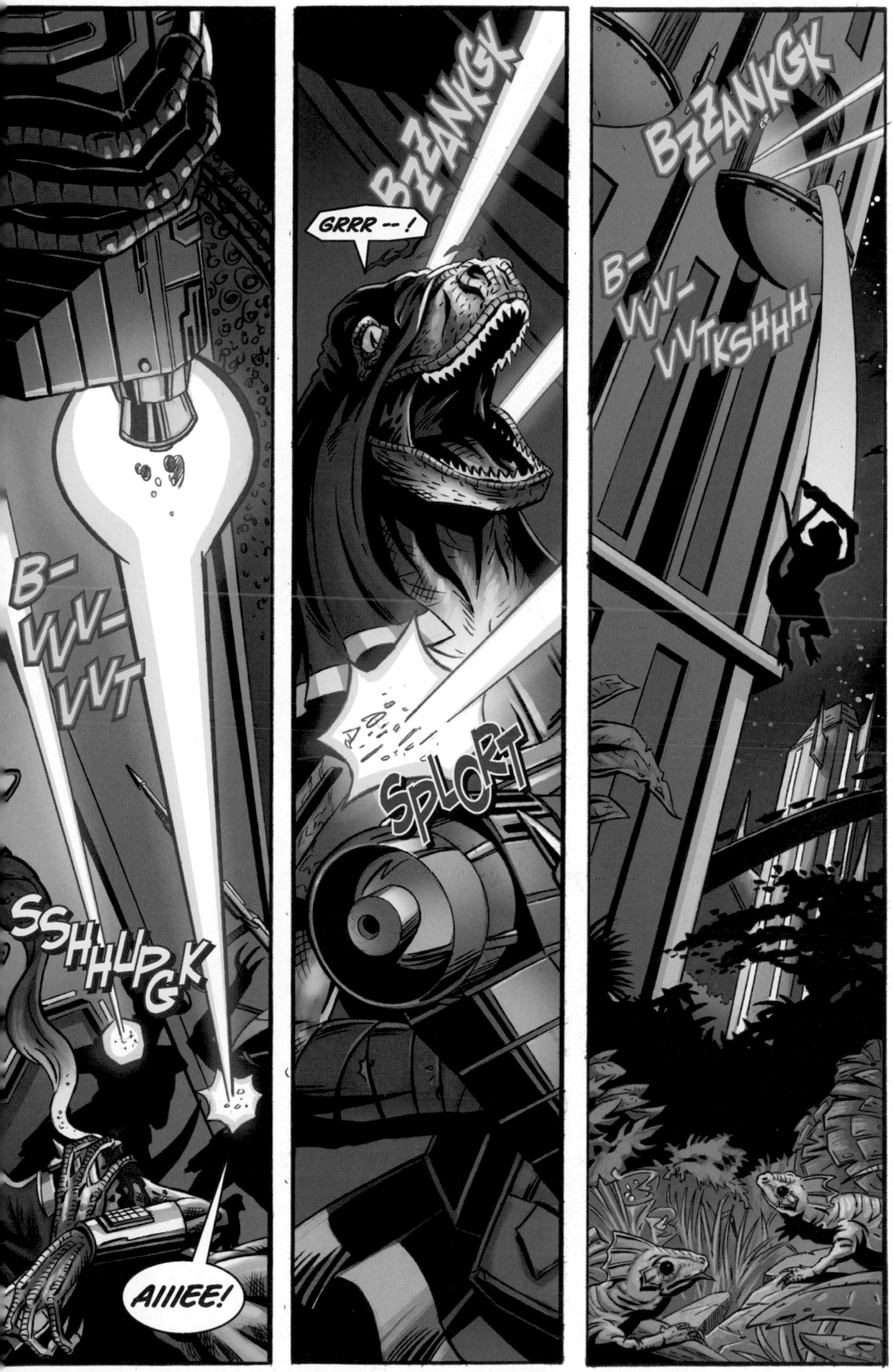
B-
VVV-
VVT
SSHHUPGK
AIIIEE!
BZZANKGK
GRRR --!
SPLORT
BZZANKGK
B-
VVV-
VVTKSHHH

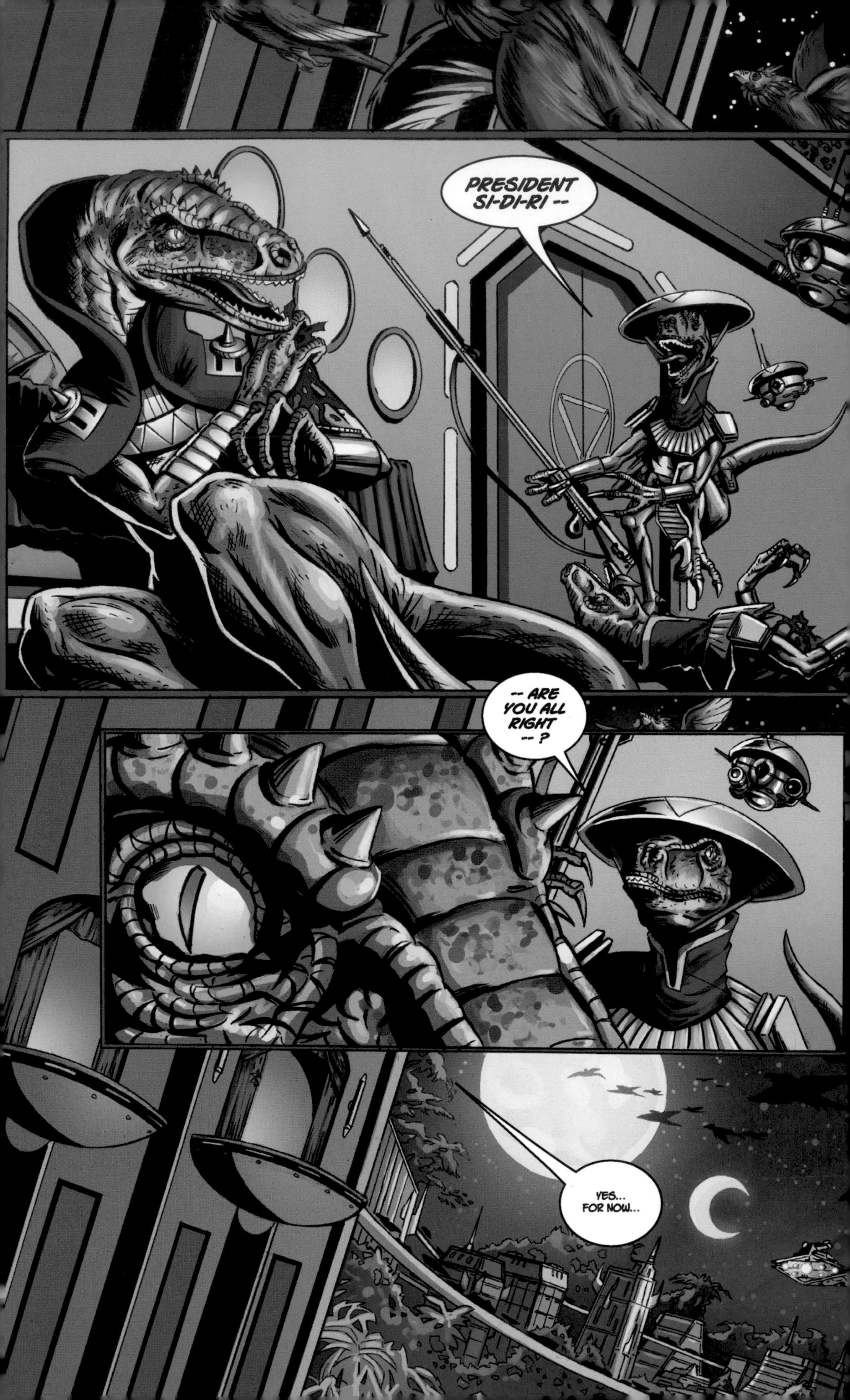
PRESIDENT SI-DI-RI --
-- ARE YOU ALL RIGHT -- ?
YES... FOR NOW...

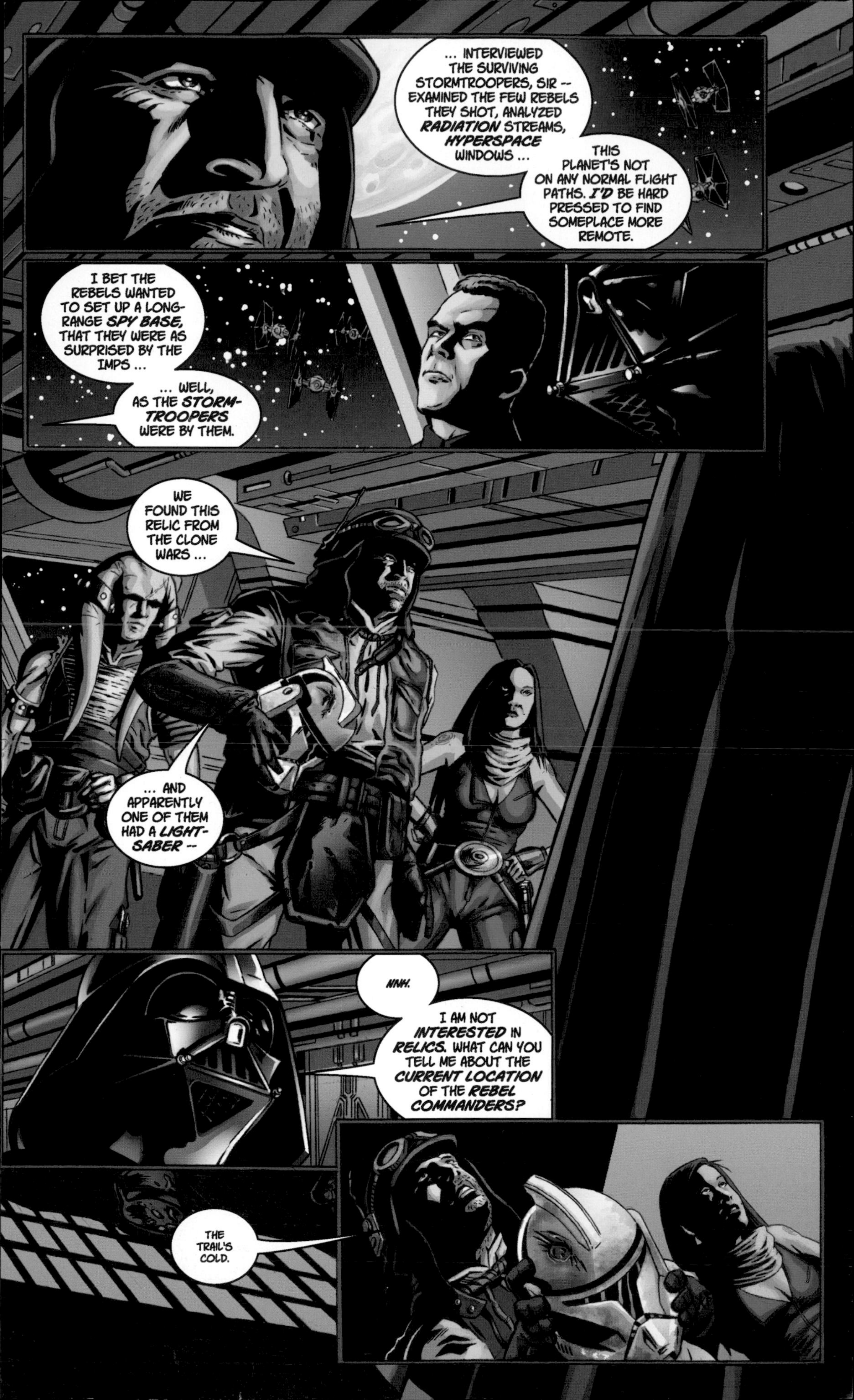
... INTERVIEWED THE SURVIVING STORMTROOPERS, SIR -- EXAMINED THE FEW REBELS THEY SHOT, ANALYZED RADIATION STREAMS, HYPERSPACE WINDOWS ...
THIS PLANET'S NOT ON ANY NORMAL FLIGHT PATHS. I'D BE HARD PRESSED TO FIND SOMEPLACE MORE REMOTE.
I BET THE REBELS WANTED TO SET UP A LONG-RANGE SPY BASE, THAT THEY WERE AS SURPRISED BY THE IMPS ...
... WELL, AS THE STORM-TROOPERS WERE BY THEM.
WE FOUND THIS RELIC FROM THE CLONE WARS ...
... AND APPARENTLY ONE OF THEM HAD A LIGHT-SABER --
NNH.
I AM NOT INTERESTED IN RELICS. WHAT CAN YOU TELL ME ABOUT THE CURRENT LOCATION OF THE REBEL COMMANDERS?
THE TRAIL'S COLD.

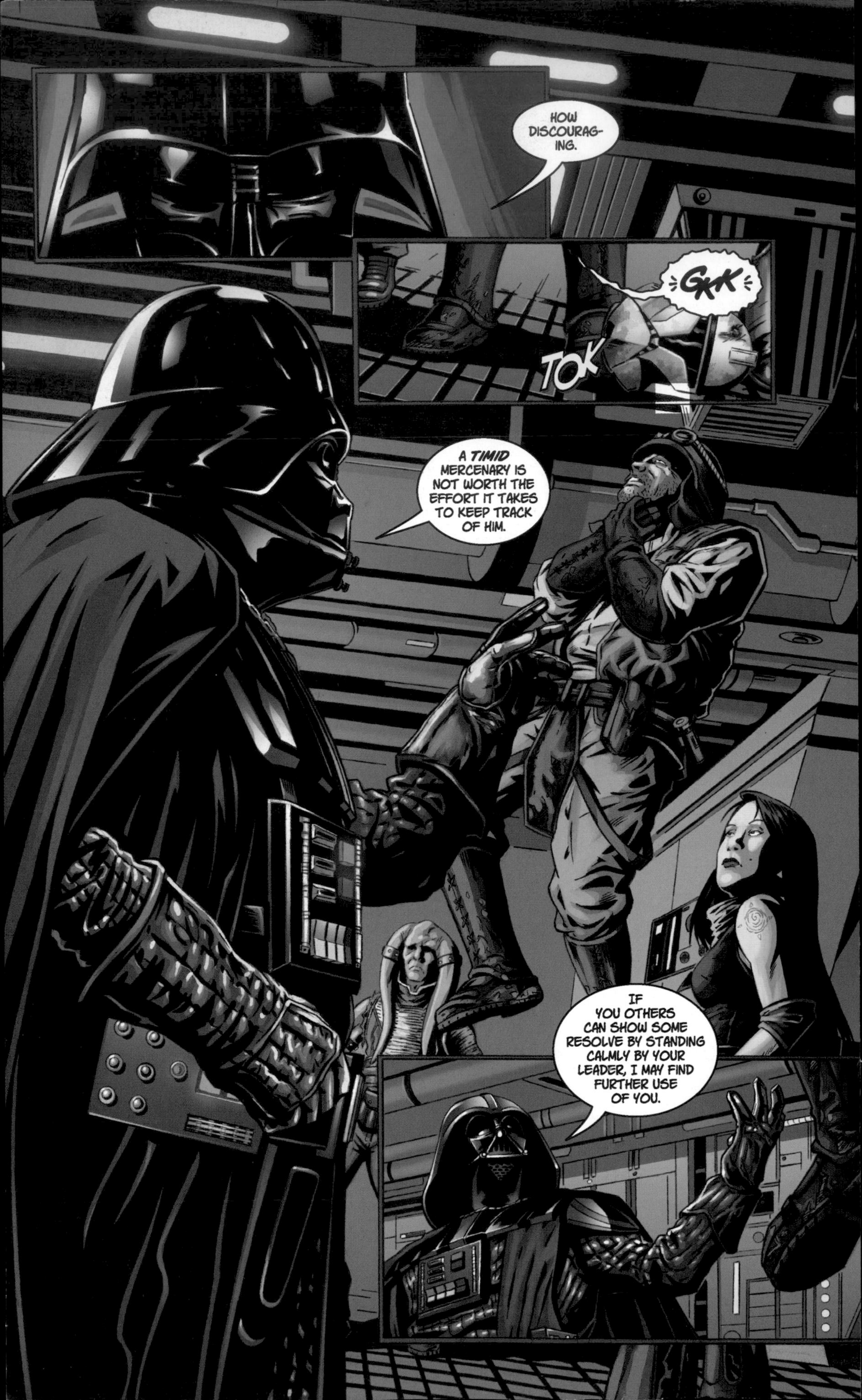
HOW DISCOURAG-ING.
GKK
TOK
A TIMID MERCENARY IS NOT WORTH THE EFFORT IT TAKES TO KEEP TRACK OF HIM.
IF YOU OTHERS CAN SHOW SOME RESOLVE BY STANDING CALMLY BY YOUR LEADER, I MAY FIND FURTHER USE OF YOU.

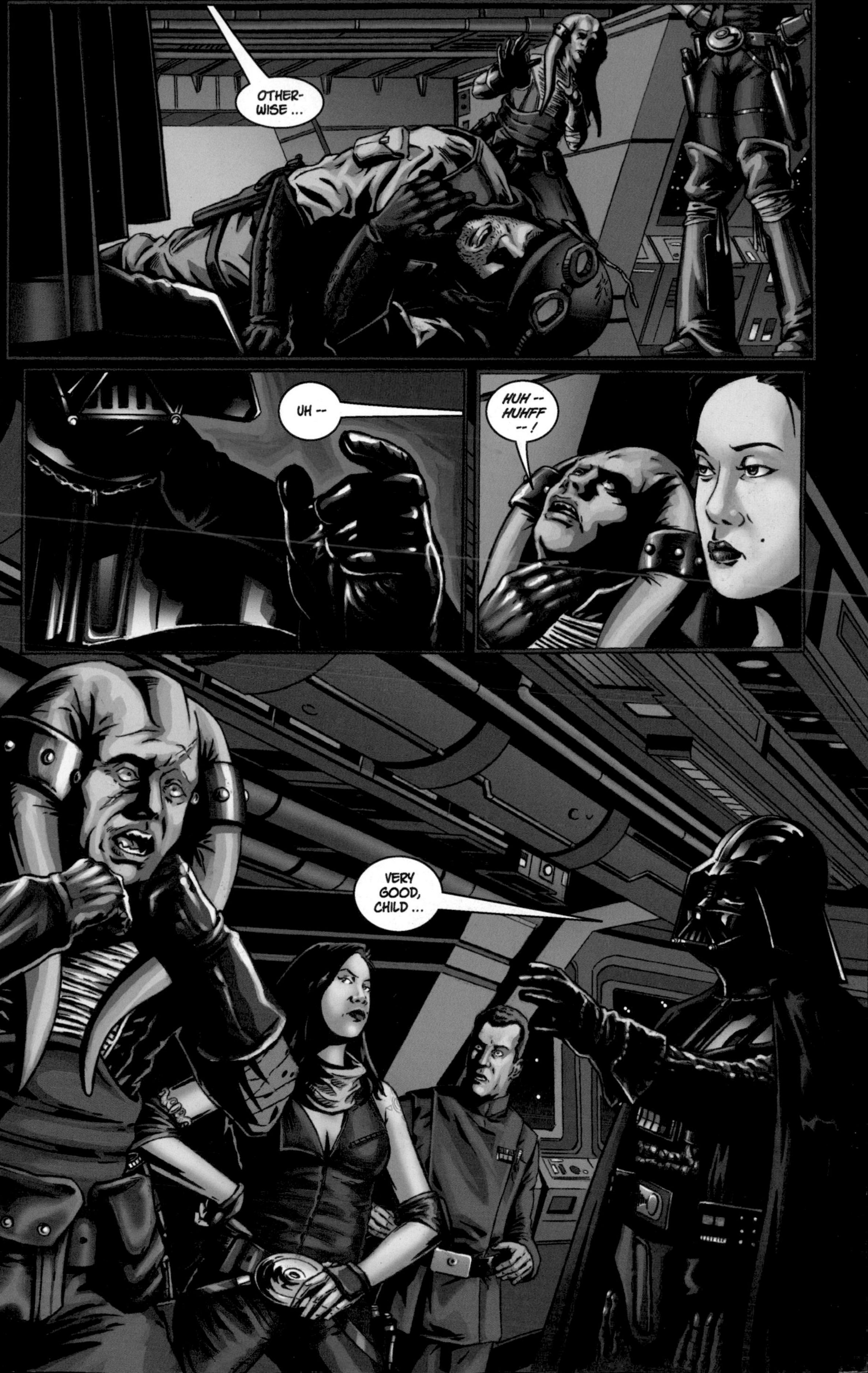
OTHER-
WISE ...
UH --
HUH --
HUHFF
-- !
VERY
GOOD,
CHILD ...

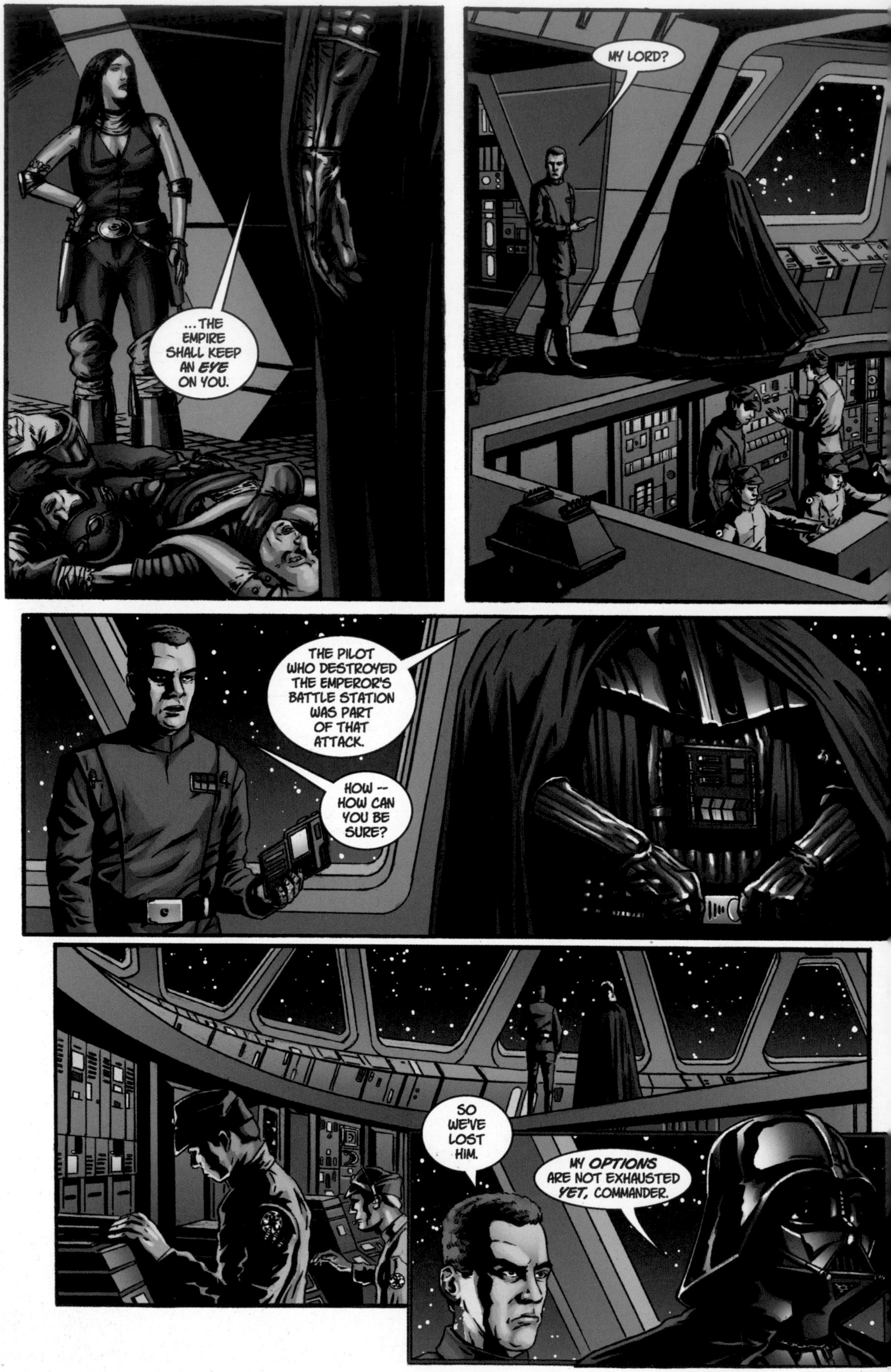
...THE EMPIRE SHALL KEEP AN EYE ON YOU.
MY LORD?
THE PILOT WHO DESTROYED THE EMPEROR'S BATTLE STATION WAS PART OF THAT ATTACK.
HOW -- HOW CAN YOU BE SURE?
SO WE'VE LOST HIM.
MY OPTIONS ARE NOT EXHAUSTED YET, COMMANDER.

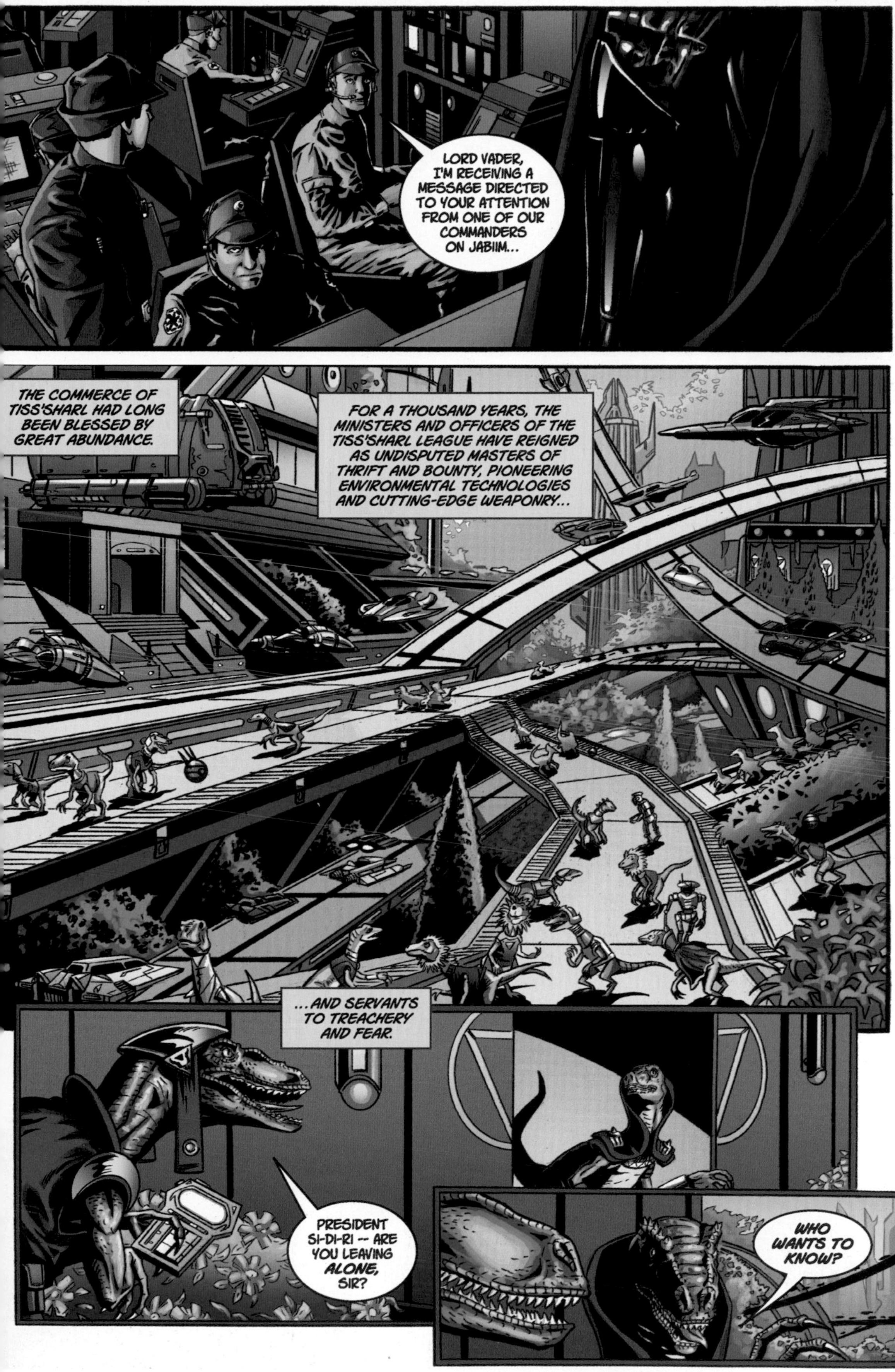
LORD VADER, I'M RECEIVING A MESSAGE DIRECTED TO YOUR ATTENTION FROM ONE OF OUR COMMANDERS ON JABIIM...
THE COMMERCE OF TISS'SHARL HAD LONG BEEN BLESSED BY GREAT ABUNDANCE.
FOR A THOUSAND YEARS, THE MINISTERS AND OFFICERS OF THE TISS'SHARL LEAGUE HAVE REIGNED AS UNDISPUTED MASTERS OF THRIFT AND BOUNTY, PIONEERING ENVIRONMENTAL TECHNOLOGIES AND CUTTING-EDGE WEAPONRY...
...AND SERVANTS TO TREACHERY AND FEAR.
PRESIDENT SI-DI-RI -- ARE YOU LEAVING ALONE, SIR?
WHO WANTS TO KNOW?

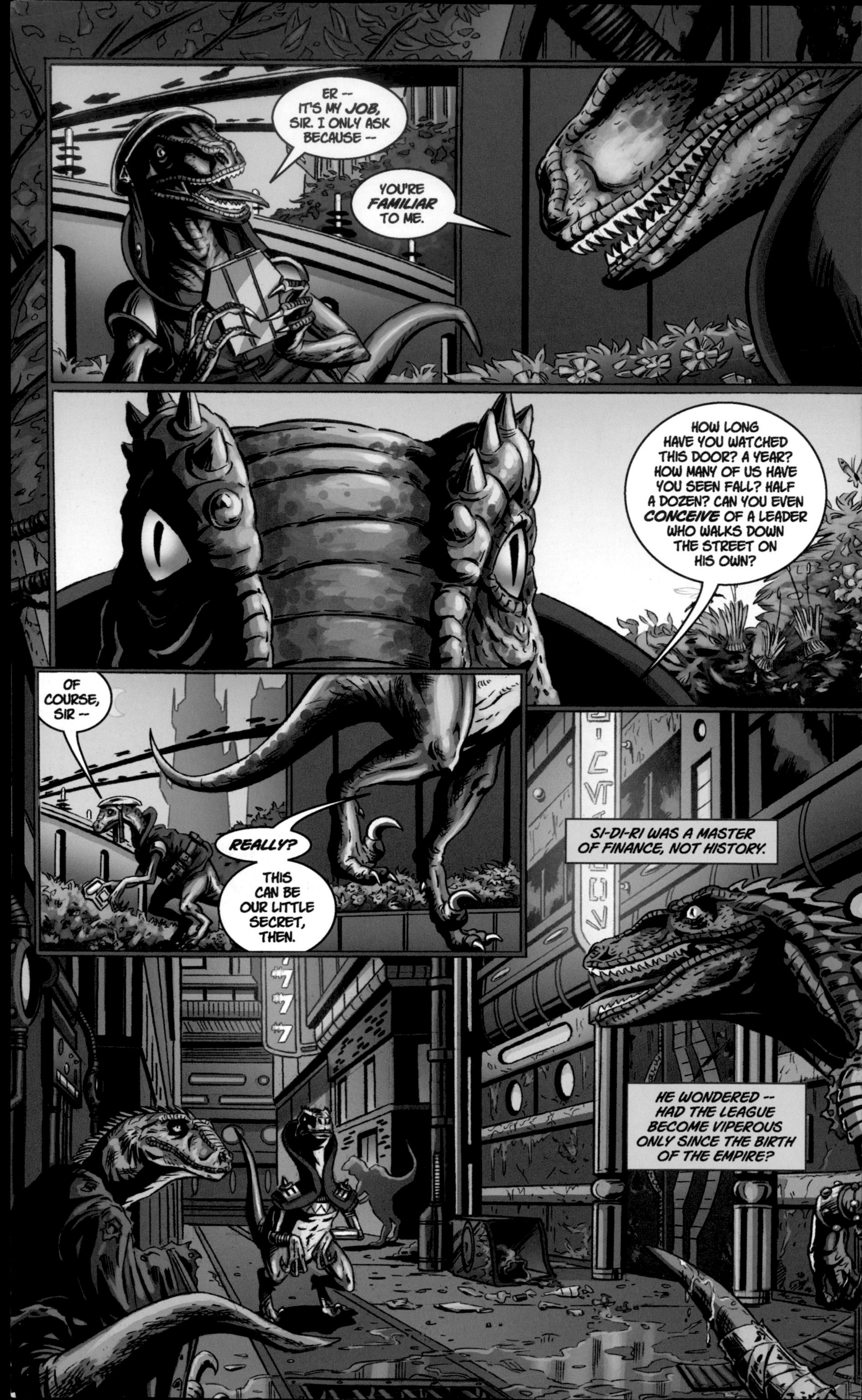
ER -- IT'S MY JOB, SIR. I ONLY ASK BECAUSE --
YOU'RE FAMILIAR TO ME.
HOW LONG HAVE YOU WATCHED THIS DOOR? A YEAR? HOW MANY OF US HAVE YOU SEEN FALL? HALF A DOZEN? CAN YOU EVEN CONCEIVE OF A LEADER WHO WALKS DOWN THE STREET ON HIS OWN?
OF COURSE, SIR --
REALLY?
THIS CAN BE OUR LITTLE SECRET, THEN.
SI-DI-RI WAS A MASTER OF FINANCE, NOT HISTORY.
HE WONDERED -- HAD THE LEAGUE BECOME VIPEROUS ONLY SINCE THE BIRTH OF THE EMPIRE?

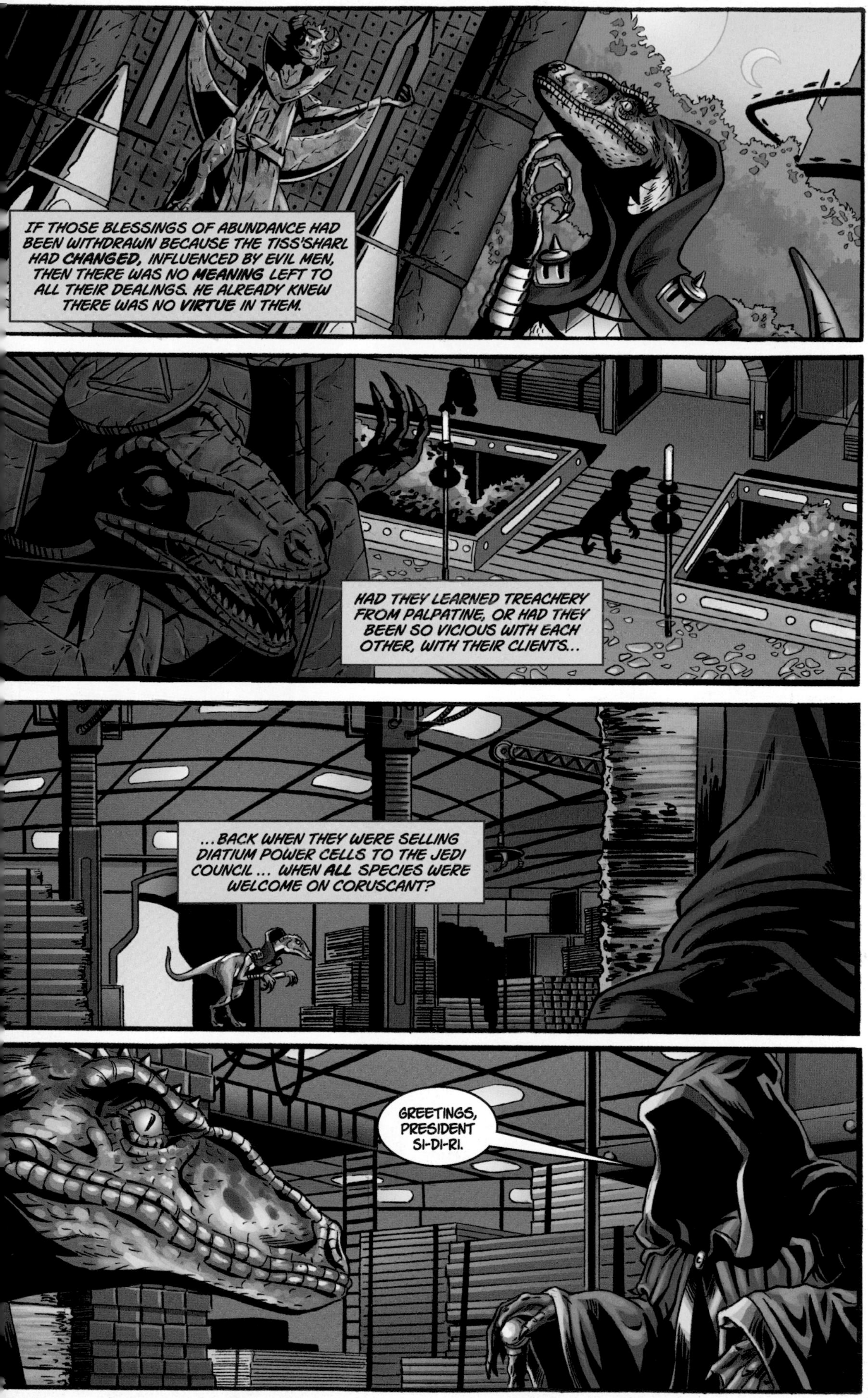
IF THOSE BLESSINGS OF ABUNDANCE HAD BEEN WITHDRAWN BECAUSE THE TISS'SHARL HAD CHANGED, INFLUENCED BY EVIL MEN, THEN THERE WAS NO MEANING LEFT TO ALL THEIR DEALINGS. HE ALREADY KNEW THERE WAS NO VIRTUE IN THEM.
HAD THEY LEARNED TREACHERY FROM PALPATINE, OR HAD THEY BEEN SO VICIOUS WITH EACH OTHER, WITH THEIR CLIENTS...
...BACK WHEN THEY WERE SELLING DIATIUM POWER CELLS TO THE JEDI COUNCIL... WHEN ALL SPECIES WERE WELCOME ON CORUSCANT?
GREETINGS, PRESIDENT SI-DI-RI.

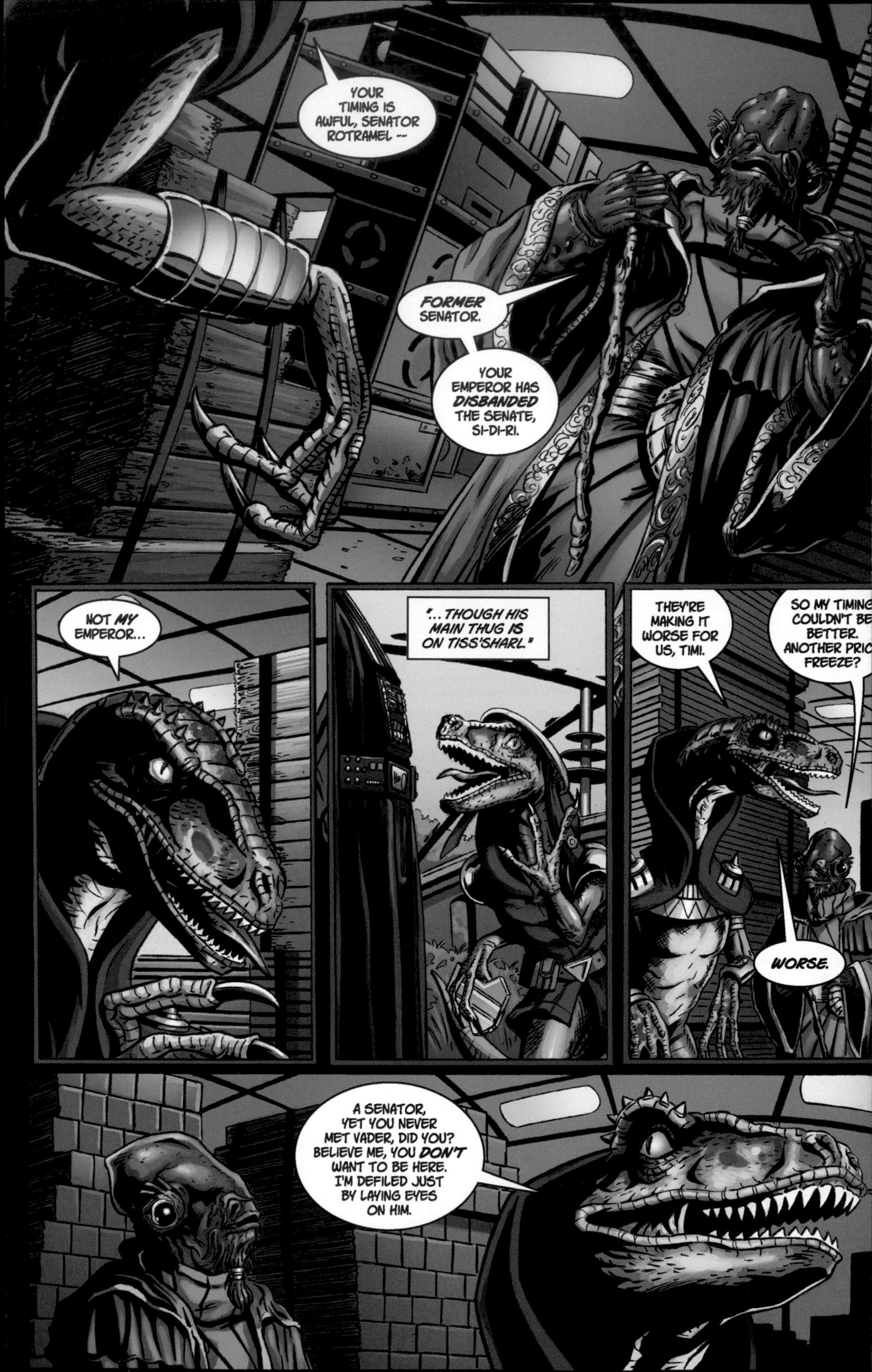
YOUR TIMING IS AWFUL, SENATOR ROTRAMEL --
FORMER SENATOR.
YOUR EMPEROR HAS DISBANDED THE SENATE, SI-DI-RI.
NOT MY EMPEROR...
"...THOUGH HIS MAIN THUG IS ON TISS'SHARL."
THEY'RE MAKING IT WORSE FOR US, TIMI.
SO MY TIMING COULDN'T BE BETTER. ANOTHER PRIC FREEZE?
WORSE.
A SENATOR, YET YOU NEVER MET VADER, DID YOU? BELIEVE ME, YOU DON'T WANT TO BE HERE. I'M DEFILED JUST BY LAYING EYES ON HIM.

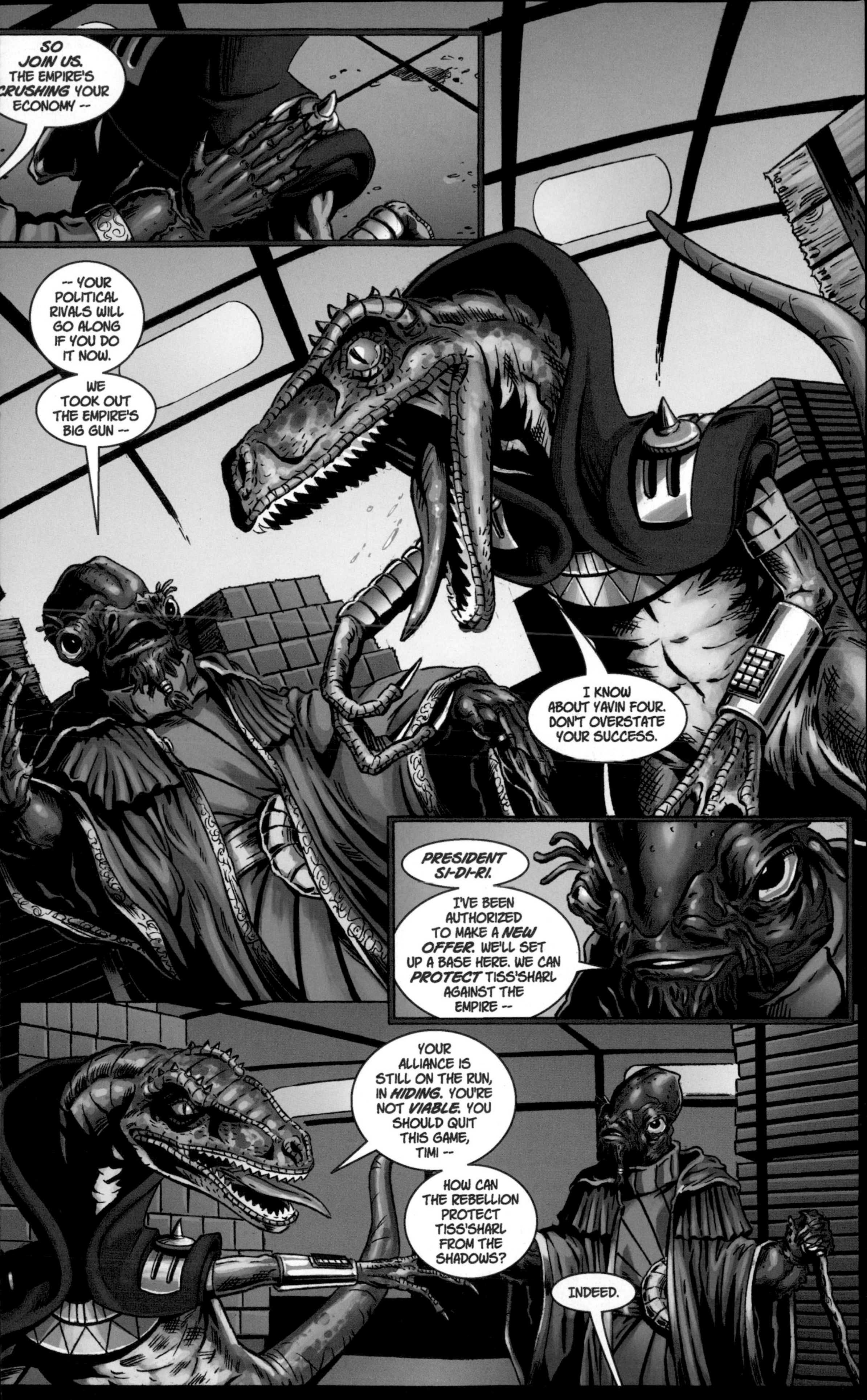
SO JOIN US. THE EMPIRE'S CRUSHING YOUR ECONOMY --
-- YOUR POLITICAL RIVALS WILL GO ALONG IF YOU DO IT NOW.
WE TOOK OUT THE EMPIRE'S BIG GUN --
I KNOW ABOUT YAVIN FOUR. DON'T OVERSTATE YOUR SUCCESS.
PRESIDENT SI-DI-RI.
I'VE BEEN AUTHORIZED TO MAKE A NEW OFFER. WE'LL SET UP A BASE HERE. WE CAN PROTECT TISS'SHARL AGAINST THE EMPIRE --
YOUR ALLIANCE IS STILL ON THE RUN, IN HIDING. YOU'RE NOT VIABLE. YOU SHOULD QUIT THIS GAME, TIMI --
HOW CAN THE REBELLION PROTECT TISS'SHARL FROM THE SHADOWS?
INDEED.

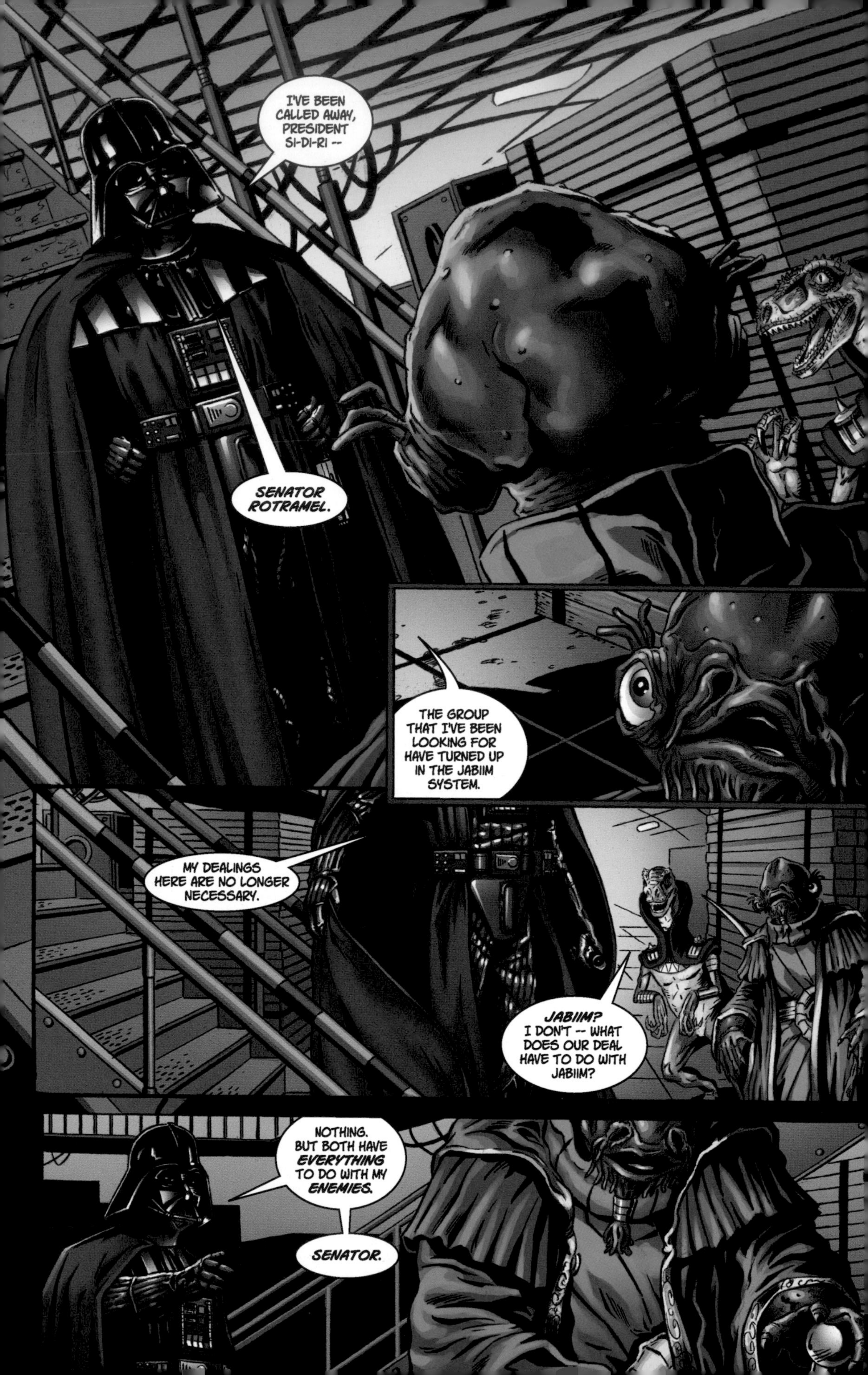
I'VE BEEN CALLED AWAY, PRESIDENT SI-DI-RI --
SENATOR ROTRAMEL.
THE GROUP THAT I'VE BEEN LOOKING FOR HAVE TURNED UP IN THE JABIIM SYSTEM.
MY DEALINGS HERE ARE NO LONGER NECESSARY.
JABIIM? I DON'T -- WHAT DOES OUR DEAL HAVE TO DO WITH JABIIM?
NOTHING. BUT BOTH HAVE EVERYTHING TO DO WITH MY ENEMIES.
SENATOR.

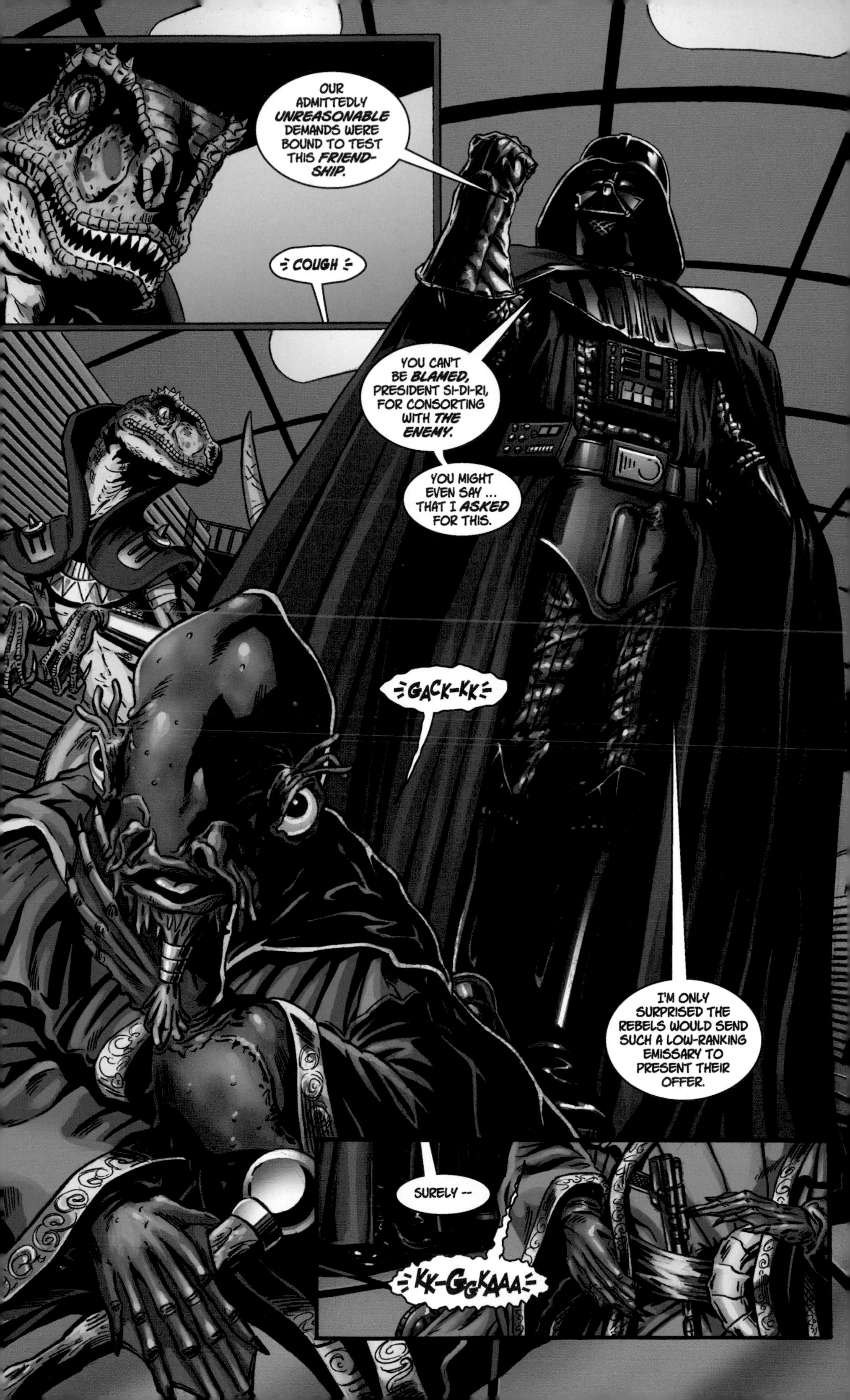
OUR ADMITTEDLY UNREASONABLE DEMANDS WERE BOUND TO TEST THIS FRIEND-SHIP.
COUGH
YOU CAN'T BE BLAMED, PRESIDENT SI-DI-RI, FOR CONSORTING WITH THE ENEMY.
YOU MIGHT EVEN SAY ... THAT I ASKED FOR THIS.
GACK-KK
I'M ONLY SURPRISED THE REBELS WOULD SEND SUCH A LOW-RANKING EMISSARY TO PRESENT THEIR OFFER.
SURELY --
KK-GGKAAA

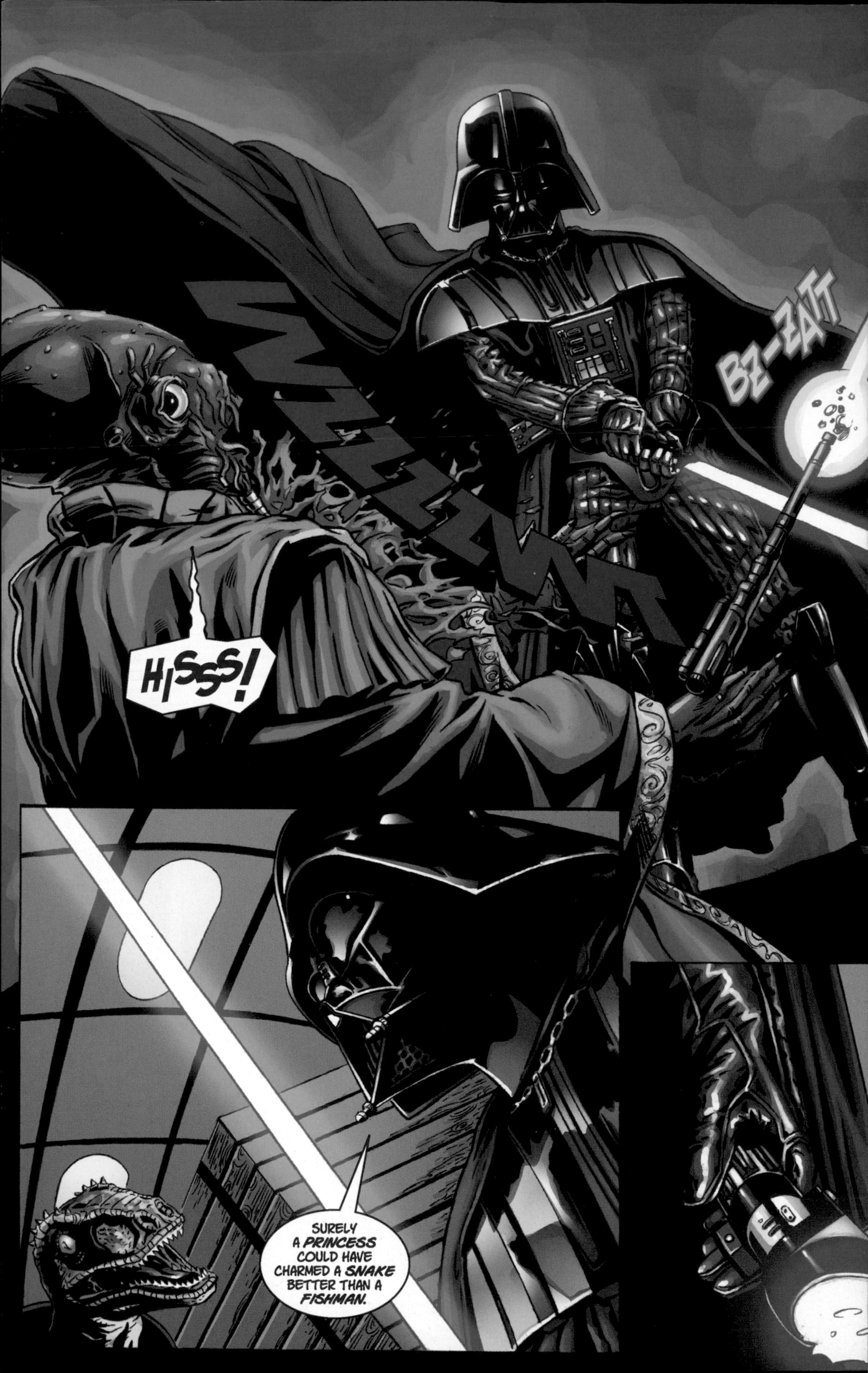
BZ-ZATT
HISSS!
SURELY A *PRINCESS* COULD HAVE CHARMED A *SNAKE* BETTER THAN A *FISHMAN.*

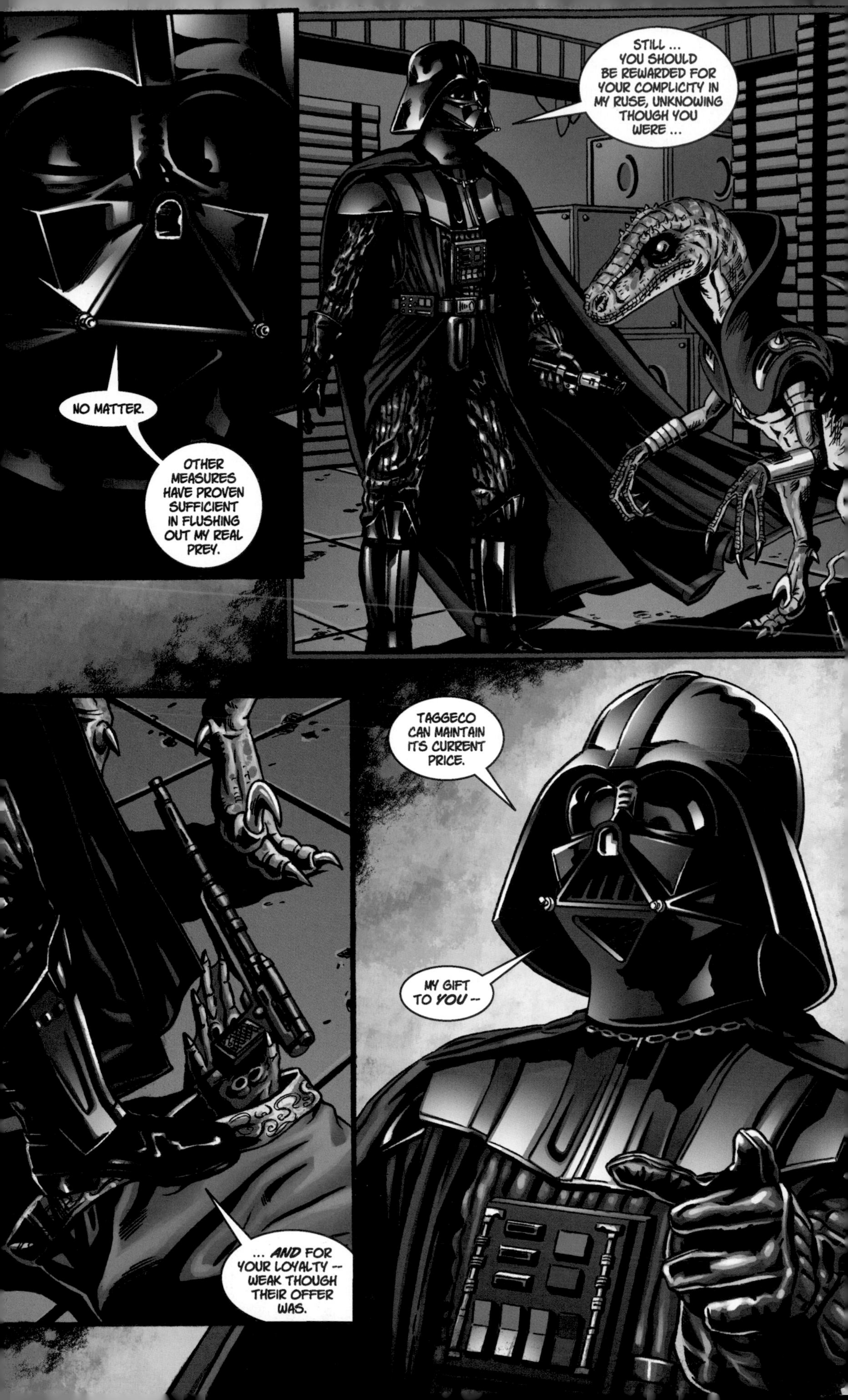
NO MATTER.
OTHER MEASURES HAVE PROVEN SUFFICIENT IN FLUSHING OUT MY REAL PREY.
STILL ... YOU SHOULD BE REWARDED FOR YOUR COMPLICITY IN MY RUSE, UNKNOWING THOUGH YOU WERE ...
... *AND* FOR YOUR LOYALTY -- WEAK THOUGH THEIR OFFER WAS.
TAGGECO CAN MAINTAIN ITS CURRENT PRICE.
MY GIFT TO *YOU* --

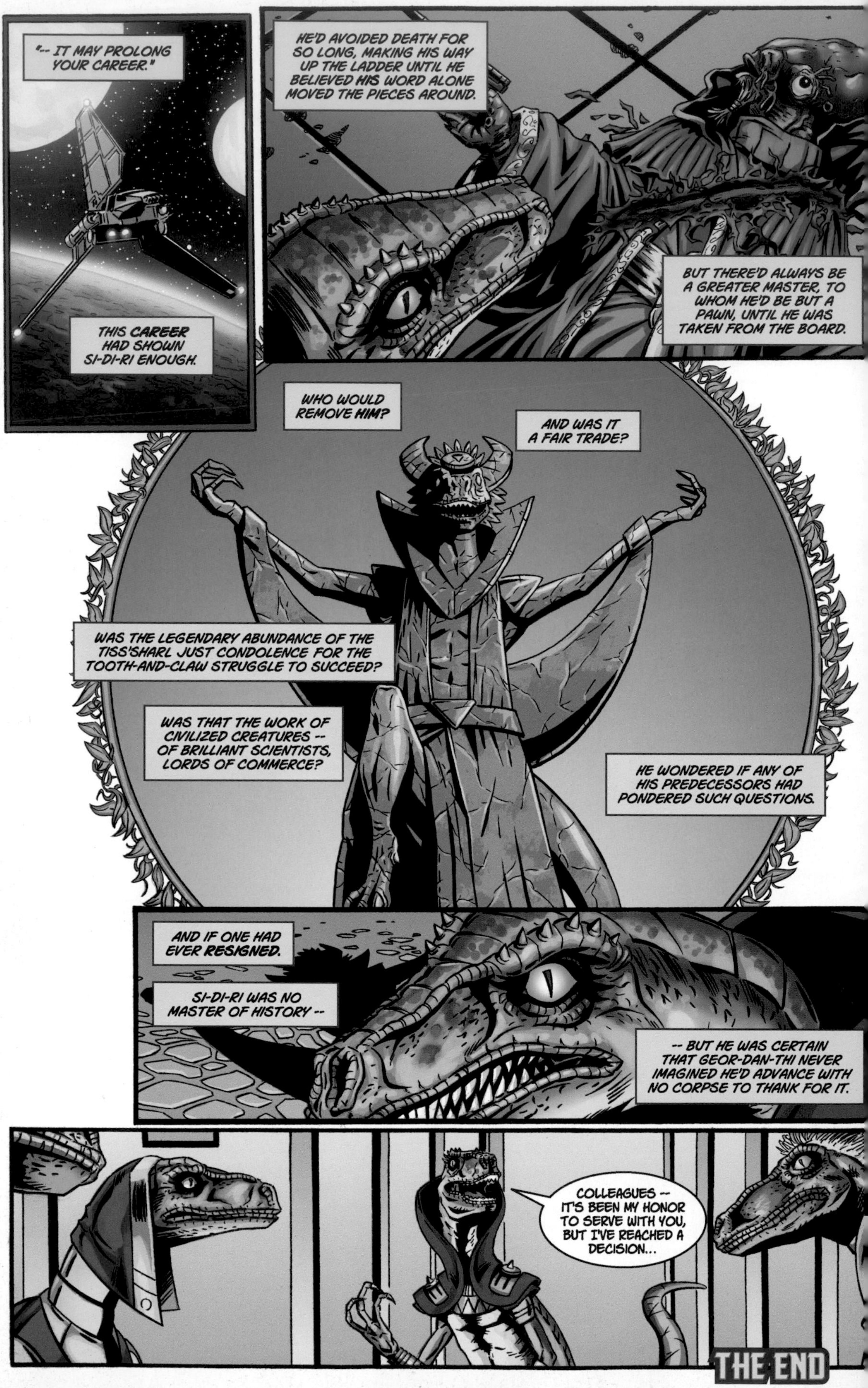
"-- IT MAY PROLONG YOUR CAREER."
THIS CAREER HAD SHOWN SI-DI-RI ENOUGH.
HE'D AVOIDED DEATH FOR SO LONG, MAKING HIS WAY UP THE LADDER UNTIL HE BELIEVED HIS WORD ALONE MOVED THE PIECES AROUND.
BUT THERE'D ALWAYS BE A GREATER MASTER, TO WHOM HE'D BE BUT A PAWN, UNTIL HE WAS TAKEN FROM THE BOARD.
WHO WOULD REMOVE HIM?
AND WAS IT A FAIR TRADE?
WAS THE LEGENDARY ABUNDANCE OF THE TISS'SHARL JUST CONDOLENCE FOR THE TOOTH-AND-CLAW STRUGGLE TO SUCCEED?
WAS THAT THE WORK OF CIVILIZED CREATURES -- OF BRILLIANT SCIENTISTS, LORDS OF COMMERCE?
HE WONDERED IF ANY OF HIS PREDECESSORS HAD PONDERED SUCH QUESTIONS.
AND IF ONE HAD EVER RESIGNED.
SI-DI-RI WAS NO MASTER OF HISTORY --
-- BUT HE WAS CERTAIN THAT GEOR-DAN-THI NEVER IMAGINED HE'D ADVANCE WITH NO CORPSE TO THANK FOR IT.
COLLEAGUES -- IT'S BEEN MY HONOR TO SERVE WITH YOU, BUT I'VE REACHED A DECISION...
THE END

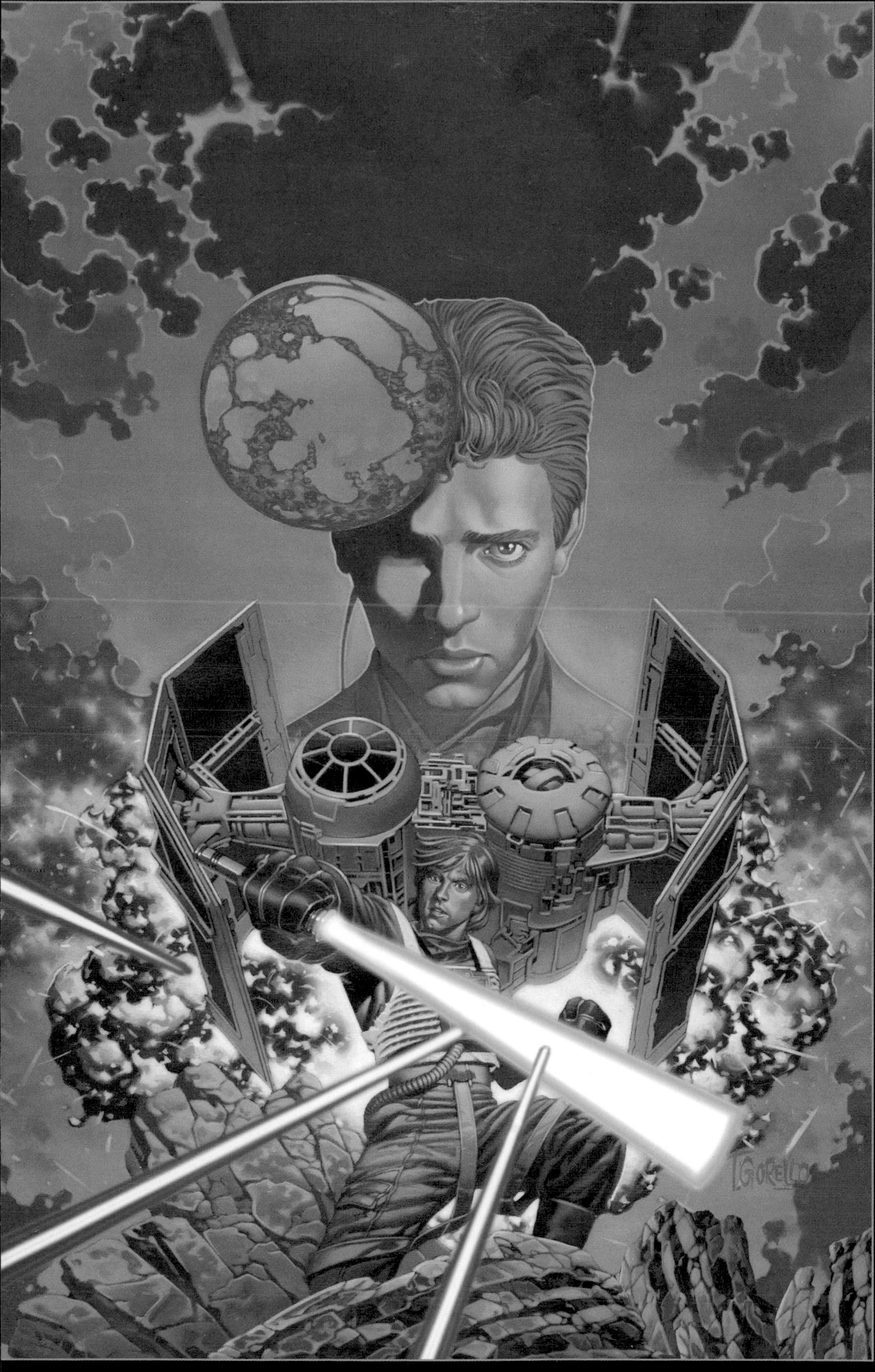
T.Giorello

ART: TOMÁS GIORELLO

IN THE SHADOWS
OF THEIR FATHERS

Script THOMAS ANDREWS
Art ADRIANA MELO,
MICHEL LaCOMBE

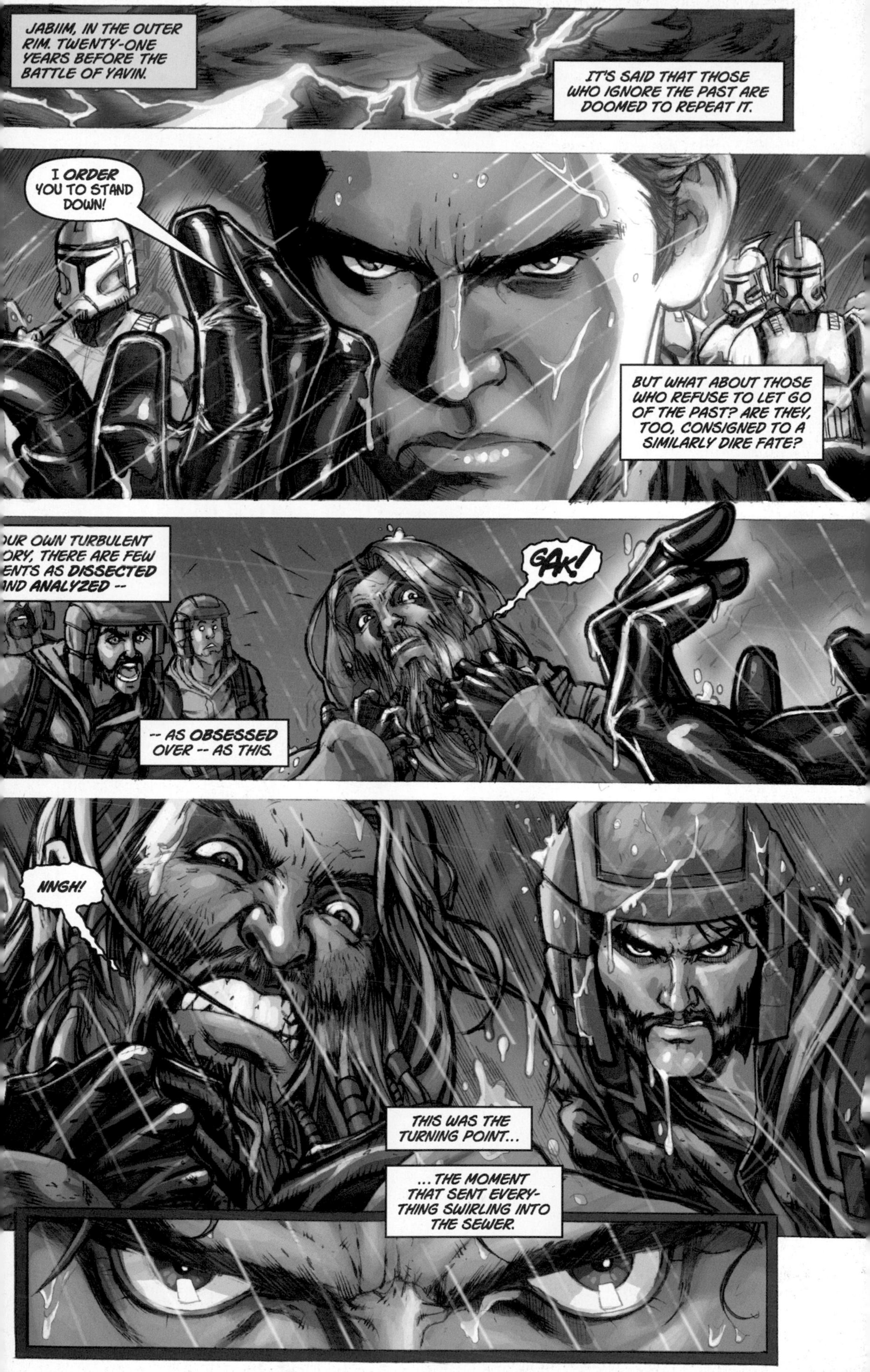
JABIIM, IN THE OUTER RIM. TWENTY-ONE YEARS BEFORE THE BATTLE OF YAVIN.
IT'S SAID THAT THOSE WHO IGNORE THE PAST ARE DOOMED TO REPEAT IT.
I ORDER YOU TO STAND DOWN!
BUT WHAT ABOUT THOSE WHO REFUSE TO LET GO OF THE PAST? ARE THEY, TOO, CONSIGNED TO A SIMILARLY DIRE FATE?
OUR OWN TURBULENT ...ORY, THERE ARE FEW ...ENTS AS DISSECTED AND ANALYZED --
GAK!
-- AS OBSESSED OVER -- AS THIS.
NNGH!
THIS WAS THE TURNING POINT...
...THE MOMENT THAT SENT EVERY-THING SWIRLING INTO THE SEWER.

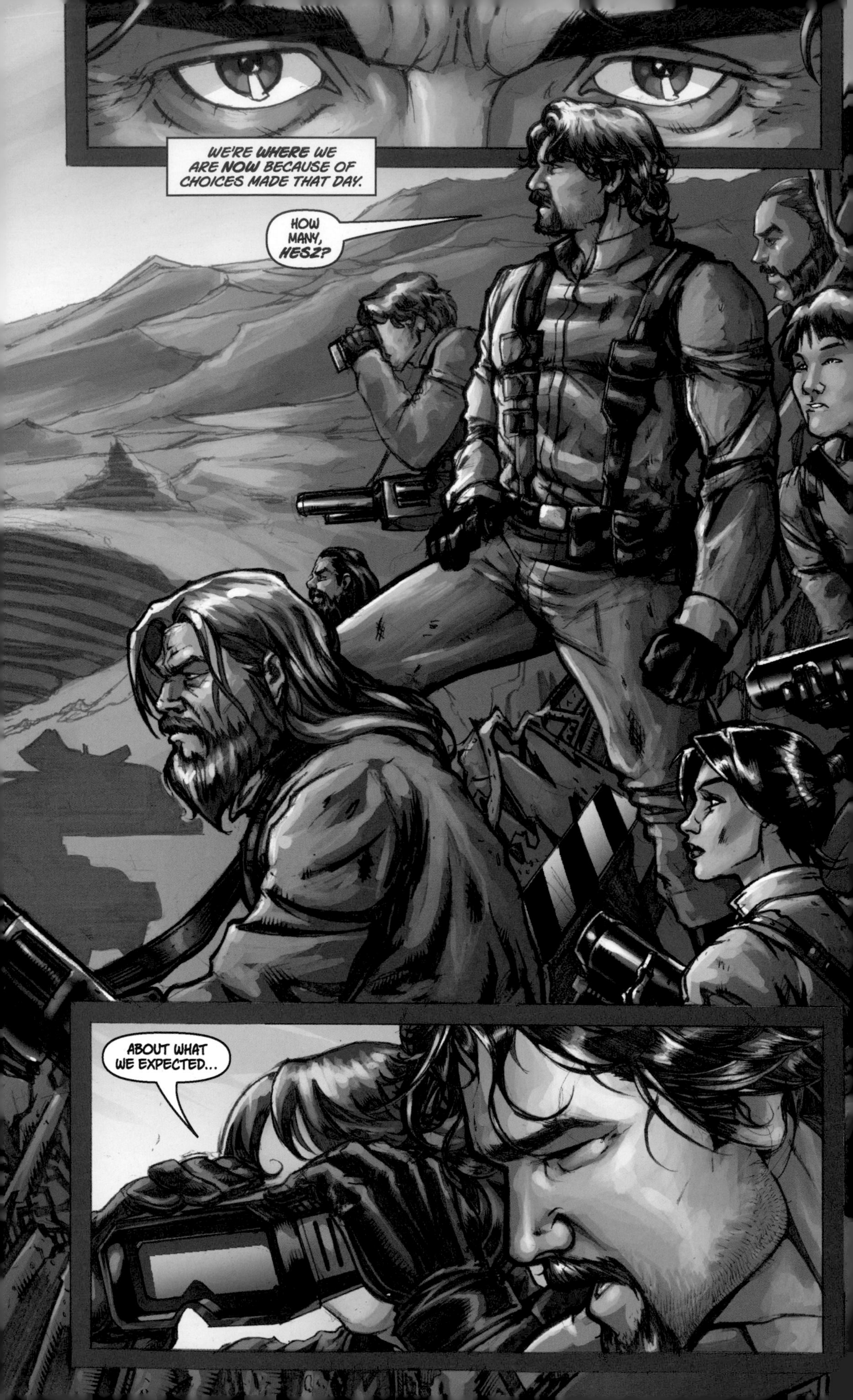
WE'RE WHERE WE ARE NOW BECAUSE OF CHOICES MADE THAT DAY.
HOW MANY, HESZ?
ABOUT WHAT WE EXPECTED...

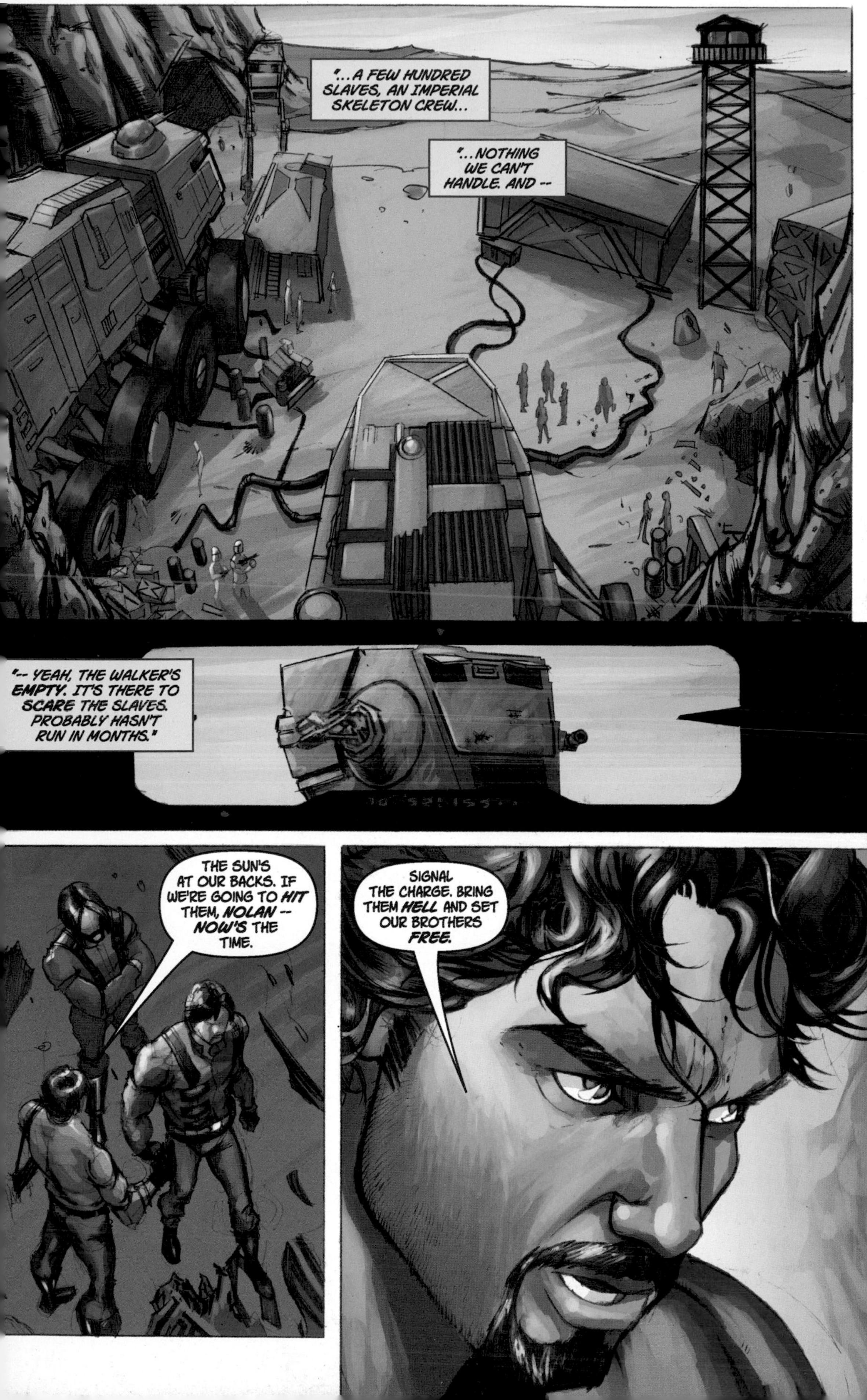
"...A FEW HUNDRED SLAVES, AN IMPERIAL SKELETON CREW...
"...NOTHING WE CAN'T HANDLE. AND --
"-- YEAH, THE WALKER'S EMPTY. IT'S THERE TO SCARE THE SLAVES. PROBABLY HASN'T RUN IN MONTHS."
THE SUN'S AT OUR BACKS. IF WE'RE GOING TO HIT THEM, NOLAN -- NOW'S THE TIME.
SIGNAL THE CHARGE. BRING THEM HELL AND SET OUR BROTHERS FREE.

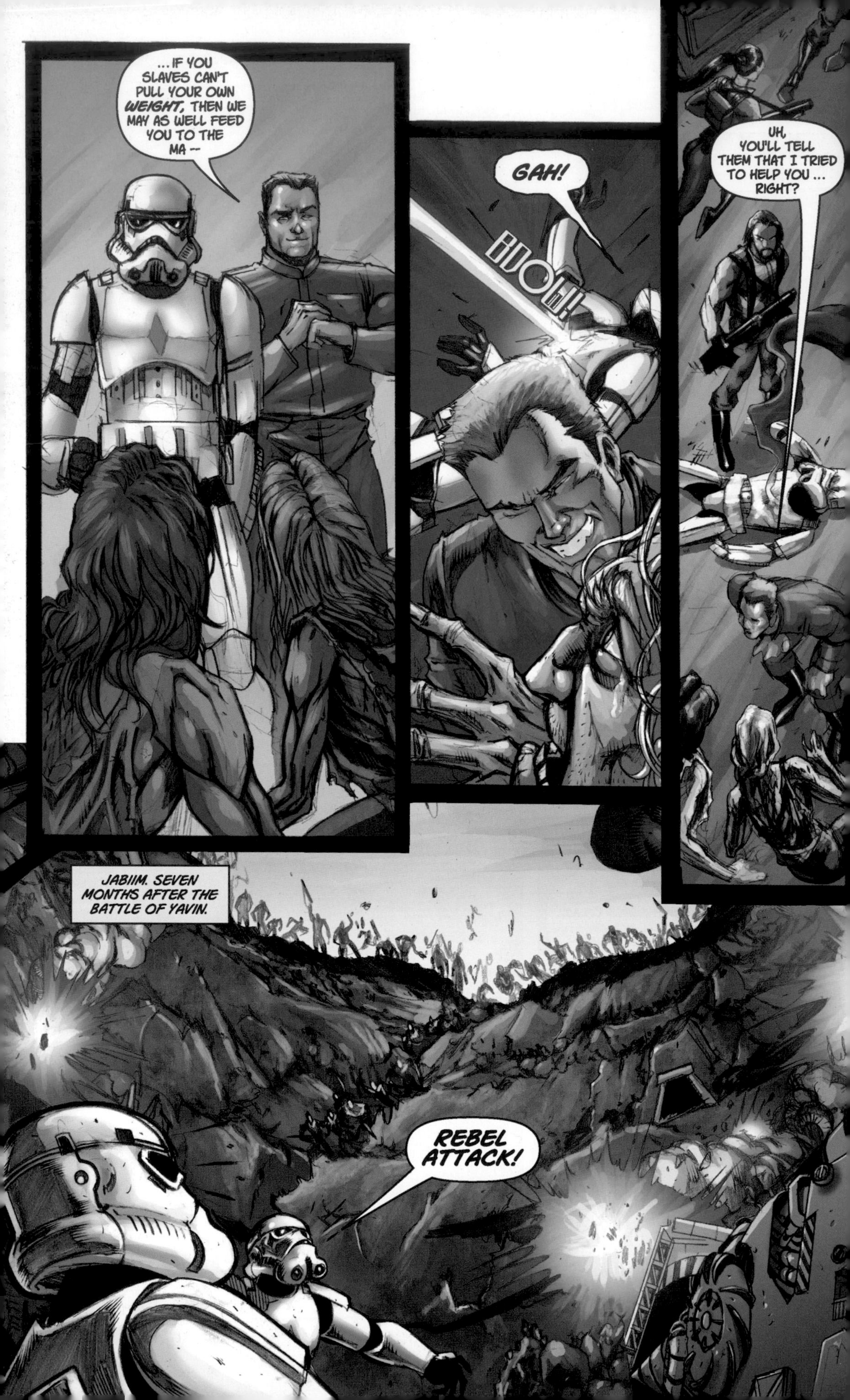

... IF YOU SLAVES CAN'T PULL YOUR OWN *WEIGHT,* THEN WE MAY AS WELL FEED YOU TO THE MA --
GAH!
UH, YOU'LL TELL THEM THAT I TRIED TO HELP YOU ... RIGHT?
JABIIM. SEVEN MONTHS AFTER THE BATTLE OF YAVIN.
REBEL ATTACK!

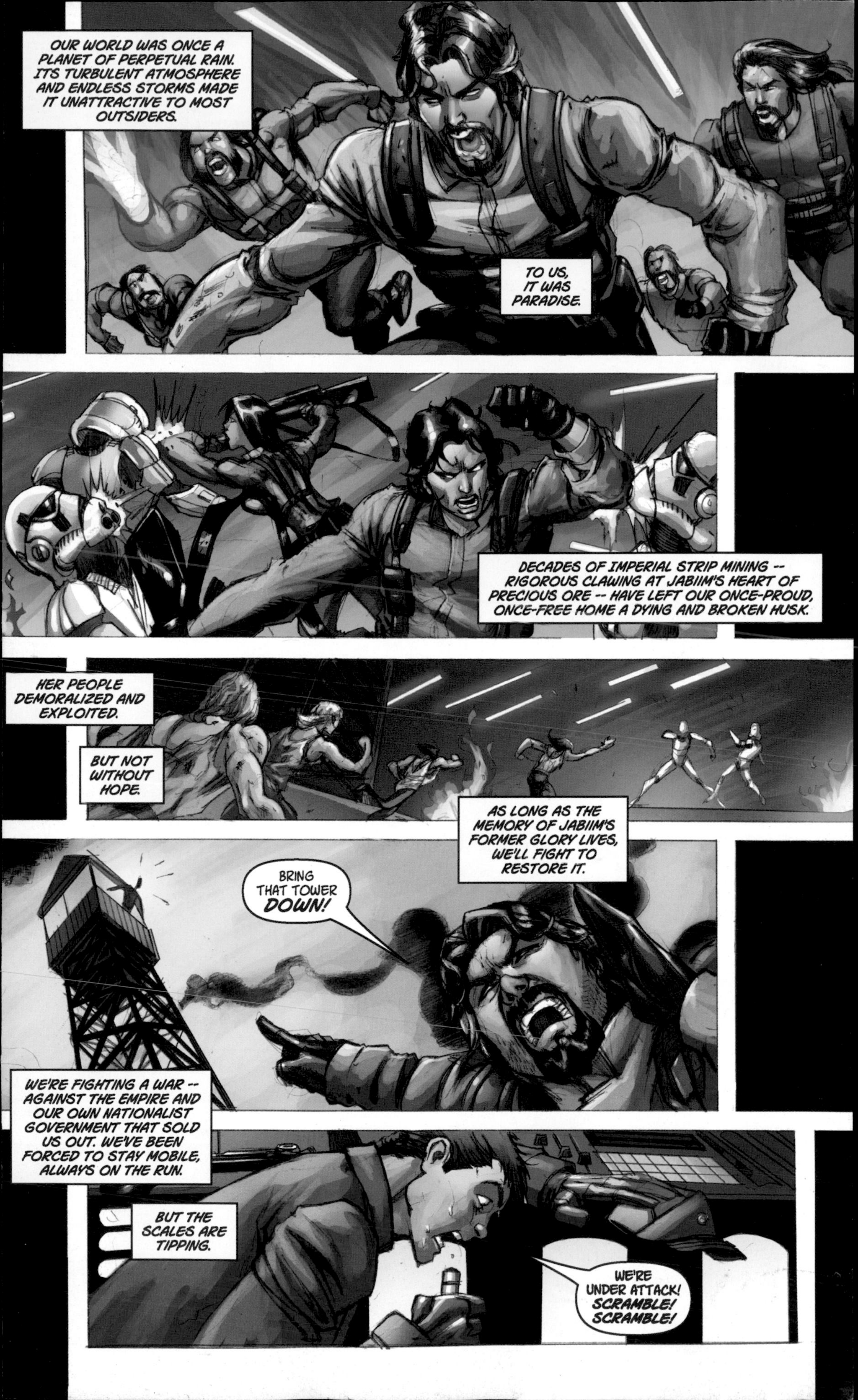
OUR WORLD WAS ONCE A PLANET OF PERPETUAL RAIN. ITS TURBULENT ATMOSPHERE AND ENDLESS STORMS MADE IT UNATTRACTIVE TO MOST OUTSIDERS.
TO US, IT WAS PARADISE.
DECADES OF IMPERIAL STRIP MINING -- RIGOROUS CLAWING AT JABIIM'S HEART OF PRECIOUS ORE -- HAVE LEFT OUR ONCE-PROUD, ONCE-FREE HOME A DYING AND BROKEN HUSK.
HER PEOPLE DEMORALIZED AND EXPLOITED.
BUT NOT WITHOUT HOPE.
AS LONG AS THE MEMORY OF JABIIM'S FORMER GLORY LIVES, WE'LL FIGHT TO RESTORE IT.
BRING THAT TOWER DOWN!
WE'RE FIGHTING A WAR -- AGAINST THE EMPIRE AND OUR OWN NATIONALIST GOVERNMENT THAT SOLD US OUT. WE'VE BEEN FORCED TO STAY MOBILE, ALWAYS ON THE RUN.
BUT THE SCALES ARE TIPPING.
WE'RE UNDER ATTACK! SCRAMBLE! SCRAMBLE!

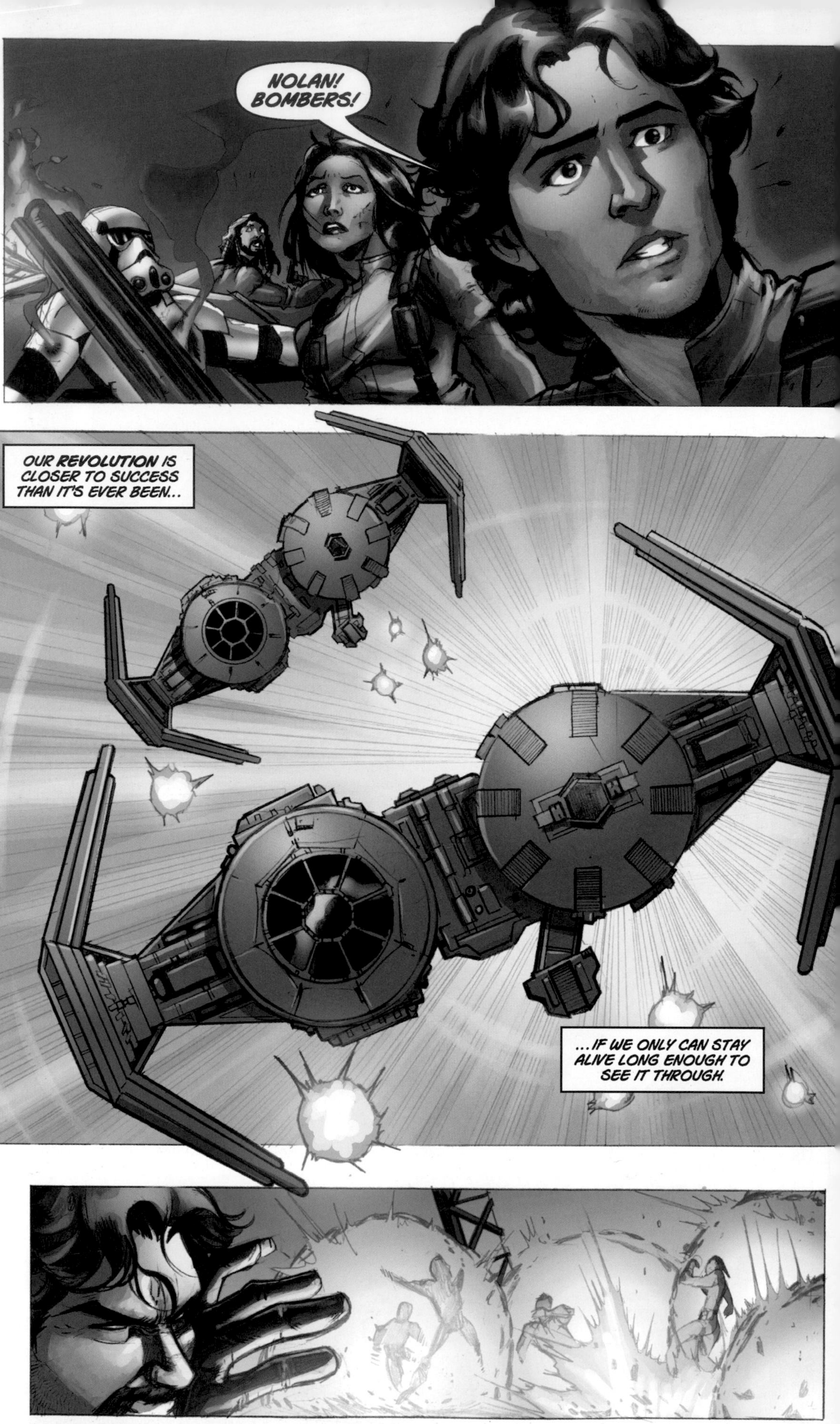
NOLAN! BOMBERS!
OUR REVOLUTION IS CLOSER TO SUCCESS THAN IT'S EVER BEEN...
...IF WE ONLY CAN STAY ALIVE LONG ENOUGH TO SEE IT THROUGH.

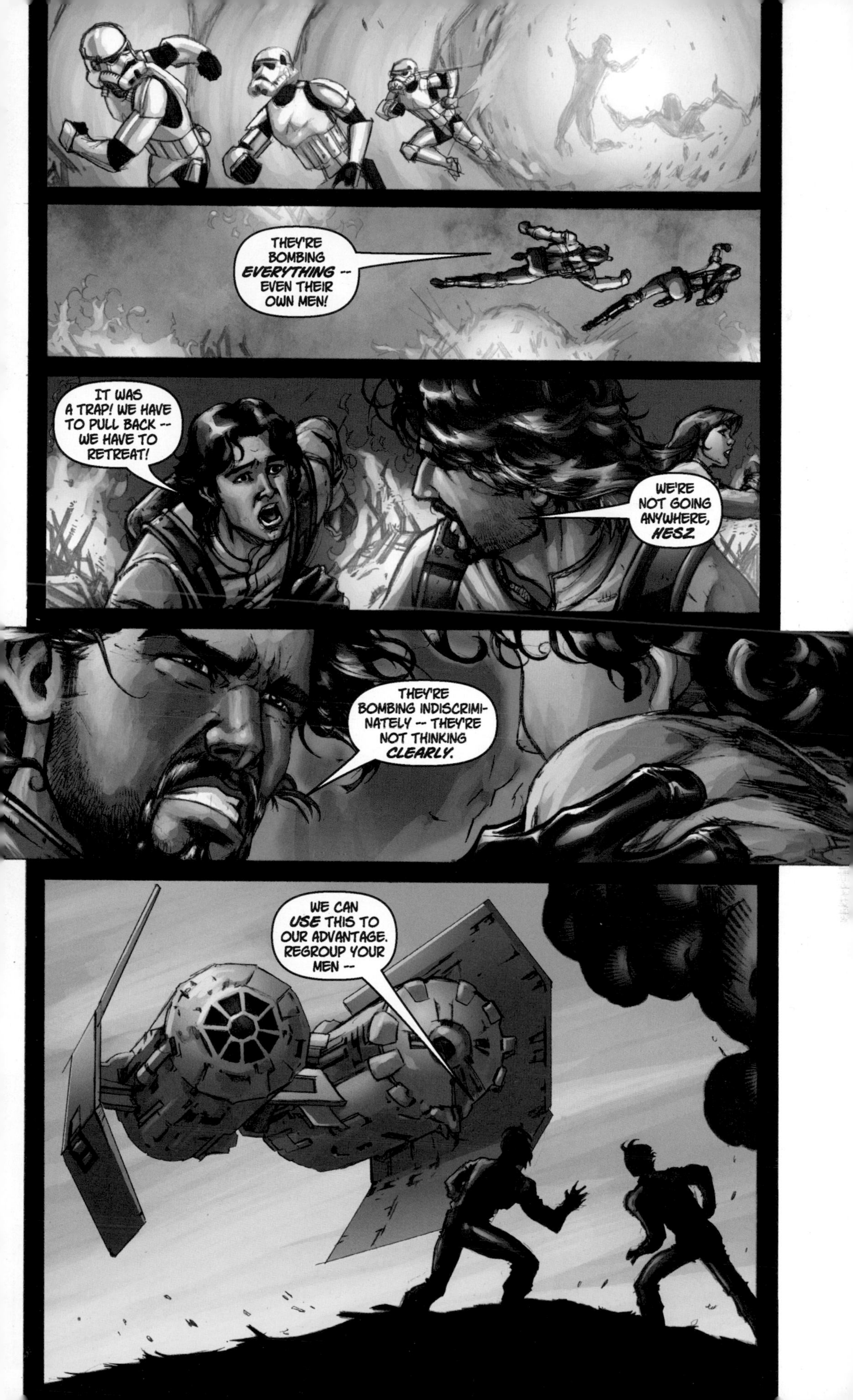

THEY'RE BOMBING EVERYTHING -- EVEN THEIR OWN MEN!
IT WAS A TRAP! WE HAVE TO PULL BACK -- WE HAVE TO RETREAT!
WE'RE NOT GOING ANYWHERE, HESZ.
THEY'RE BOMBING INDISCRIMI-NATELY -- THEY'RE NOT THINKING CLEARLY.
WE CAN USE THIS TO OUR ADVANTAGE. REGROUP YOUR MEN --

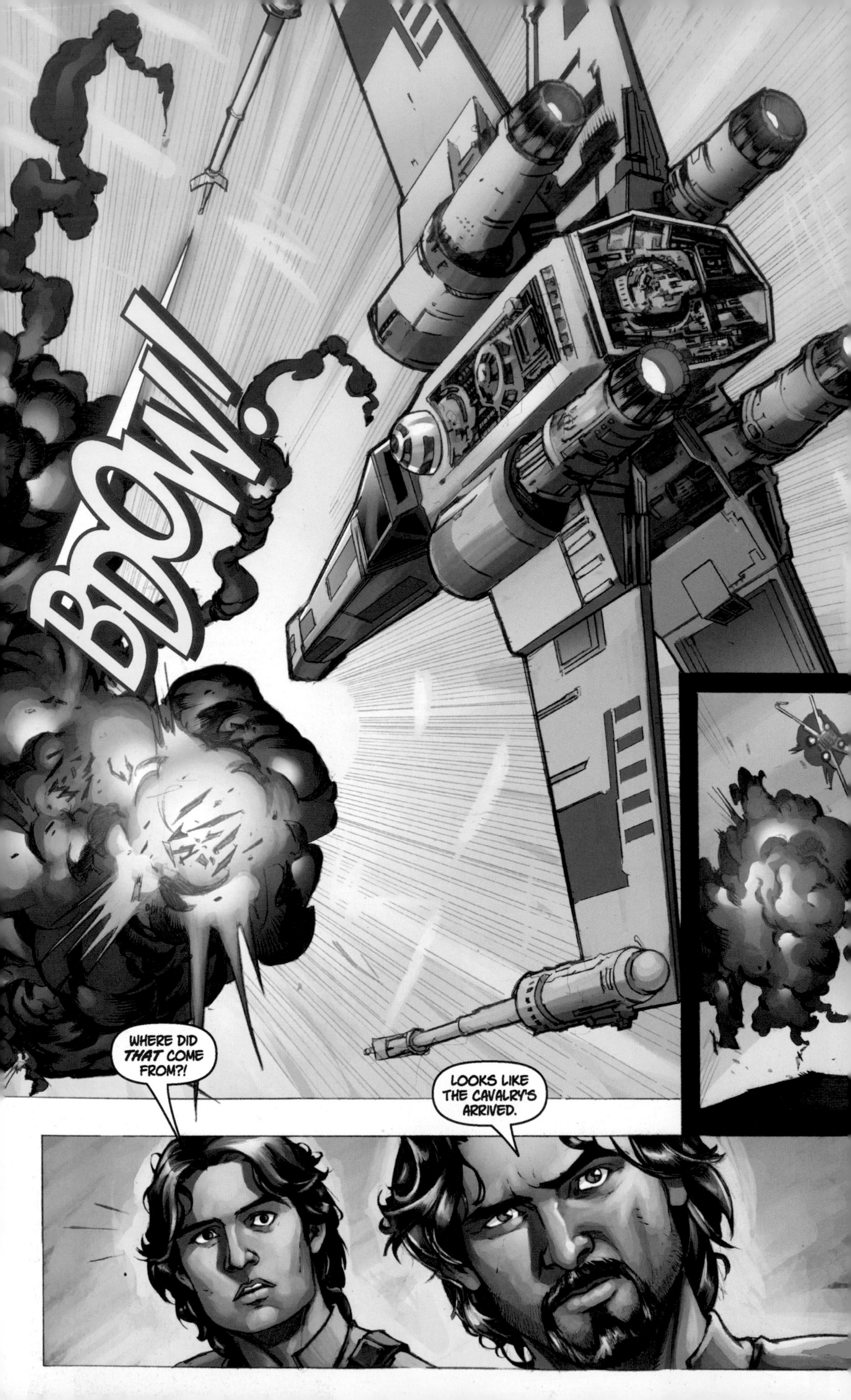
BDOW!
WHERE DID *THAT* COME FROM?!
LOOKS LIKE THE CAVALRY'S ARRIVED.

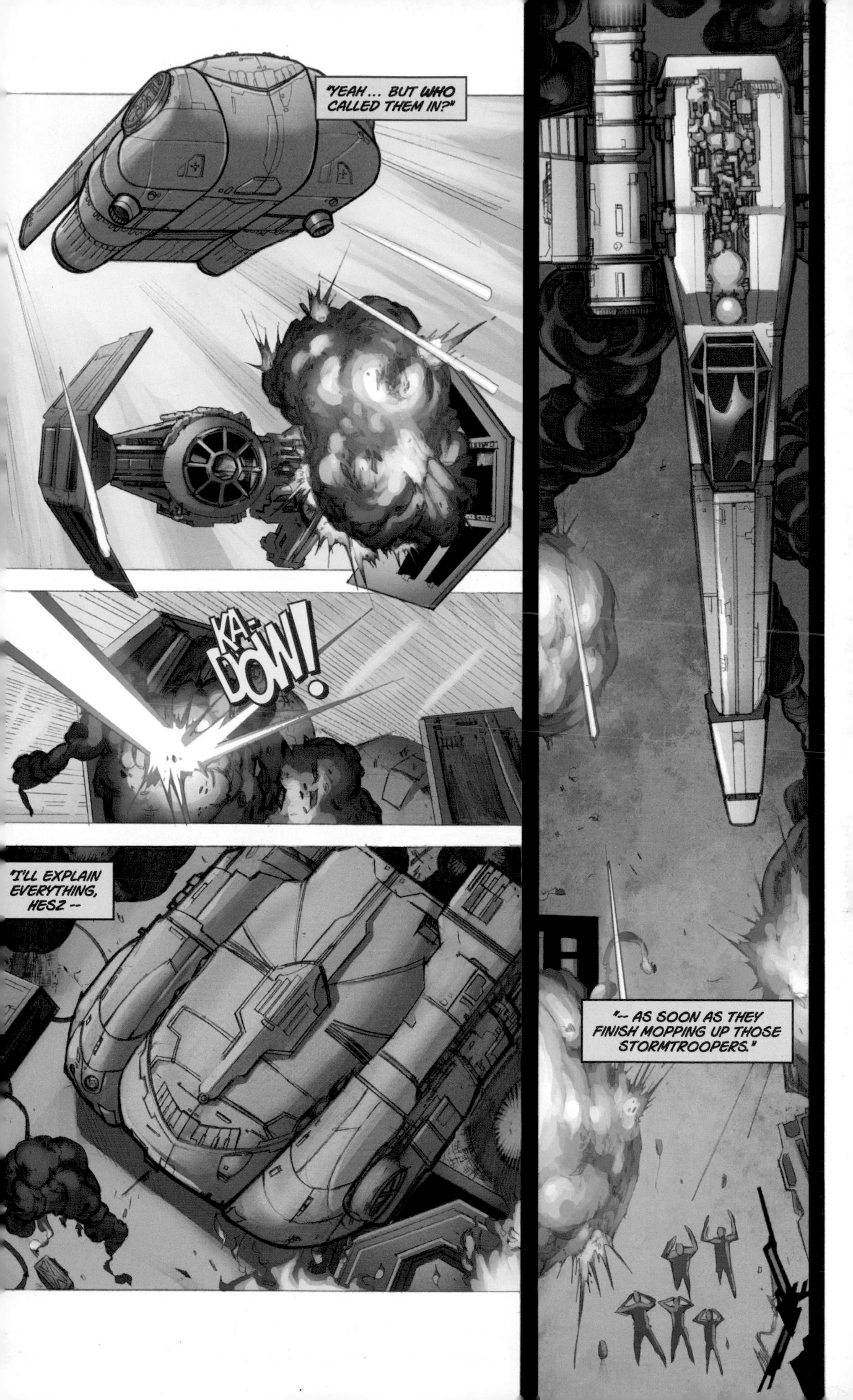
"YEAH ... BUT WHO CALLED THEM IN?"
KA-DOW!
"I'LL EXPLAIN EVERYTHING, HESZ --
"-- AS SOON AS THEY FINISH MOPPING UP THOSE STORMTROOPERS."

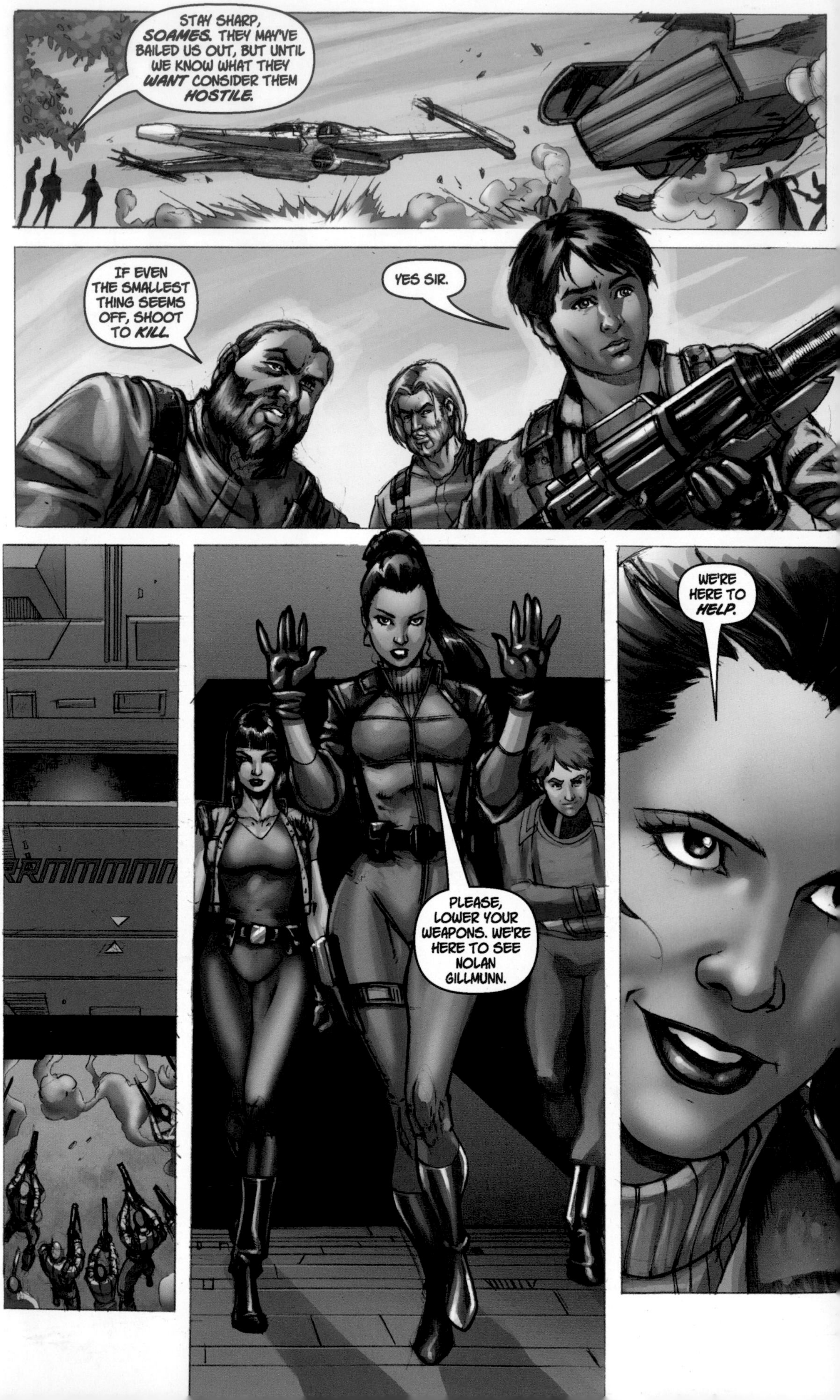
STAY SHARP, SOAMES. THEY MAY'VE BAILED US OUT, BUT UNTIL WE KNOW WHAT THEY WANT CONSIDER THEM HOSTILE.
IF EVEN THE SMALLEST THING SEEMS OFF, SHOOT TO KILL.
YES SIR.
RRMMMMMM
PLEASE, LOWER YOUR WEAPONS. WE'RE HERE TO SEE NOLAN GILLMUNN.
WE'RE HERE TO HELP.

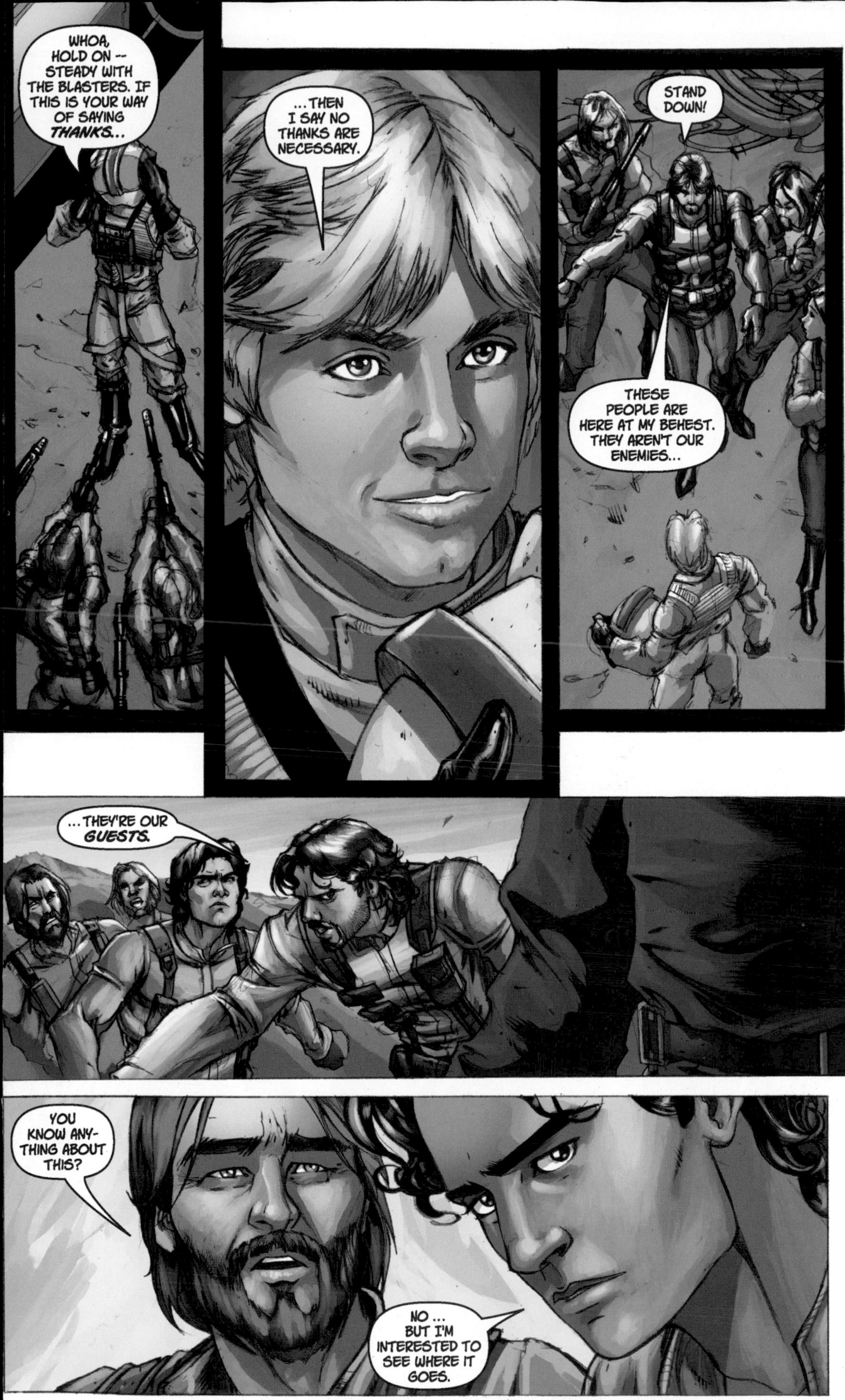
WHOA, HOLD ON -- STEADY WITH THE BLASTERS. IF THIS IS YOUR WAY OF SAYING *THANKS*...
...THEN I SAY NO THANKS ARE NECESSARY.
STAND DOWN!
THESE PEOPLE ARE HERE AT MY BEHEST. THEY AREN'T OUR ENEMIES...
...THEY'RE OUR *GUESTS.*
YOU KNOW ANY-THING ABOUT THIS?
NO ... BUT I'M INTERESTED TO SEE WHERE IT GOES.

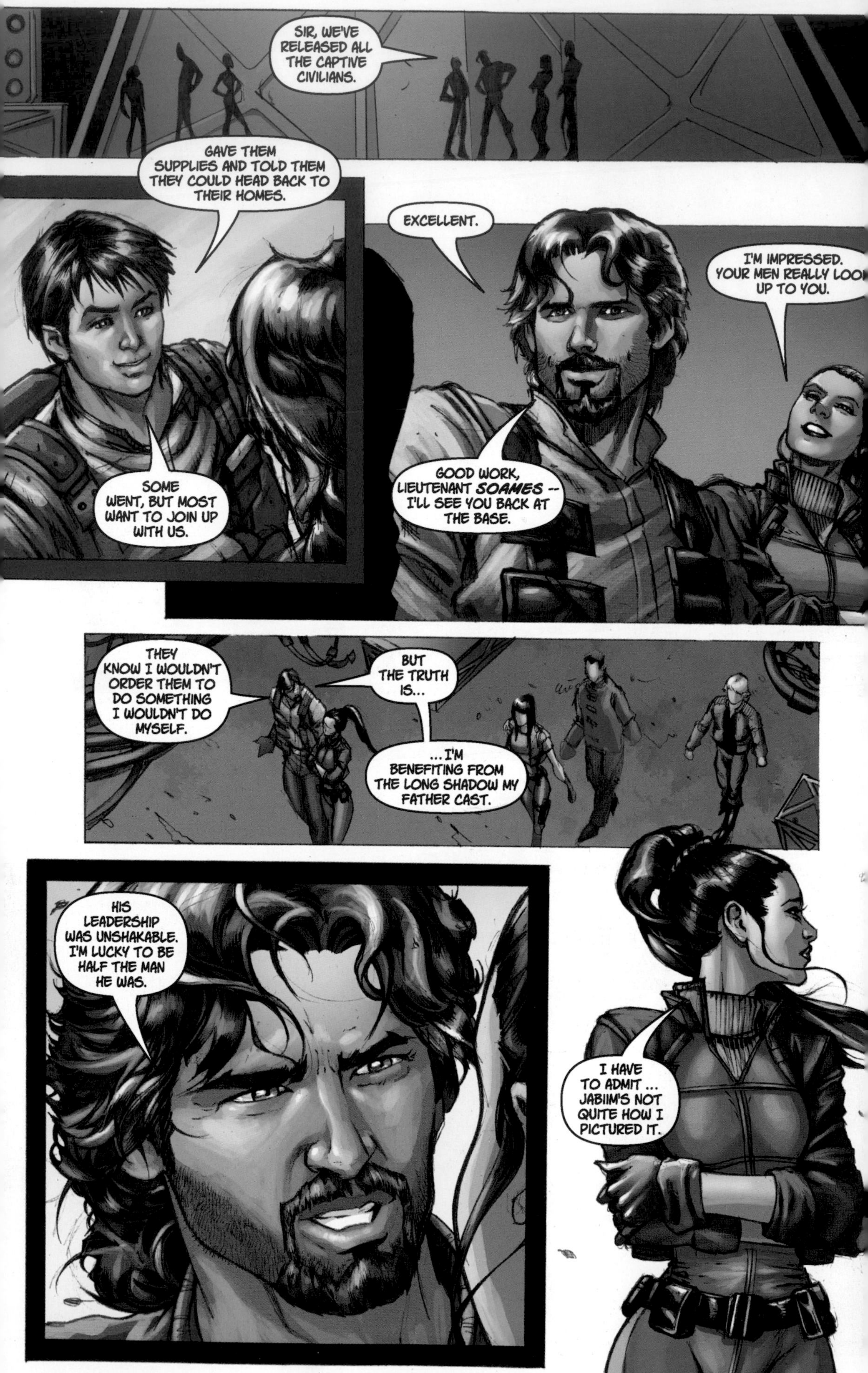
SIR, WE'VE RELEASED ALL THE CAPTIVE CIVILIANS.
GAVE THEM SUPPLIES AND TOLD THEM THEY COULD HEAD BACK TO THEIR HOMES.
SOME WENT, BUT MOST WANT TO JOIN UP WITH US.
EXCELLENT.
GOOD WORK, LIEUTENANT SOAMES -- I'LL SEE YOU BACK AT THE BASE.
I'M IMPRESSED. YOUR MEN REALLY LOOK UP TO YOU.
THEY KNOW I WOULDN'T ORDER THEM TO DO SOMETHING I WOULDN'T DO MYSELF.
BUT THE TRUTH IS...
...I'M BENEFITING FROM THE LONG SHADOW MY FATHER CAST.
HIS LEADERSHIP WAS UNSHAKABLE. I'M LUCKY TO BE HALF THE MAN HE WAS.
I HAVE TO ADMIT ... JABIIM'S NOT QUITE HOW I PICTURED IT.

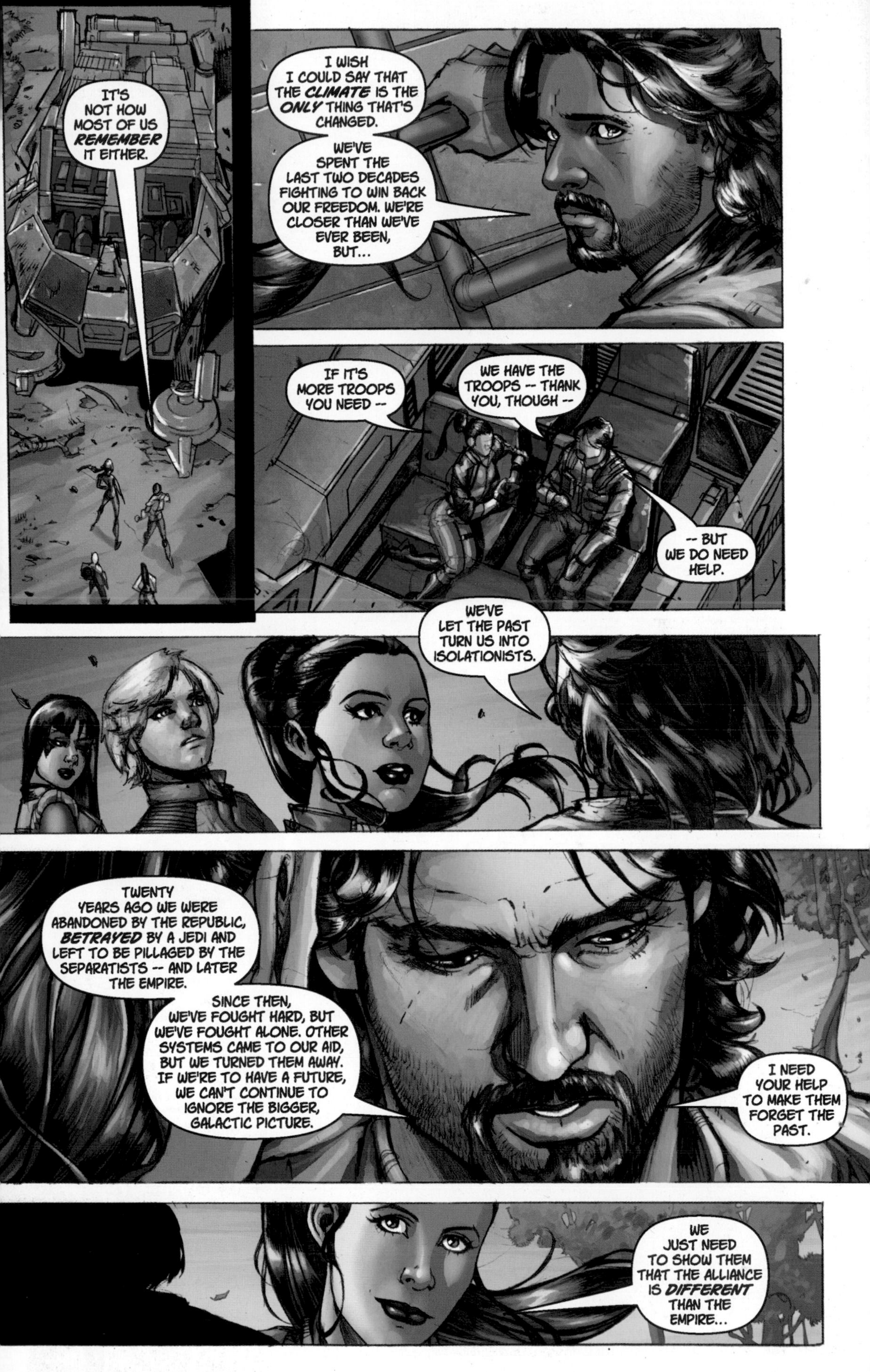
IT'S NOT HOW MOST OF US REMEMBER IT EITHER.
I WISH I COULD SAY THAT THE CLIMATE IS THE ONLY THING THAT'S CHANGED.
WE'VE SPENT THE LAST TWO DECADES FIGHTING TO WIN BACK OUR FREEDOM. WE'RE CLOSER THAN WE'VE EVER BEEN, BUT...
IF IT'S MORE TROOPS YOU NEED --
WE HAVE THE TROOPS -- THANK YOU, THOUGH --
-- BUT WE DO NEED HELP.
WE'VE LET THE PAST TURN US INTO ISOLATIONISTS.
TWENTY YEARS AGO WE WERE ABANDONED BY THE REPUBLIC, BETRAYED BY A JEDI AND LEFT TO BE PILLAGED BY THE SEPARATISTS -- AND LATER THE EMPIRE.
SINCE THEN, WE'VE FOUGHT HARD, BUT WE'VE FOUGHT ALONE. OTHER SYSTEMS CAME TO OUR AID, BUT WE TURNED THEM AWAY. IF WE'RE TO HAVE A FUTURE, WE CAN'T CONTINUE TO IGNORE THE BIGGER, GALACTIC PICTURE.
I NEED YOUR HELP TO MAKE THEM FORGET THE PAST.
WE JUST NEED TO SHOW THEM THAT THE ALLIANCE IS DIFFERENT THAN THE EMPIRE...

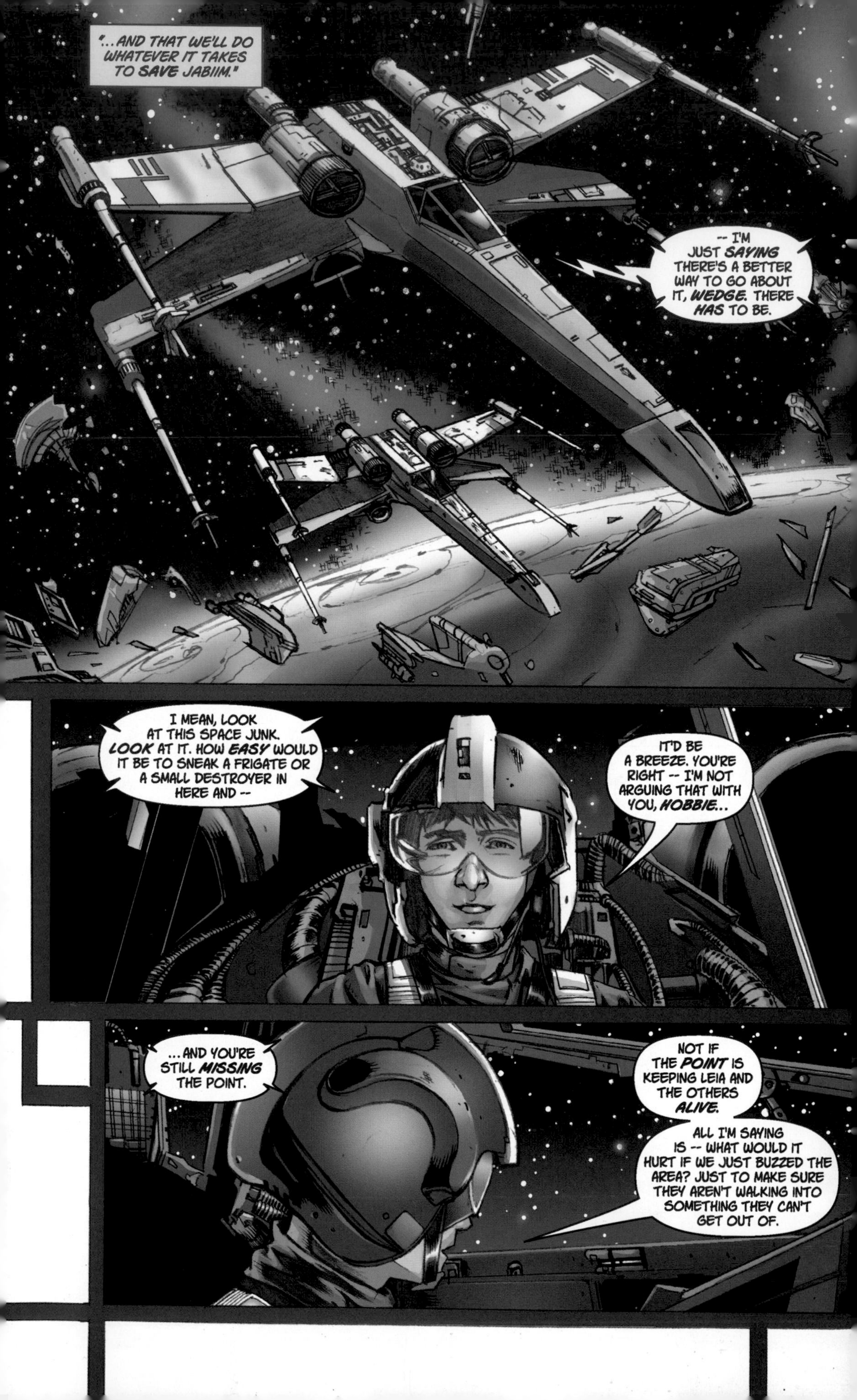
"...AND THAT WE'LL DO WHATEVER IT TAKES TO SAVE JABIIM."
-- I'M JUST SAYING THERE'S A BETTER WAY TO GO ABOUT IT, WEDGE. THERE HAS TO BE.
I MEAN, LOOK AT THIS SPACE JUNK. LOOK AT IT. HOW EASY WOULD IT BE TO SNEAK A FRIGATE OR A SMALL DESTROYER IN HERE AND --
IT'D BE A BREEZE. YOU'RE RIGHT -- I'M NOT ARGUING THAT WITH YOU, HOBBIE...
...AND YOU'RE STILL MISSING THE POINT.
NOT IF THE POINT IS KEEPING LEIA AND THE OTHERS ALIVE.
ALL I'M SAYING IS -- WHAT WOULD IT HURT IF WE JUST BUZZED THE AREA? JUST TO MAKE SURE THEY AREN'T WALKING INTO SOMETHING THEY CAN'T GET OUT OF.

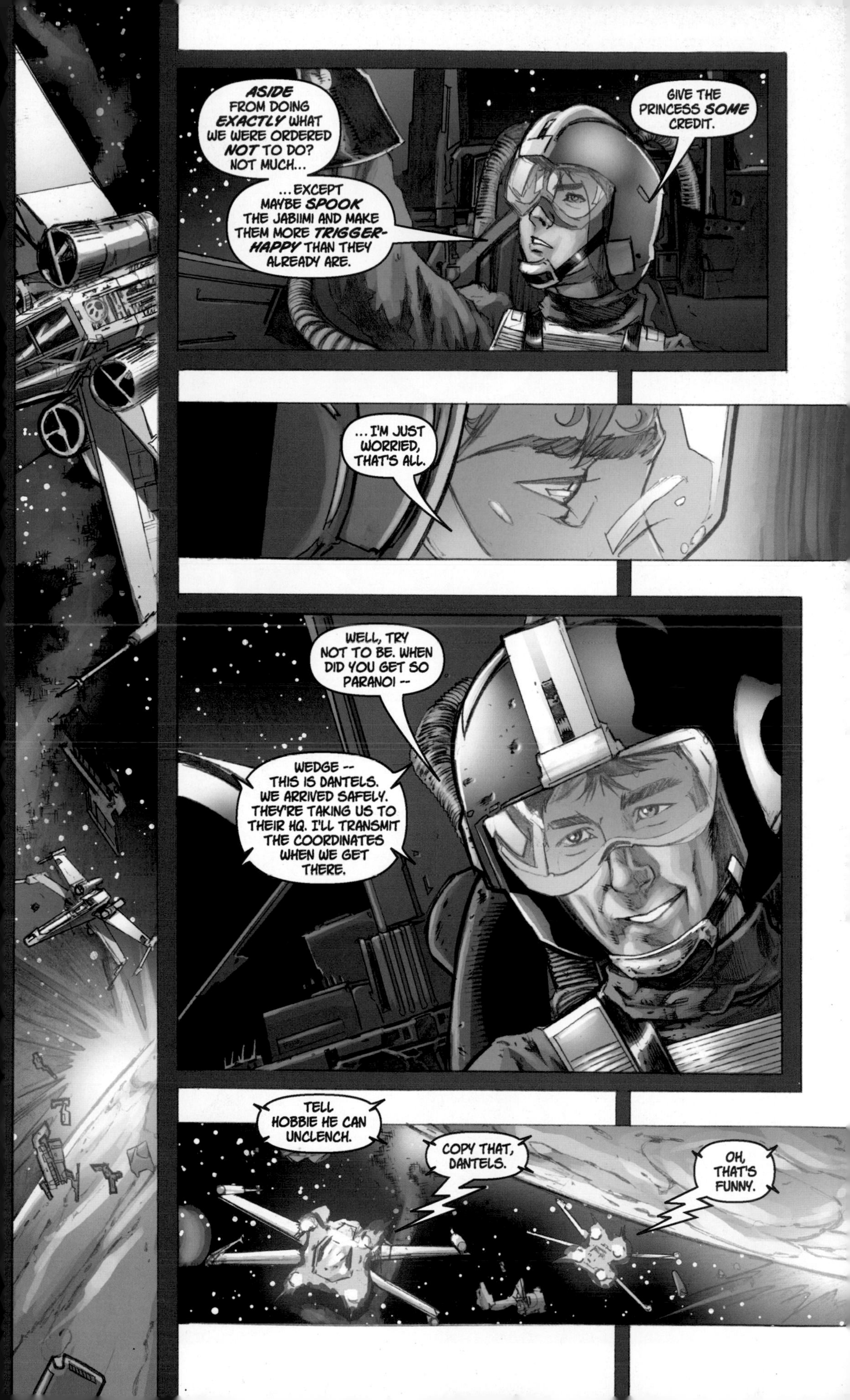
ASIDE FROM DOING EXACTLY WHAT WE WERE ORDERED NOT TO DO? NOT MUCH...
...EXCEPT MAYBE SPOOK THE JABIIMI AND MAKE THEM MORE TRIGGER-HAPPY THAN THEY ALREADY ARE.
GIVE THE PRINCESS SOME CREDIT.
...I'M JUST WORRIED, THAT'S ALL.
WELL, TRY NOT TO BE. WHEN DID YOU GET SO PARANOI --
WEDGE -- THIS IS DANTELS. WE ARRIVED SAFELY. THEY'RE TAKING US TO THEIR HQ. I'LL TRANSMIT THE COORDINATES WHEN WE GET THERE.
TELL HOBBIE HE CAN UNCLENCH.
COPY THAT, DANTELS.
OH, THAT'S FUNNY.

THE REBELS' SHIPS ARE SQUARED AWAY. WE STASHED THE X-WING IN THE FREIGHTER'S HOLD, AND BACKED THE LADY'S FREIGHTER INTO A MINE ENTRANCE.

THE IMPS COULD BE STANDING ON THEM AND THEY WOULDN'T SEE THEM.

NOLAN... I KNOW WHAT YOU'RE TRYING TO DO BY BRINGING THE REBELS HERE...

...BUT I DON'T UNDERSTAND WHY I WAS LEFT OUT OF THE LOOP.

YOU'RE GOING TO HAVE A HARD ENOUGH TIME WITH THE OTHERS WITHOUT RISKING A BREAKDOWN IN YOUR CHAIN OF COMMAND.

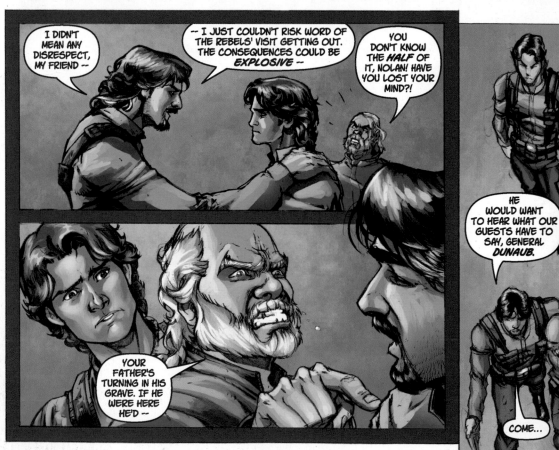

I DIDN'T MEAN ANY DISRESPECT, MY FRIEND --

-- I JUST COULDN'T RISK WORD OF THE REBELS' VISIT GETTING OUT. THE CONSEQUENCES COULD BE EXPLOSIVE --

YOU DON'T KNOW THE HALF OF IT, NOLAN! HAVE YOU LOST YOUR MIND?!

HE WOULD WANT TO HEAR WHAT OUR GUESTS HAVE TO SAY, GENERAL DUNAUB.

YOUR FATHER'S TURNING IN HIS GRAVE. IF HE WERE HERE HE'D --

COME...

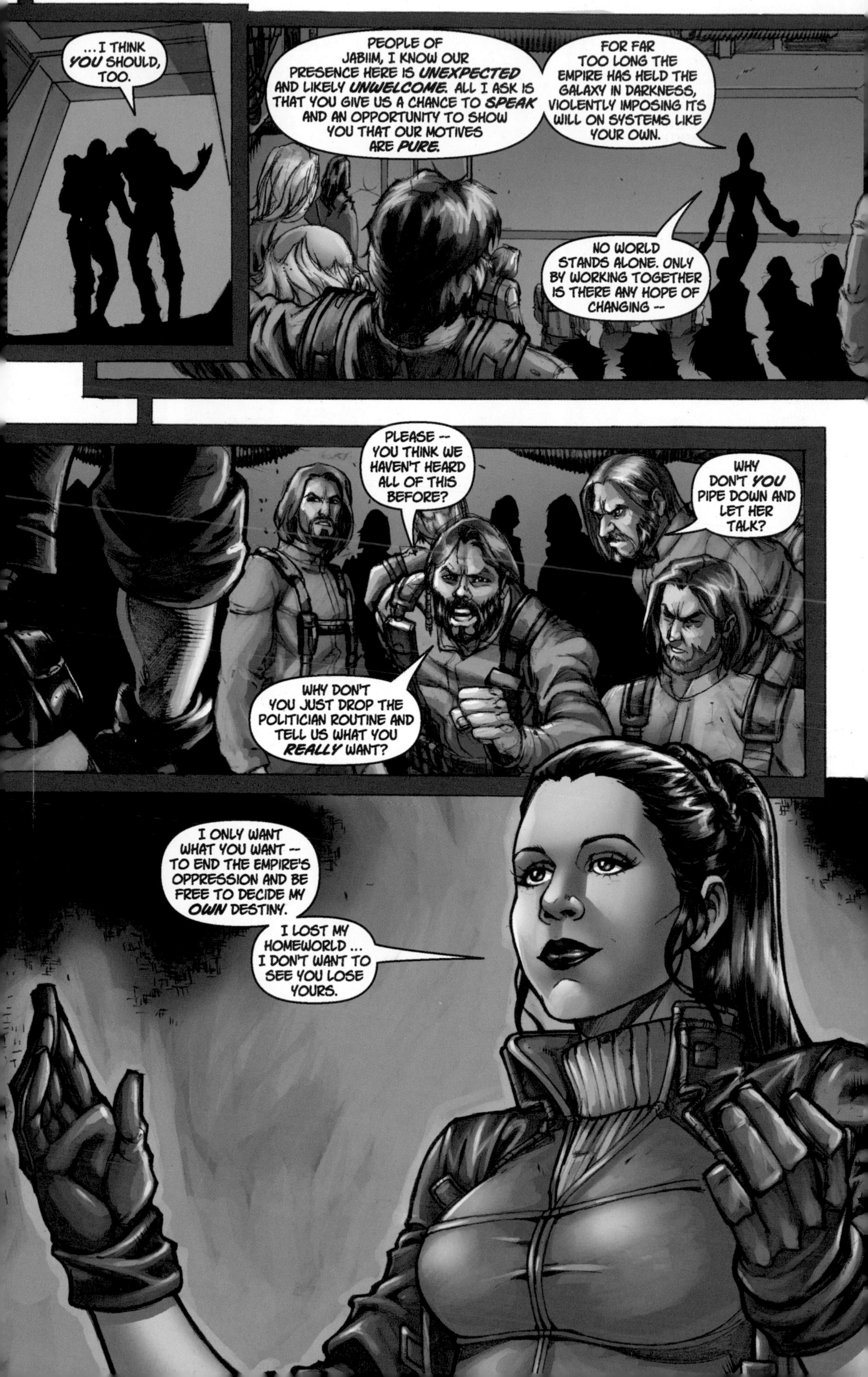
... I THINK *YOU* SHOULD, TOO.
PEOPLE OF JABIIM, I KNOW OUR PRESENCE HERE IS *UNEXPECTED* AND LIKELY *UNWELCOME*. ALL I ASK IS THAT YOU GIVE US A CHANCE TO *SPEAK* AND AN OPPORTUNITY TO SHOW YOU THAT OUR MOTIVES ARE *PURE*.
FOR FAR TOO LONG THE EMPIRE HAS HELD THE GALAXY IN DARKNESS, VIOLENTLY IMPOSING ITS WILL ON SYSTEMS LIKE YOUR OWN.
NO WORLD STANDS ALONE. ONLY BY WORKING TOGETHER IS THERE ANY HOPE OF CHANGING --
PLEASE -- YOU THINK WE HAVEN'T HEARD ALL OF THIS BEFORE?
WHY DON'T *YOU* PIPE DOWN AND LET HER TALK?
WHY DON'T YOU JUST DROP THE POLITICIAN ROUTINE AND TELL US WHAT YOU *REALLY* WANT?
I ONLY WANT WHAT YOU WANT -- TO END THE EMPIRE'S OPPRESSION AND BE FREE TO DECIDE MY *OWN* DESTINY.
I LOST MY HOMEWORLD ... I DON'T WANT TO SEE YOU LOSE YOURS.

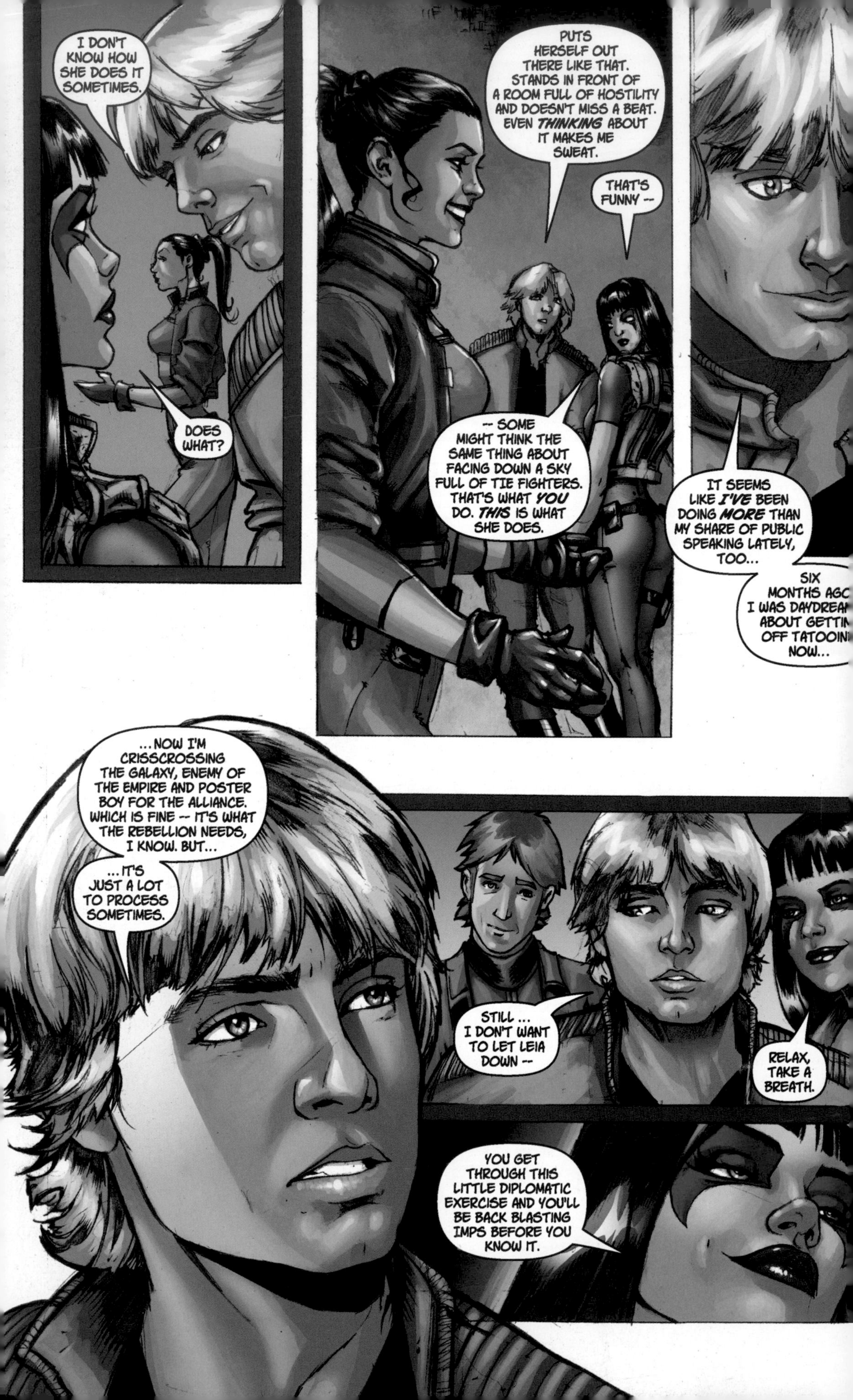
I DON'T KNOW HOW SHE DOES IT SOMETIMES.
DOES WHAT?
PUTS HERSELF OUT THERE LIKE THAT. STANDS IN FRONT OF A ROOM FULL OF HOSTILITY AND DOESN'T MISS A BEAT. EVEN *THINKING* ABOUT IT MAKES ME SWEAT.
THAT'S FUNNY --
-- SOME MIGHT THINK THE SAME THING ABOUT FACING DOWN A SKY FULL OF TIE FIGHTERS. THAT'S WHAT *YOU* DO. *THIS* IS WHAT SHE DOES.
IT SEEMS LIKE *I'VE* BEEN DOING *MORE* THAN MY SHARE OF PUBLIC SPEAKING LATELY, TOO...
...NOW I'M CRISSCROSSING THE GALAXY, ENEMY OF THE EMPIRE AND POSTER BOY FOR THE ALLIANCE. WHICH IS FINE -- IT'S WHAT THE REBELLION NEEDS, I KNOW. BUT...
...IT'S JUST A LOT TO PROCESS SOMETIMES.
STILL ... I DON'T WANT TO LET LEIA DOWN --
RELAX, TAKE A BREATH.
YOU GET THROUGH THIS LITTLE DIPLOMATIC EXERCISE AND YOU'LL BE BACK BLASTING IMPS BEFORE YOU KNOW IT.

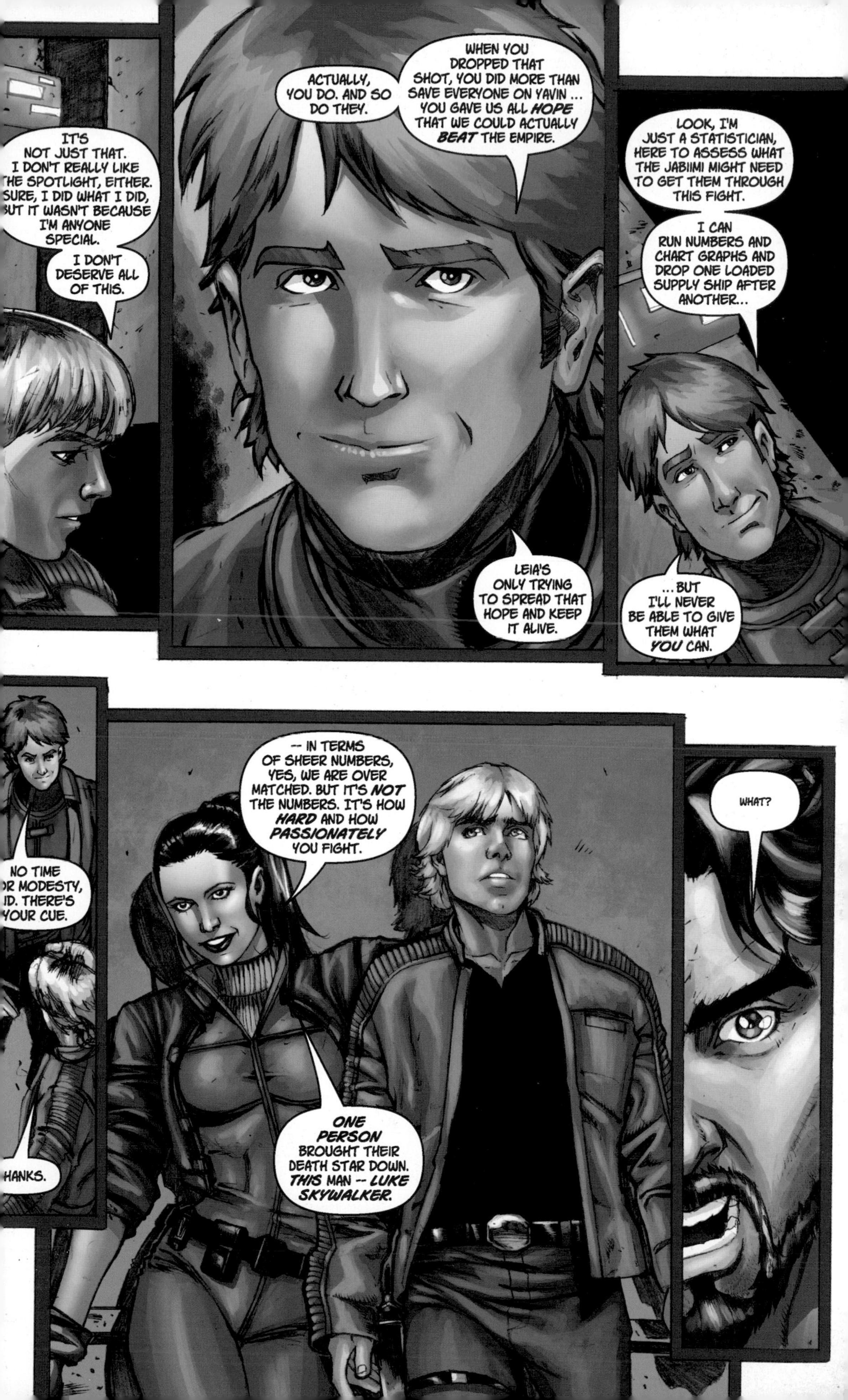

IT'S NOT JUST THAT. I DON'T REALLY LIKE THE SPOTLIGHT, EITHER. SURE, I DID WHAT I DID, UT IT WASN'T BECAUSE I'M ANYONE SPECIAL.
I DON'T DESERVE ALL OF THIS.
ACTUALLY, YOU DO. AND SO DO THEY.
WHEN YOU DROPPED THAT SHOT, YOU DID MORE THAN SAVE EVERYONE ON YAVIN ... YOU GAVE US ALL *HOPE* THAT WE COULD ACTUALLY *BEAT* THE EMPIRE.
LEIA'S ONLY TRYING TO SPREAD THAT HOPE AND KEEP IT ALIVE.
LOOK, I'M JUST A STATISTICIAN, HERE TO ASSESS WHAT THE JABIIMI MIGHT NEED TO GET THEM THROUGH THIS FIGHT.
I CAN RUN NUMBERS AND CHART GRAPHS AND DROP ONE LOADED SUPPLY SHIP AFTER ANOTHER...
... BUT I'LL NEVER BE ABLE TO GIVE THEM WHAT *YOU* CAN.
NO TIME OR MODESTY, ID. THERE'S YOUR CUE.
HANKS.
-- IN TERMS OF SHEER NUMBERS, YES, WE ARE OVER MATCHED. BUT IT'S *NOT* THE NUMBERS. IT'S HOW *HARD* AND HOW *PASSIONATELY* YOU FIGHT.
ONE PERSON BROUGHT THEIR DEATH STAR DOWN. *THIS* MAN -- *LUKE SKYWALKER*.
WHAT?

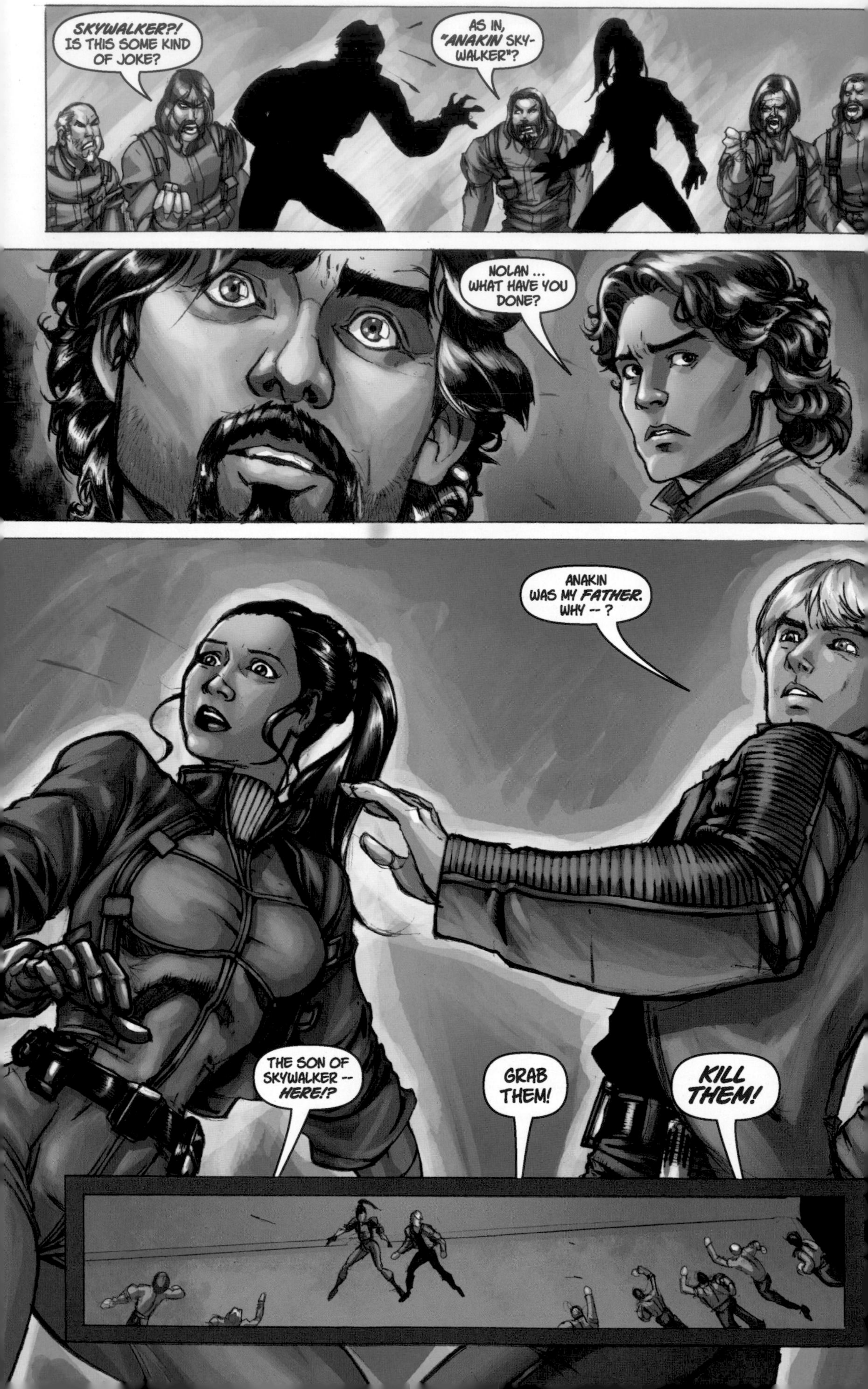
SKYWALKER?! IS THIS SOME KIND OF JOKE?
AS IN, "ANAKIN SKY-WALKER"?
NOLAN ... WHAT HAVE YOU DONE?
ANAKIN WAS MY FATHER. WHY -- ?
THE SON OF SKYWALKER -- HERE!?
GRAB THEM!
KILL THEM!

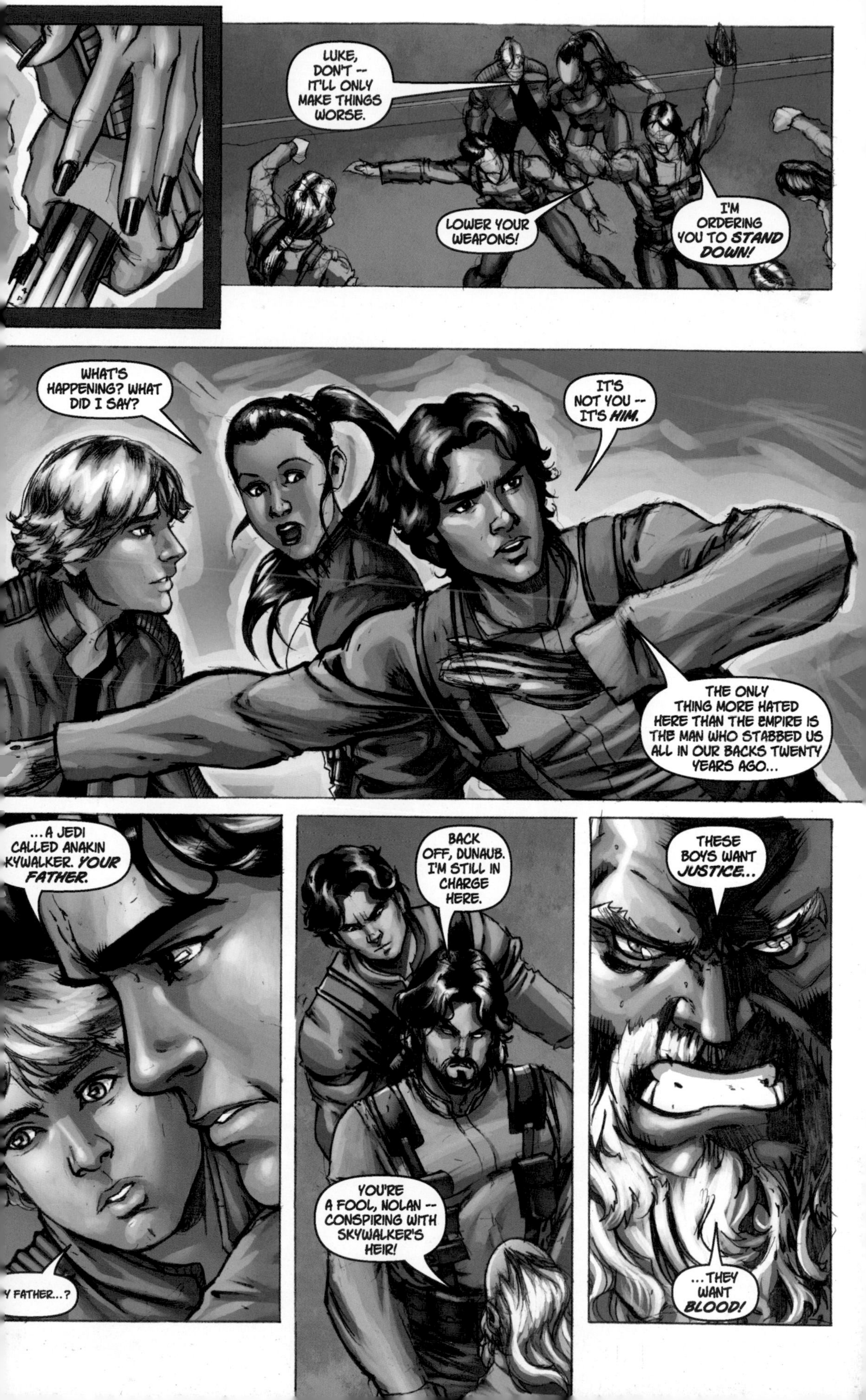
LUKE, DON'T -- IT'LL ONLY MAKE THINGS WORSE.
LOWER YOUR WEAPONS!
I'M ORDERING YOU TO STAND DOWN!
WHAT'S HAPPENING? WHAT DID I SAY?
IT'S NOT YOU -- IT'S HIM.
THE ONLY THING MORE HATED HERE THAN THE EMPIRE IS THE MAN WHO STABBED US ALL IN OUR BACKS TWENTY YEARS AGO...
...A JEDI CALLED ANAKIN SKYWALKER. YOUR FATHER.
FATHER...?
BACK OFF, DUNAUB. I'M STILL IN CHARGE HERE.
YOU'RE A FOOL, NOLAN -- CONSPIRING WITH SKYWALKER'S HEIR!
THESE BOYS WANT JUSTICE...
...THEY WANT BLOOD!

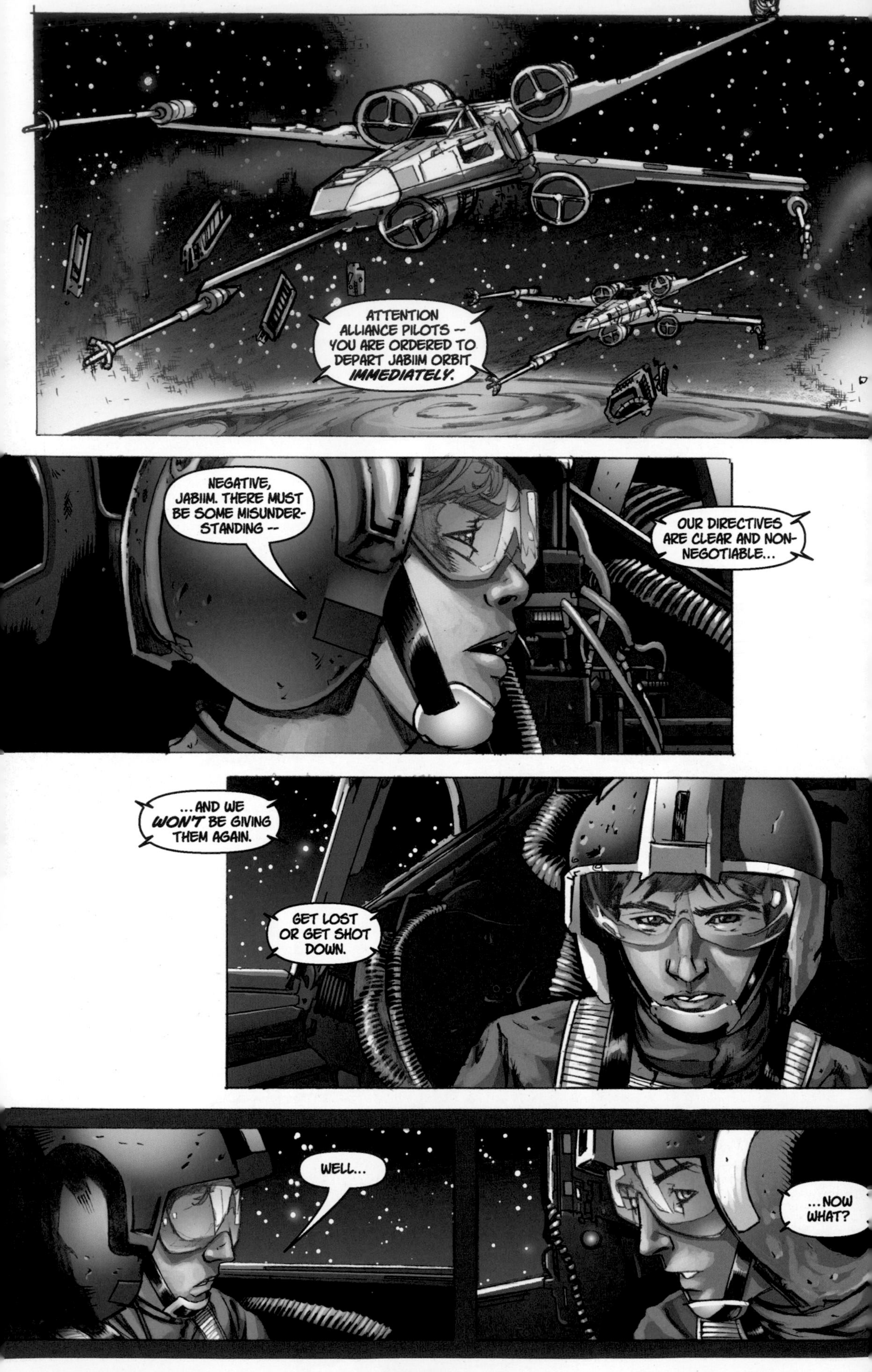
ATTENTION ALLIANCE PILOTS -- YOU ARE ORDERED TO DEPART JABIIM ORBIT IMMEDIATELY.
NEGATIVE, JABIIM. THERE MUST BE SOME MISUNDER-STANDING --
OUR DIRECTIVES ARE CLEAR AND NON-NEGOTIABLE...
...AND WE WON'T BE GIVING THEM AGAIN.
GET LOST OR GET SHOT DOWN.
WELL...
...NOW WHAT?

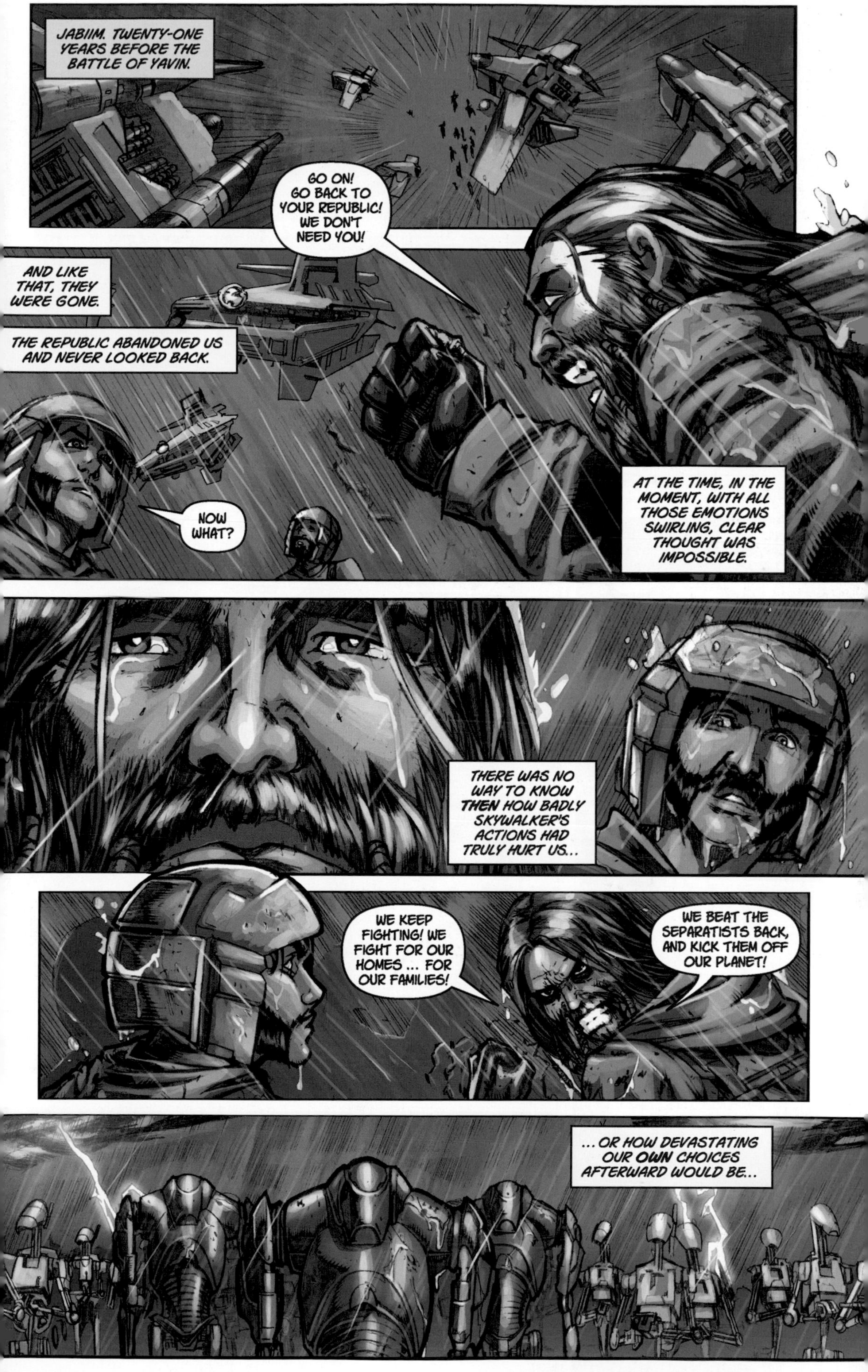
JABIIM. TWENTY-ONE YEARS BEFORE THE BATTLE OF YAVIN.
GO ON! GO BACK TO YOUR REPUBLIC! WE DON'T NEED YOU!
AND LIKE THAT, THEY WERE GONE.
THE REPUBLIC ABANDONED US AND NEVER LOOKED BACK.
NOW WHAT?
AT THE TIME, IN THE MOMENT, WITH ALL THOSE EMOTIONS SWIRLING, CLEAR THOUGHT WAS IMPOSSIBLE.
THERE WAS NO WAY TO KNOW THEN HOW BADLY SKYWALKER'S ACTIONS HAD TRULY HURT US...
WE KEEP FIGHTING! WE FIGHT FOR OUR HOMES ... FOR OUR FAMILIES!
WE BEAT THE SEPARATISTS BACK, AND KICK THEM OFF OUR PLANET!
... OR HOW DEVASTATING OUR OWN CHOICES AFTERWARD WOULD BE...

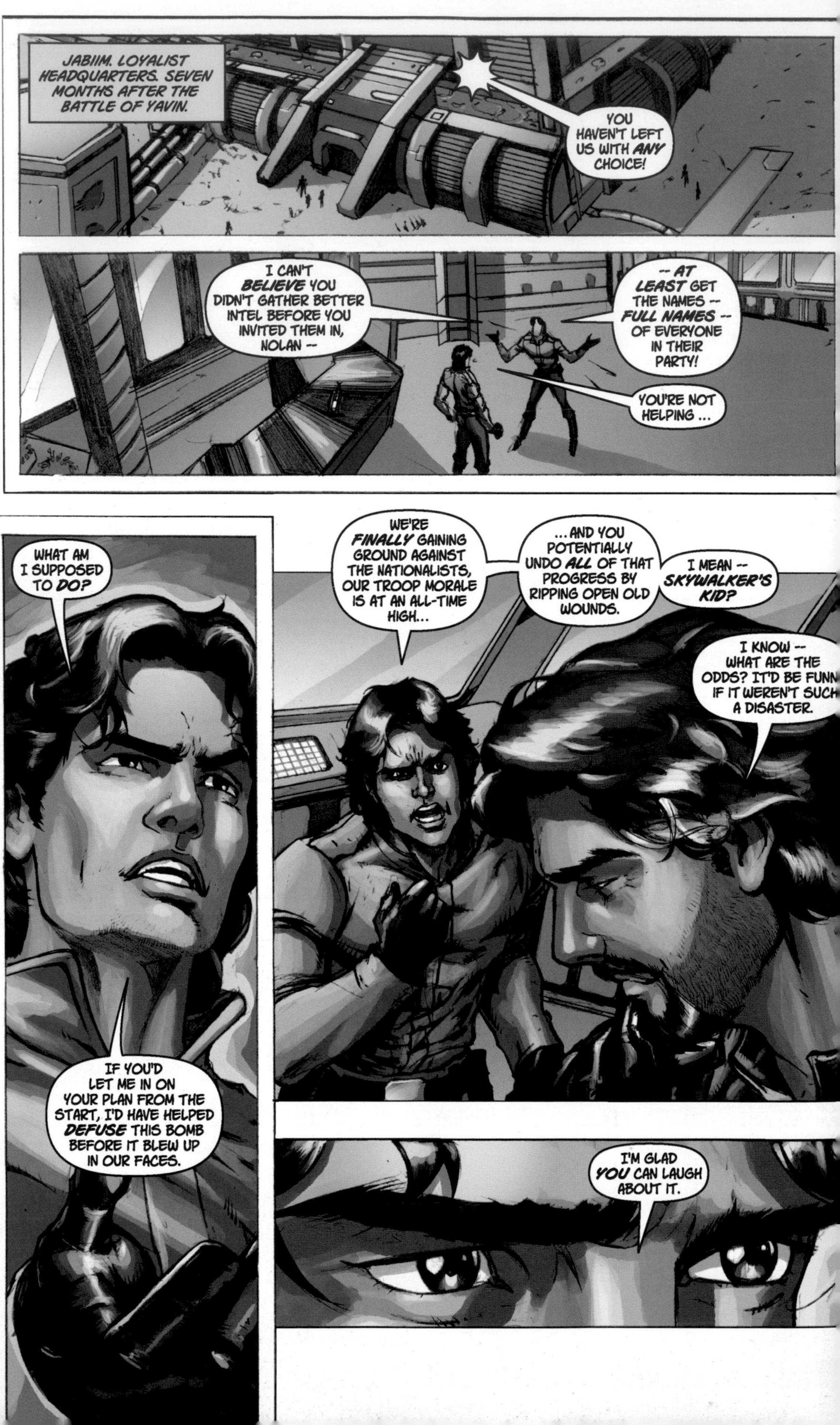
JABIIM. LOYALIST HEADQUARTERS. SEVEN MONTHS AFTER THE BATTLE OF YAVIN.
YOU HAVEN'T LEFT US WITH ANY CHOICE!
I CAN'T BELIEVE YOU DIDN'T GATHER BETTER INTEL BEFORE YOU INVITED THEM IN, NOLAN --
-- AT LEAST GET THE NAMES -- FULL NAMES -- OF EVERYONE IN THEIR PARTY!
YOU'RE NOT HELPING ...
WHAT AM I SUPPOSED TO DO?
IF YOU'D LET ME IN ON YOUR PLAN FROM THE START, I'D HAVE HELPED DEFUSE THIS BOMB BEFORE IT BLEW UP IN OUR FACES.
WE'RE FINALLY GAINING GROUND AGAINST THE NATIONALISTS, OUR TROOP MORALE IS AT AN ALL-TIME HIGH...
...AND YOU POTENTIALLY UNDO ALL OF THAT PROGRESS BY RIPPING OPEN OLD WOUNDS.
I MEAN -- SKYWALKER'S KID?
I KNOW -- WHAT ARE THE ODDS? IT'D BE FUNN IF IT WEREN'T SUCH A DISASTER.
I'M GLAD YOU CAN LAUGH ABOUT IT.

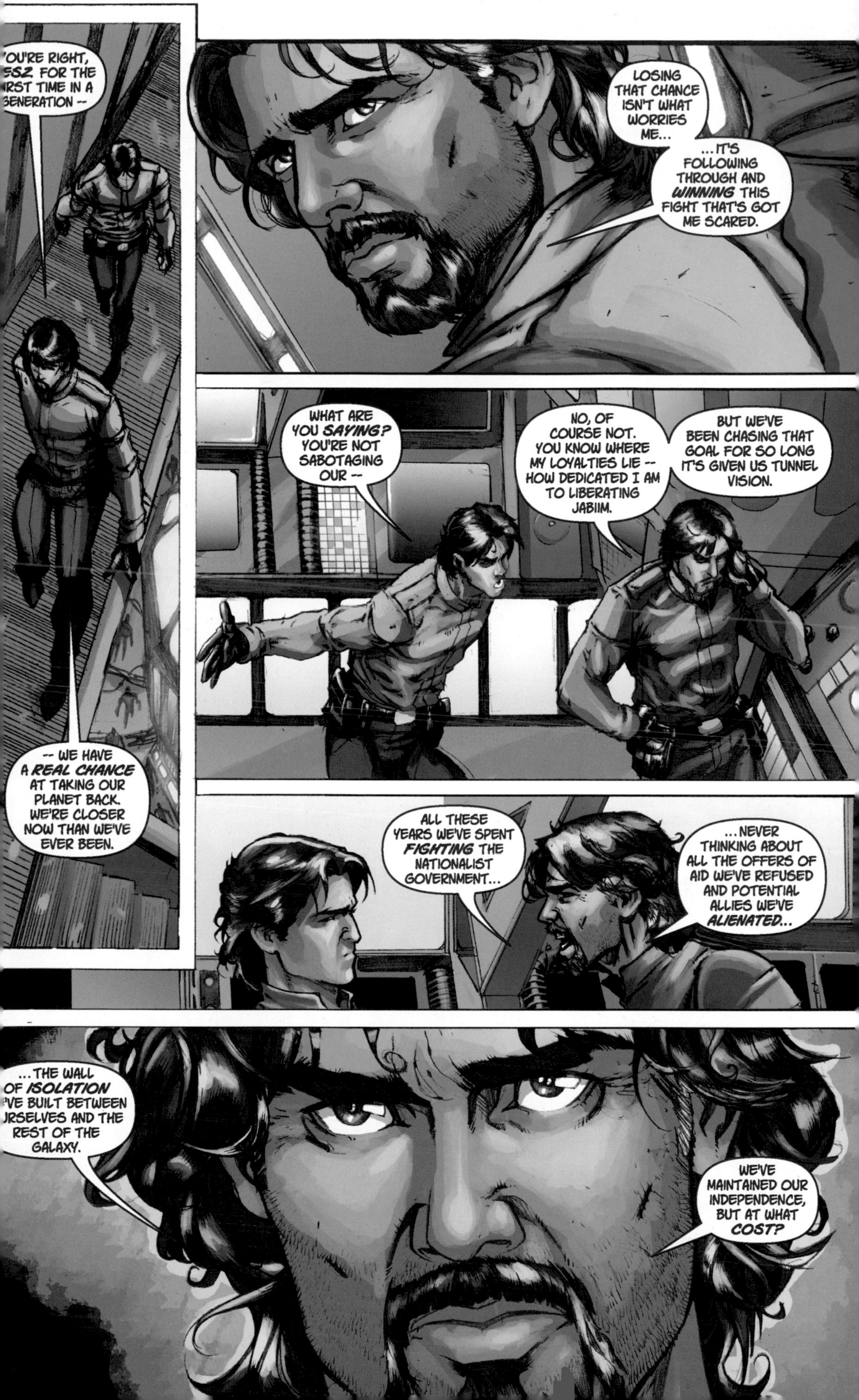
OU'RE RIGHT, ESZ. FOR THE IRST TIME IN A ENERATION --
LOSING THAT CHANCE ISN'T WHAT WORRIES ME...
...IT'S FOLLOWING THROUGH AND *WINNING* THIS FIGHT THAT'S GOT ME SCARED.
-- WE HAVE A *REAL CHANCE* AT TAKING OUR PLANET BACK. WE'RE CLOSER NOW THAN WE'VE EVER BEEN.
WHAT ARE YOU *SAYING?* YOU'RE NOT SABOTAGING OUR --
NO, OF COURSE NOT. YOU KNOW WHERE MY LOYALTIES LIE -- HOW DEDICATED I AM TO LIBERATING JABIIM.
BUT WE'VE BEEN CHASING THAT GOAL FOR SO LONG IT'S GIVEN US TUNNEL VISION.
ALL THESE YEARS WE'VE SPENT *FIGHTING* THE NATIONALIST GOVERNMENT...
...NEVER THINKING ABOUT ALL THE OFFERS OF AID WE'VE REFUSED AND POTENTIAL ALLIES WE'VE *ALIENATED*...
...THE WALL OF *ISOLATION* 'VE BUILT BETWEEN URSELVES AND THE REST OF THE GALAXY.
WE'VE MAINTAINED OUR INDEPENDENCE, BUT AT WHAT *COST?*

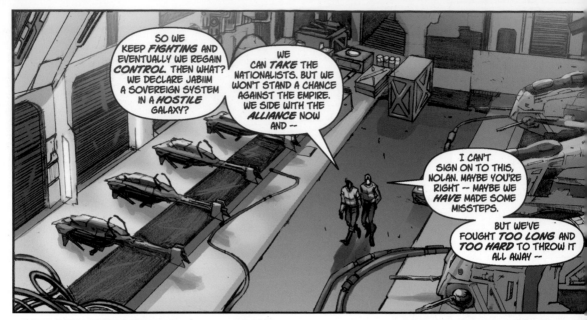

SO WE KEEP *FIGHTING* AND EVENTUALLY WE REGAIN *CONTROL.* THEN WHAT? WE DECLARE JABIIM A *SOVEREIGN* SYSTEM IN A *HOSTILE* GALAXY?

WE CAN *TAKE* THE NATIONALISTS. BUT WE WON'T STAND A CHANCE AGAINST THE EMPIRE. WE SIDE WITH THE *ALLIANCE* NOW AND --

I CAN'T SIGN ON TO THIS, NOLAN. MAYBE YOU'RE RIGHT -- MAYBE WE *HAVE* MADE SOME MISSTEPS.

BUT WE'VE FOUGHT *TOO LONG* AND *TOO HARD* TO THROW IT ALL AWAY --

-- ON THE *HOPE* THAT THINGS WILL BE *DIFFERENT* WITH THE ALLIANCE THAN THEY WERE WITH THE REPUBLIC.

YOU OF ALL PEOPLE SHOULD KNOW THAT.

THAT'S WHY YOU SHOULD *TRUST* ME.

I'VE NEVER LED US ASTRAY, AND I'M NOT ABOUT TO. BUT IF WE WANT *ANY* SHOT AT A FUTURE, WE HAVE TO *SEIZE* THIS *OPPORTUNITY* THAT SENATOR ORGANA IS GIVING US.

YOU'RE RIGHT.

THE REBELS *ARE* GIVING US AN OPPORTUNITY.

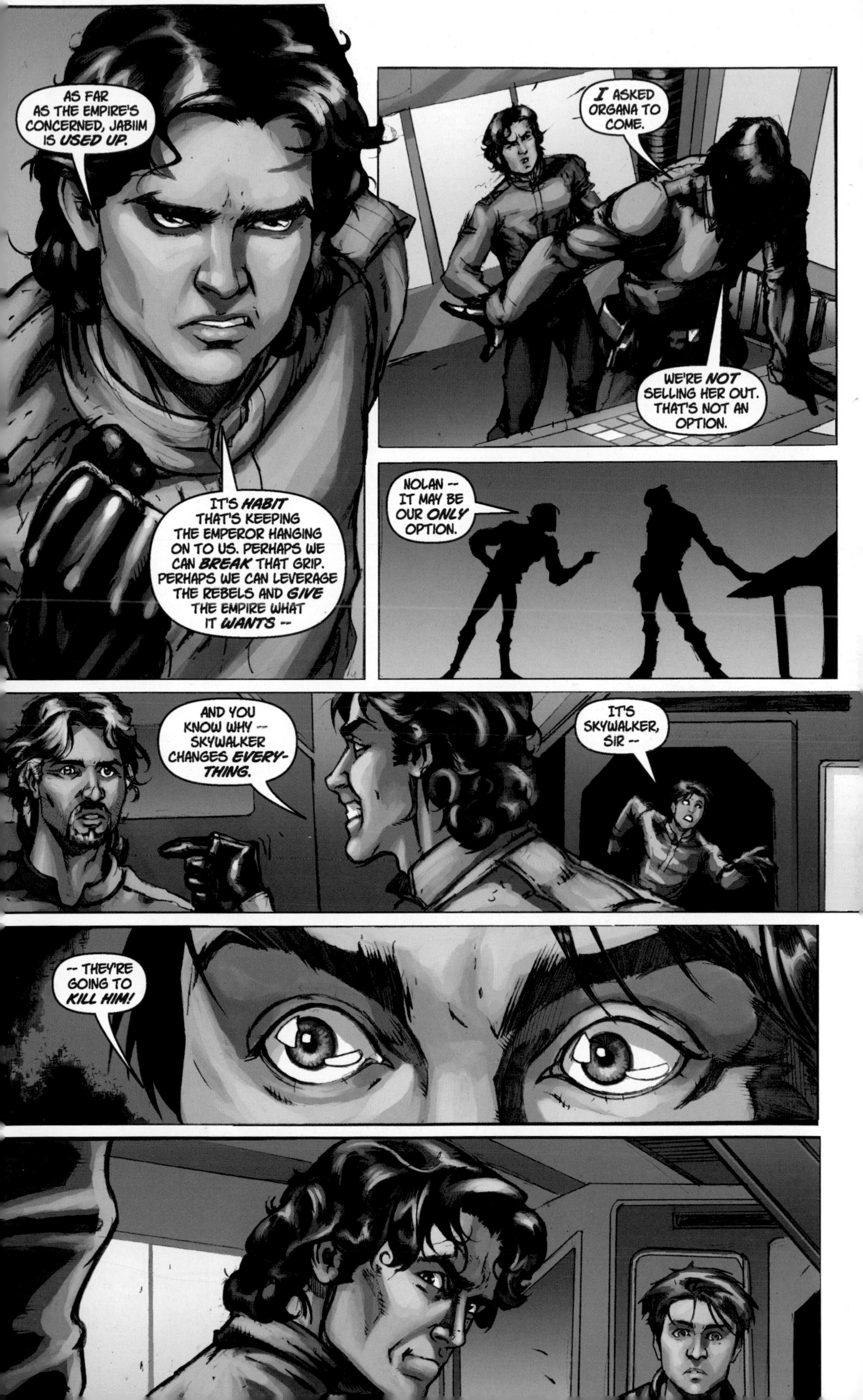
AS FAR AS THE EMPIRE'S CONCERNED, JABIIM IS USED UP.
IT'S HABIT THAT'S KEEPING THE EMPEROR HANGING ON TO US. PERHAPS WE CAN BREAK THAT GRIP. PERHAPS WE CAN LEVERAGE THE REBELS AND GIVE THE EMPIRE WHAT IT WANTS --
I ASKED ORGANA TO COME.
WE'RE NOT SELLING HER OUT. THAT'S NOT AN OPTION.
NOLAN -- IT MAY BE OUR ONLY OPTION.
AND YOU KNOW WHY -- SKYWALKER CHANGES EVERY-THING.
IT'S SKYWALKER, SIR --
-- THEY'RE GOING TO KILL HIM!

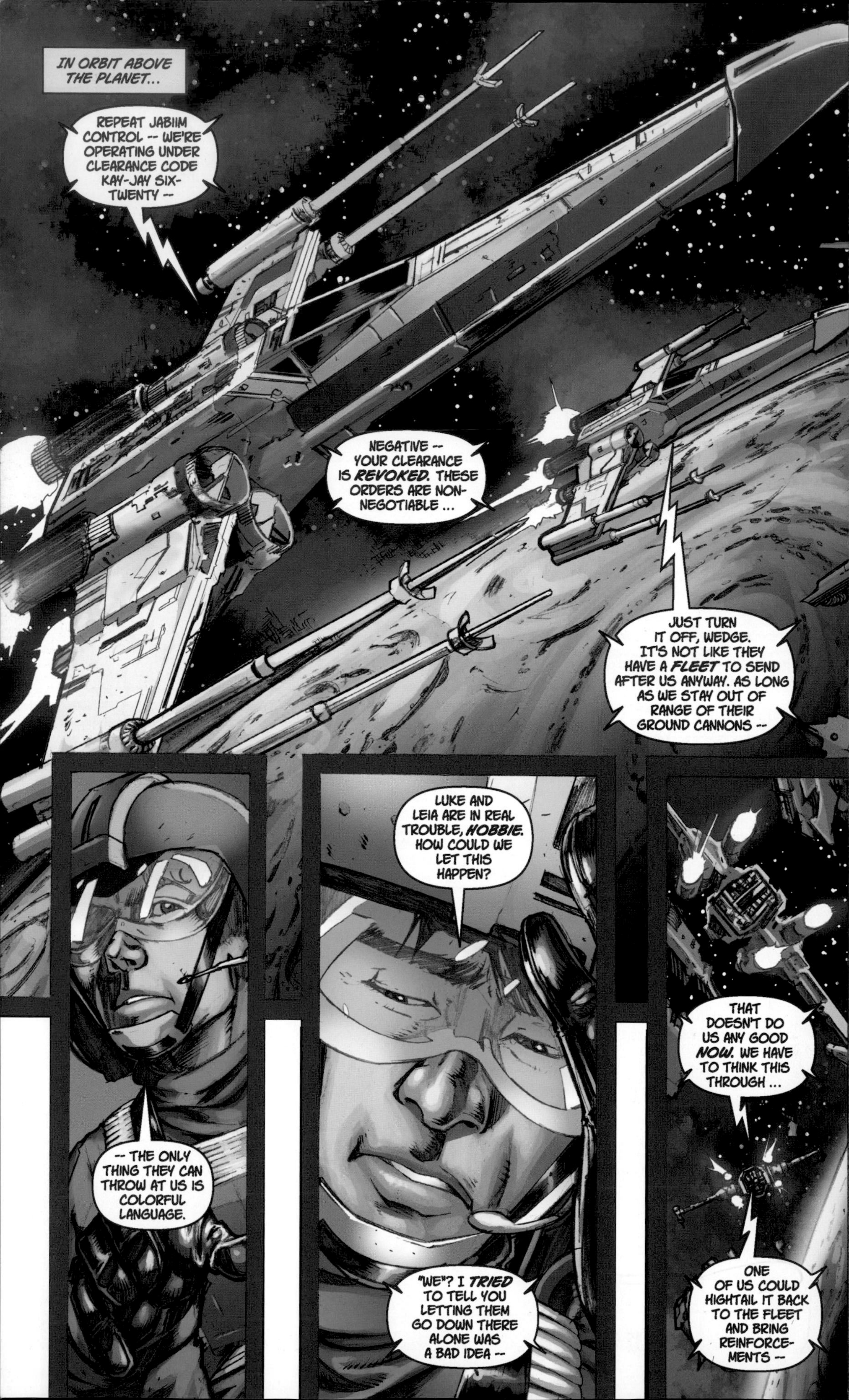

IN ORBIT ABOVE THE PLANET...
REPEAT JABIIM CONTROL -- WE'RE OPERATING UNDER CLEARANCE CODE KAY-JAY SIX-TWENTY --
NEGATIVE -- YOUR CLEARANCE IS REVOKED. THESE ORDERS ARE NON-NEGOTIABLE ...
JUST TURN IT OFF, WEDGE. IT'S NOT LIKE THEY HAVE A FLEET TO SEND AFTER US ANYWAY. AS LONG AS WE STAY OUT OF RANGE OF THEIR GROUND CANNONS --
-- THE ONLY THING THEY CAN THROW AT US IS COLORFUL LANGUAGE.
LUKE AND LEIA ARE IN REAL TROUBLE, HOBBIE. HOW COULD WE LET THIS HAPPEN?
"WE"? I TRIED TO TELL YOU LETTING THEM GO DOWN THERE ALONE WAS A BAD IDEA --
THAT DOESN'T DO US ANY GOOD NOW. WE HAVE TO THINK THIS THROUGH ...
ONE OF US COULD HIGHTAIL IT BACK TO THE FLEET AND BRING REINFORCE-MENTS --

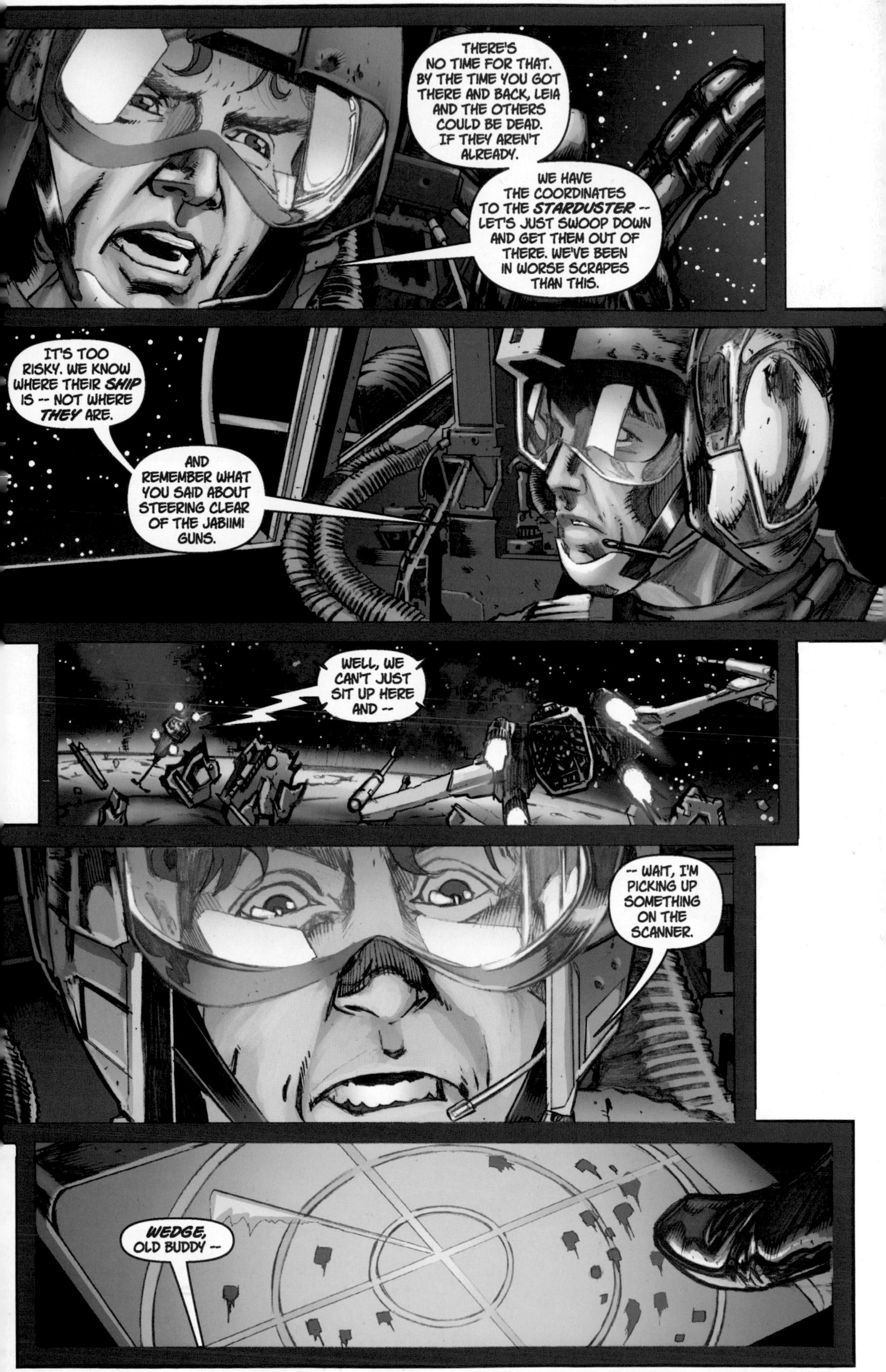
THERE'S NO TIME FOR THAT. BY THE TIME YOU GOT THERE AND BACK, LEIA AND THE OTHERS COULD BE DEAD. IF THEY AREN'T ALREADY.
WE HAVE THE COORDINATES TO THE *STARDUSTER* -- LET'S JUST SWOOP DOWN AND GET THEM OUT OF THERE. WE'VE BEEN IN WORSE SCRAPES THAN THIS.
IT'S TOO RISKY. WE KNOW WHERE THEIR *SHIP* IS -- NOT WHERE *THEY* ARE.
AND REMEMBER WHAT YOU SAID ABOUT STEERING CLEAR OF THE JABIIMI GUNS.
WELL, WE CAN'T JUST SIT UP HERE AND --
-- WAIT, I'M PICKING UP SOMETHING ON THE SCANNER.
WEDGE, OLD BUDDY --

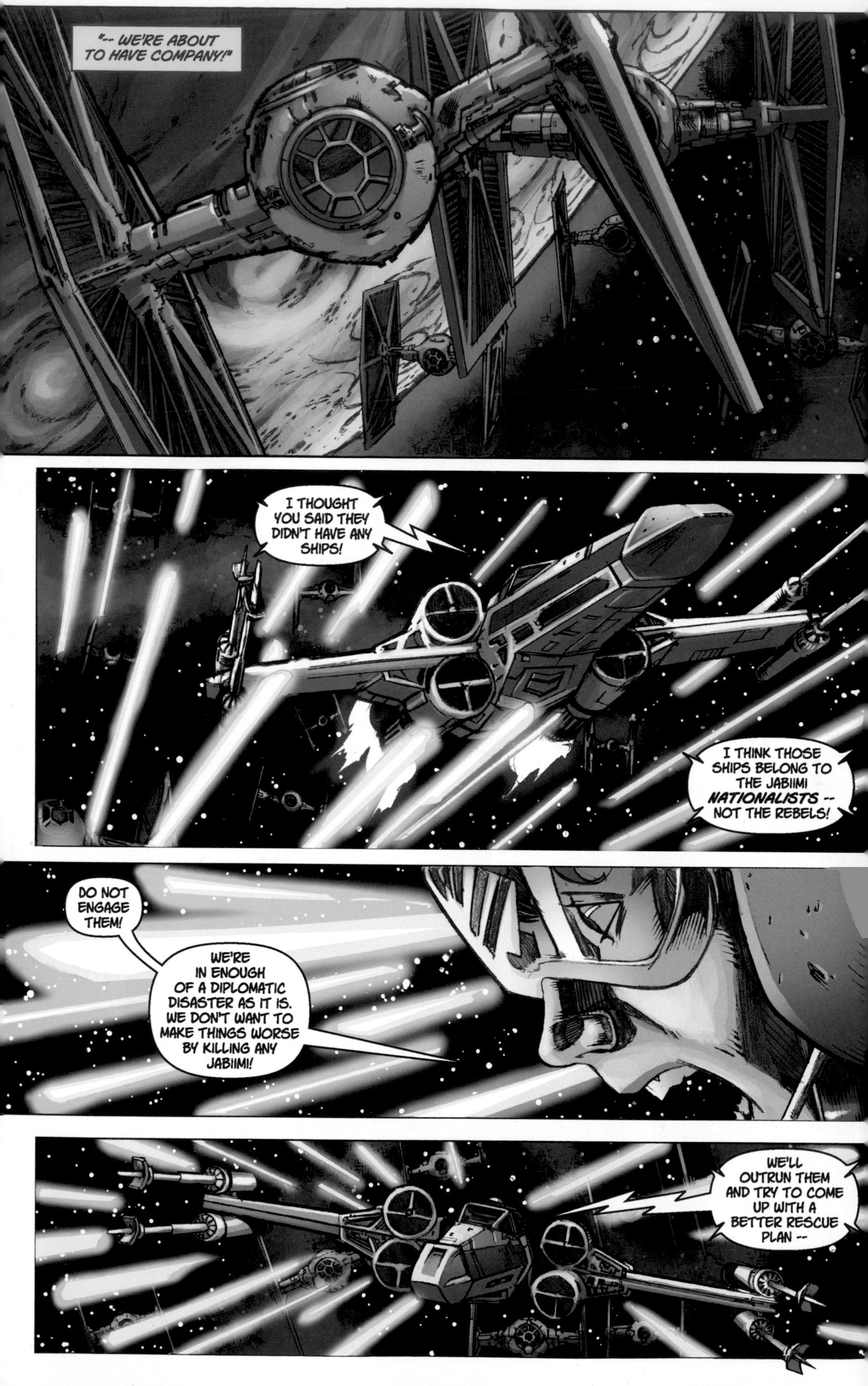
"-- WE'RE ABOUT TO HAVE COMPANY!"
I THOUGHT YOU SAID THEY DIDN'T HAVE ANY SHIPS!
I THINK THOSE SHIPS BELONG TO THE JABIIMI *NATIONALISTS* -- NOT THE REBELS!
DO NOT ENGAGE THEM!
WE'RE IN ENOUGH OF A DIPLOMATIC DISASTER AS IT IS. WE DON'T WANT TO MAKE THINGS WORSE BY KILLING ANY JABIIMI!
WE'LL OUTRUN THEM AND TRY TO COME UP WITH A BETTER RESCUE PLAN --

"ND HOPE THAT
FIA AND THE
ERS CAN HOLD
T 'TIL WE DO."

-- THE WAY I SEE IT, YOU *KEEP* TALKING AND IT'S ONLY GOING TO GET YOU IN *DEEPER*.

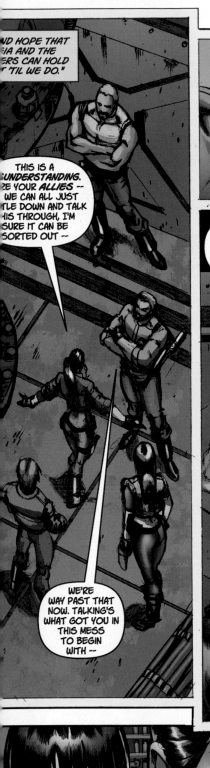

THIS IS A *MISUNDERSTANDING. *RE YOUR *ALLIES* -- WE CAN ALL JUST *LE DOWN AND TALK HIS THROUGH, I'M SURE IT CAN BE SORTED OUT --

WE'RE WAY PAST THAT NOW. TALKING'S WHAT GOT YOU IN THIS MESS TO BEGIN WITH --

YOU JUST *SIT TIGHT* UNTIL WE FIGURE OUT WHAT TO DO WITH YOU. *LUSCEN* HERE WILL KEEP YOU COMPANY.

DON'T EVEN *THINK* OF TRYING ANYTHING FUNNY WITH HIM --

-- I WATCHED HIM TAKE DOWN A SQUAD OF IMPERIAL COMMANDOS WITH NOTHING MORE THAN THE BUTT OF AN EMPTY BLASTER RIFLE.

TRUST ME -- HE WON'T BREAK A *SWEAT* WITH YOU.

WASN'T EVEN MY BLASTER.

YOU CAN'T KEEP US LOCKED UP FOREVER.

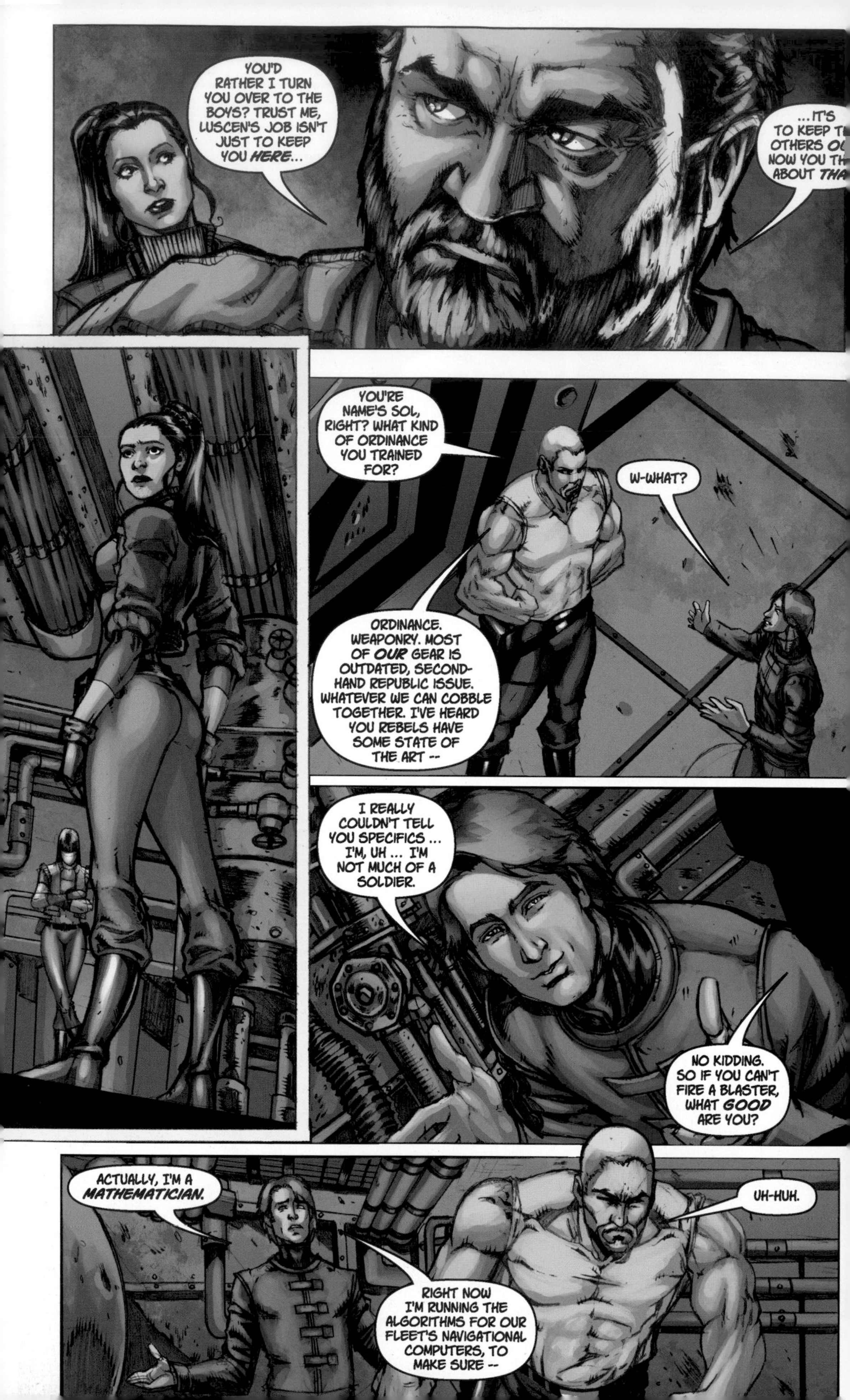
YOU'D RATHER I TURN YOU OVER TO THE BOYS? TRUST ME, LUSCEN'S JOB ISN'T JUST TO KEEP YOU HERE...
...IT'S TO KEEP T OTHERS O NOW YOU TH ABOUT THA
YOU'RE NAME'S SOL, RIGHT? WHAT KIND OF ORDINANCE YOU TRAINED FOR?
W-WHAT?
ORDINANCE. WEAPONRY. MOST OF OUR GEAR IS OUTDATED, SECOND-HAND REPUBLIC ISSUE. WHATEVER WE CAN COBBLE TOGETHER. I'VE HEARD YOU REBELS HAVE SOME STATE OF THE ART --
I REALLY COULDN'T TELL YOU SPECIFICS ... I'M, UH ... I'M NOT MUCH OF A SOLDIER.
NO KIDDING. SO IF YOU CAN'T FIRE A BLASTER, WHAT GOOD ARE YOU?
ACTUALLY, I'M A MATHEMATICIAN.
UH-HUH.
RIGHT NOW I'M RUNNING THE ALGORITHMS FOR OUR FLEET'S NAVIGATIONAL COMPUTERS, TO MAKE SURE --

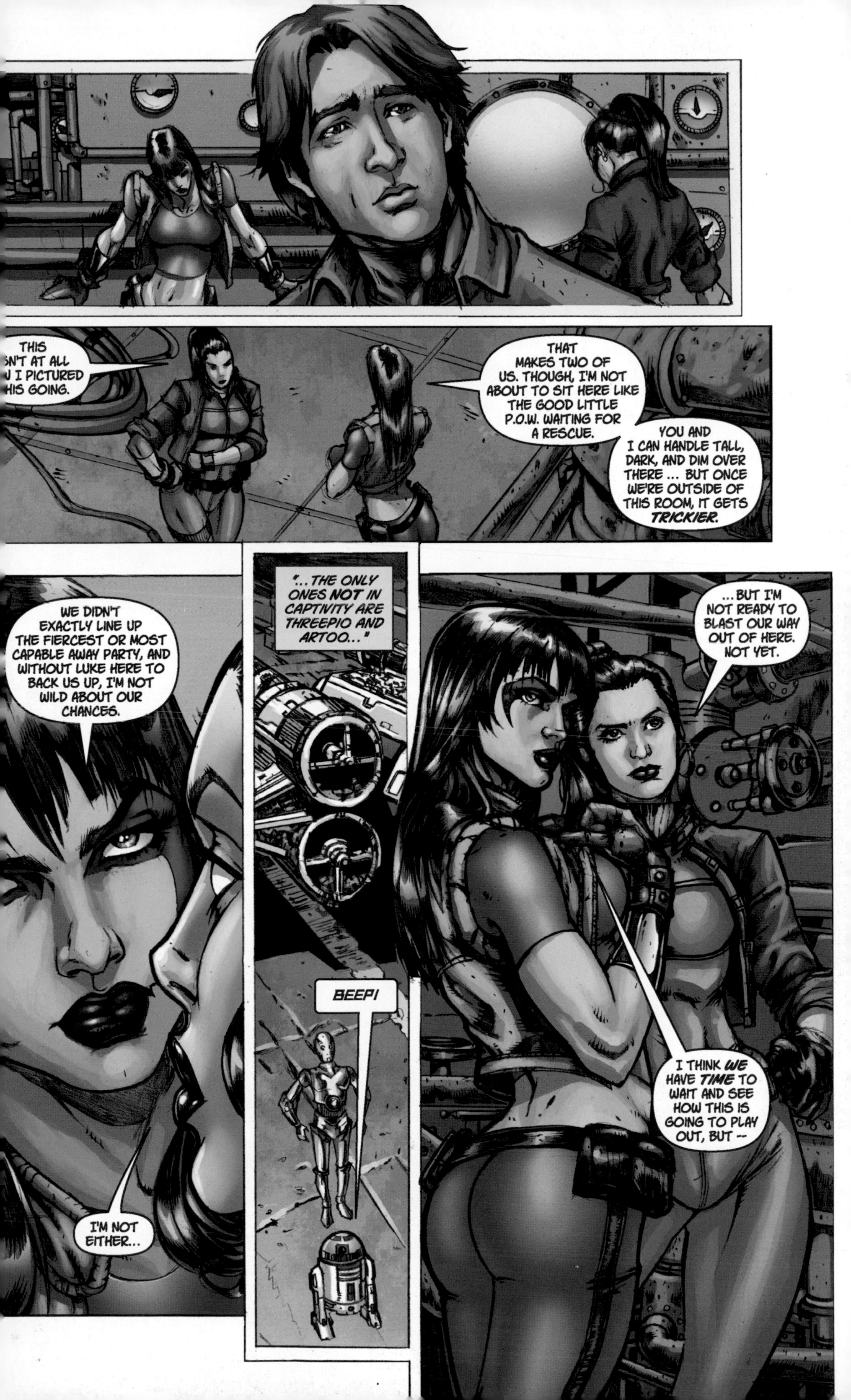
THIS ...SN'T AT ALL ...U I PICTURED ...THIS GOING.
THAT MAKES TWO OF US. THOUGH, I'M NOT ABOUT TO SIT HERE LIKE THE GOOD LITTLE P.O.W. WAITING FOR A RESCUE.
YOU AND I CAN HANDLE TALL, DARK, AND DIM OVER THERE ... BUT ONCE WE'RE OUTSIDE OF THIS ROOM, IT GETS TRICKIER.
WE DIDN'T EXACTLY LINE UP THE FIERCEST OR MOST CAPABLE AWAY PARTY, AND WITHOUT LUKE HERE TO BACK US UP, I'M NOT WILD ABOUT OUR CHANCES.
I'M NOT EITHER...
"...THE ONLY ONES NOT IN CAPTIVITY ARE THREEPIO AND ARTOO..."
BEEP!
...BUT I'M NOT READY TO BLAST OUR WAY OUT OF HERE. NOT YET.
I THINK WE HAVE TIME TO WAIT AND SEE HOW THIS IS GOING TO PLAY OUT, BUT --

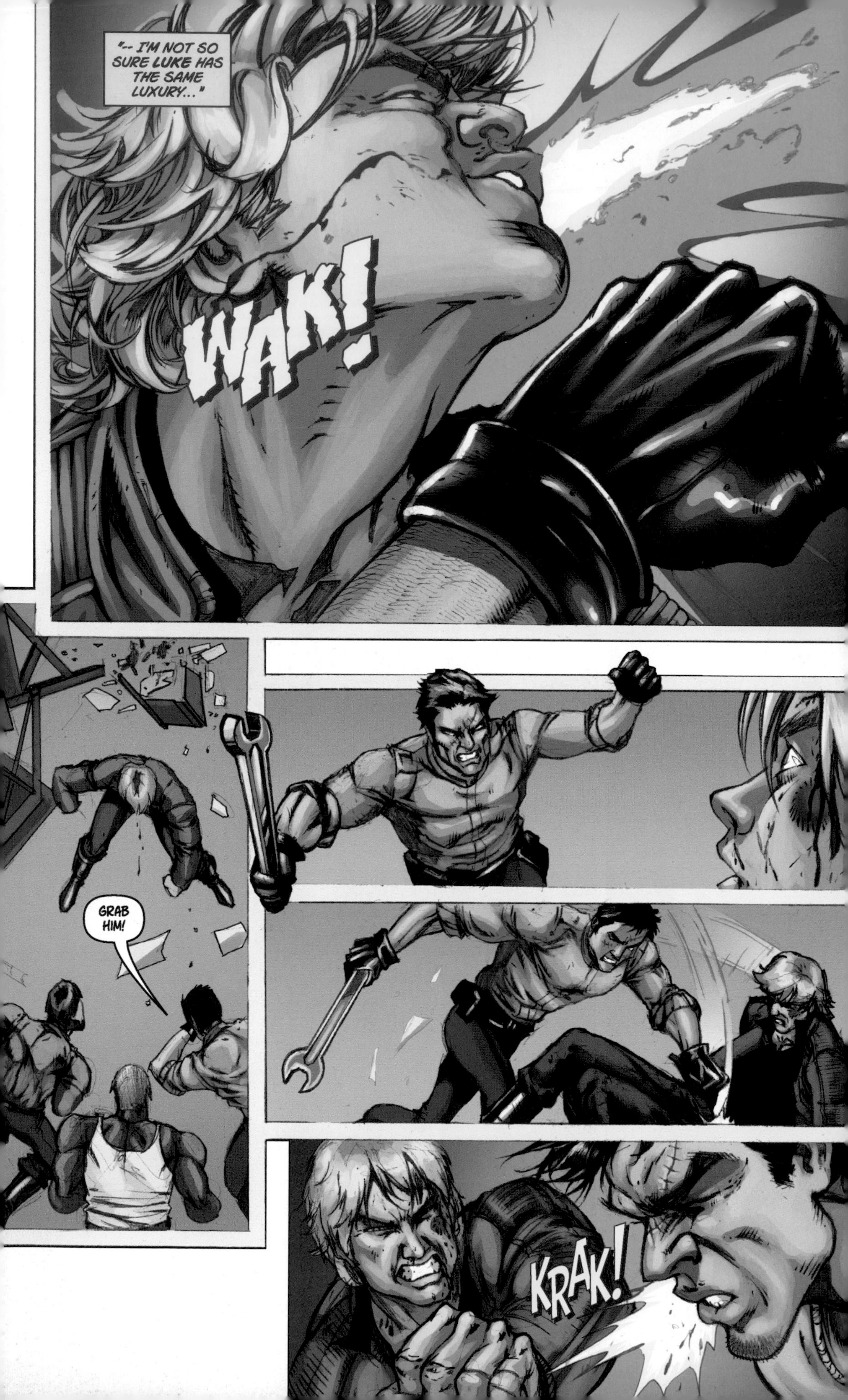
"-- I'M NOT SO SURE LUKE HAS THE SAME LUXURY..."
WAK!
GRAB HIM!
KRAK!

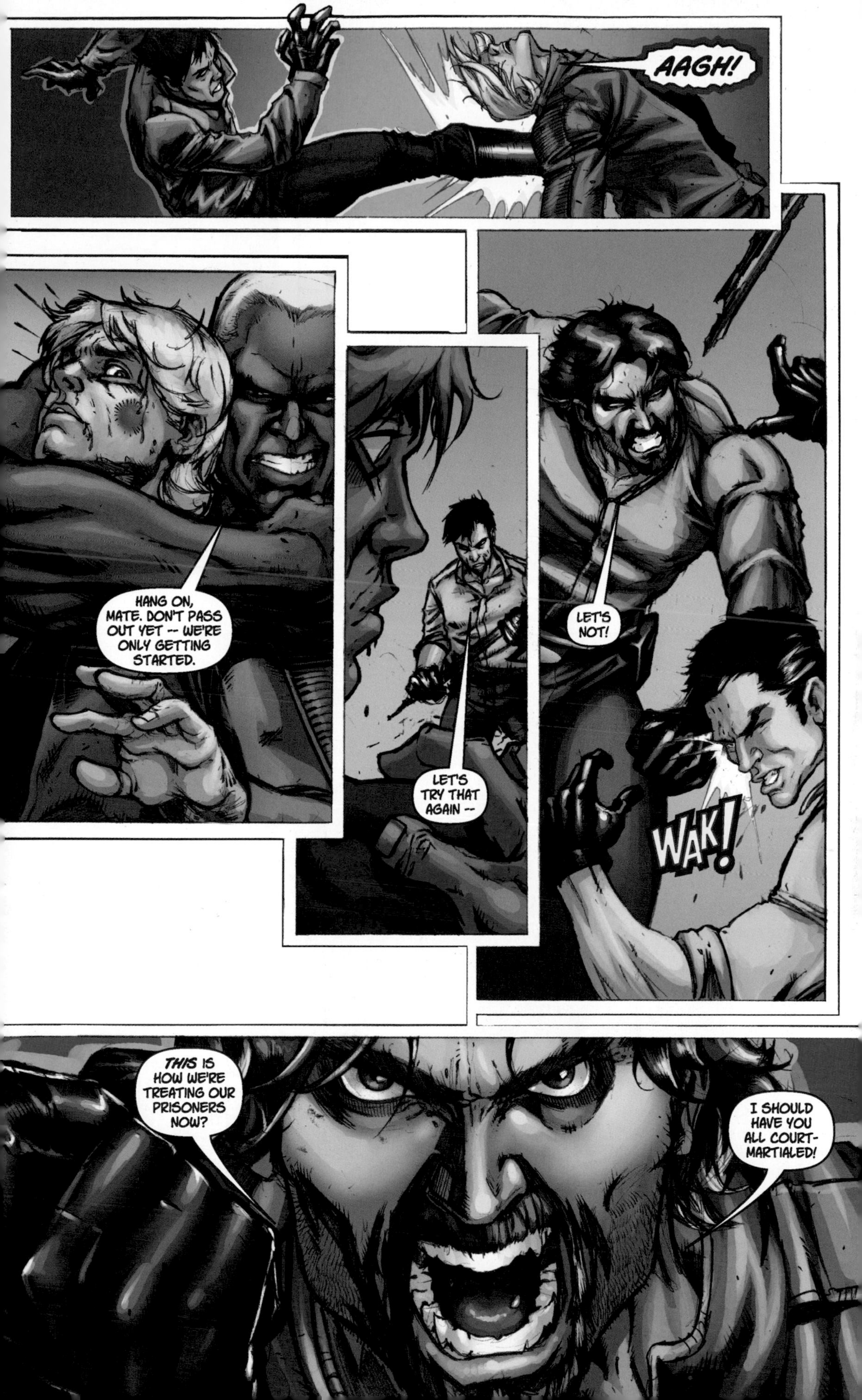
AAGH!
HANG ON, MATE. DON'T PASS OUT YET -- WE'RE ONLY GETTING STARTED.
LET'S TRY THAT AGAIN --
LET'S NOT!
WAK!
THIS IS HOW WE'RE TREATING OUR PRISONERS NOW?
I SHOULD HAVE YOU ALL COURT-MARTIALED!

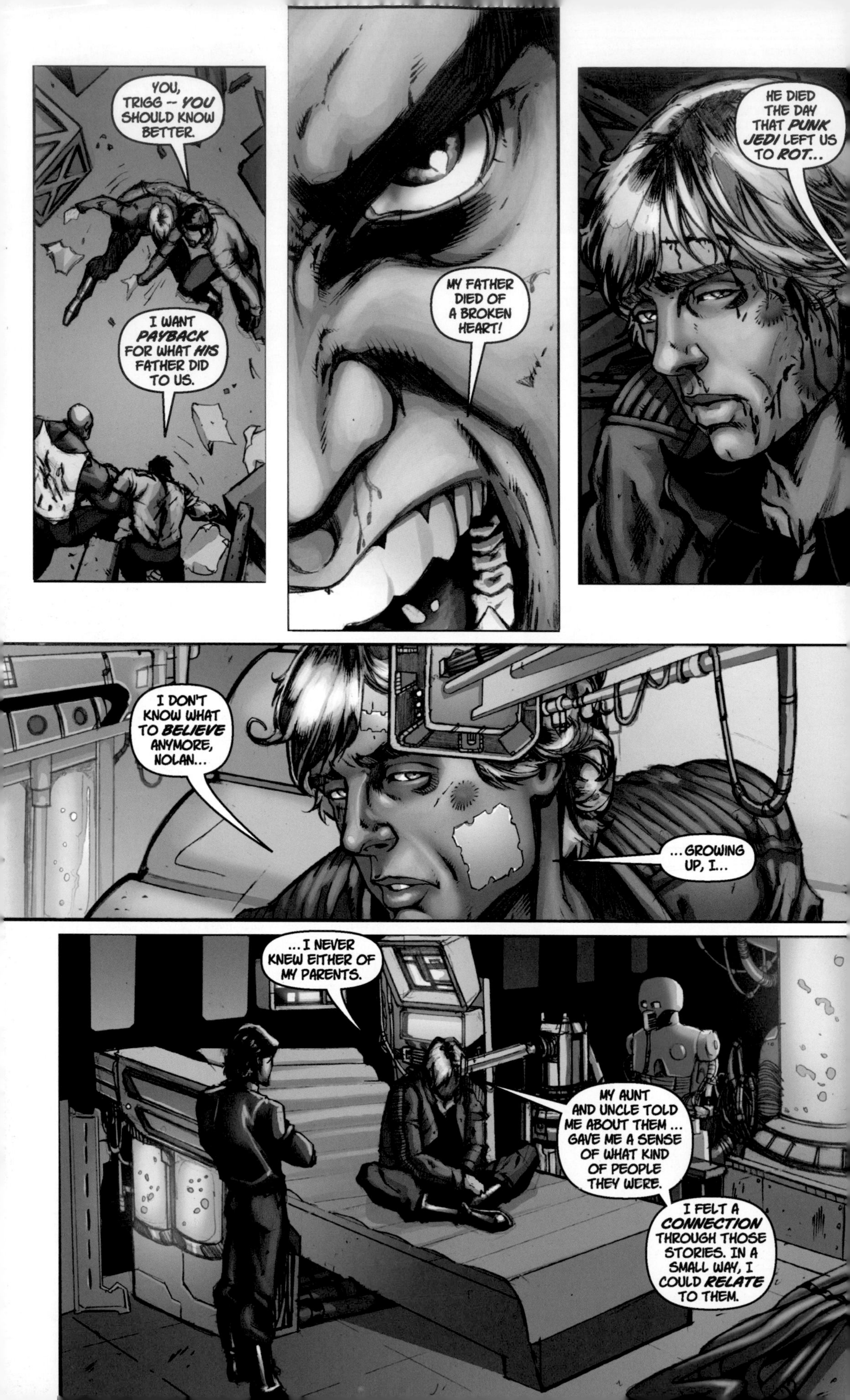
YOU, TRIGG -- YOU SHOULD KNOW BETTER.
I WANT PAYBACK FOR WHAT HIS FATHER DID TO US.
MY FATHER DIED OF A BROKEN HEART!
HE DIED THE DAY THAT PUNK JEDI LEFT US TO ROT...
I DON'T KNOW WHAT TO BELIEVE ANYMORE, NOLAN...
...GROWING UP, I...
...I NEVER KNEW EITHER OF MY PARENTS.
MY AUNT AND UNCLE TOLD ME ABOUT THEM ... GAVE ME A SENSE OF WHAT KIND OF PEOPLE THEY WERE.
I FELT A CONNECTION THROUGH THOSE STORIES. IN A SMALL WAY, I COULD RELATE TO THEM.

THEN, A FEW MONTHS AGO, I FOUND OUT THAT MOST OF THOSE STORIES WEREN'T EVEN TRUE. THAT MY FATHER WAS A *GREATER* MAN THAN I'D EVER IMAGINED ...

... AND, IN THEIR OWN STRANGE WAY, THAT MY AUNT AND UNCLE WERE *PROTECTING* ME FROM HIS LEGACY. OR FROM THE PRESSURE OF LIVING UP TO IT ... I GUESS I'LL NEVER KNOW.

BUT NOW ... WITH ALL I'VE BEEN TOLD SINCE I'VE BEEN HERE ...

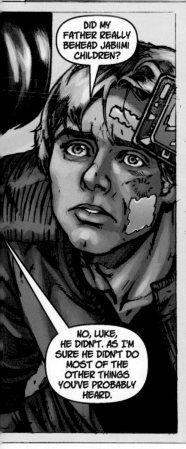

DID MY FATHER REALLY BEHEAD JABIIMI CHILDREN?

NO, LUKE, HE DIDN'T. AS I'M SURE HE DIDN'T DO MOST OF THE OTHER THINGS YOU'VE PROBABLY HEARD.

UNFORTUNATELY, THE YEARS HAVEN'T BEEN KIND TO ANAKIN'S LEGEND. STORIES HAVE BEEN PASSED DOWN, THEIR DETAILS DISTORTED AND EXAGGERATED WITH EACH TELLING.

YOUR FATHER WAS MANY THINGS, NOT ALL OF THEM FLATTERING. HIS SINS LEFT A LASTING SCAR ON MY PEOPLE...

...BUT HE WASN'T A MONSTER.

IT'S IRONIC. DESPITE THE TURMOIL AND ANGUISH THAT ANAKIN LEFT BEHIND, HIS *BETRAYAL* WAS WHAT UNITED THE JABIIMI AND HELPED THEM FIGHT ON.

OUR HATRED OF HIM FUELED OUR DESIRE FOR INDEPENDENCE, BUT THAT EVENTUALLY GREW INTO A DISTRUST OF *ALL* OUTSIDERS.

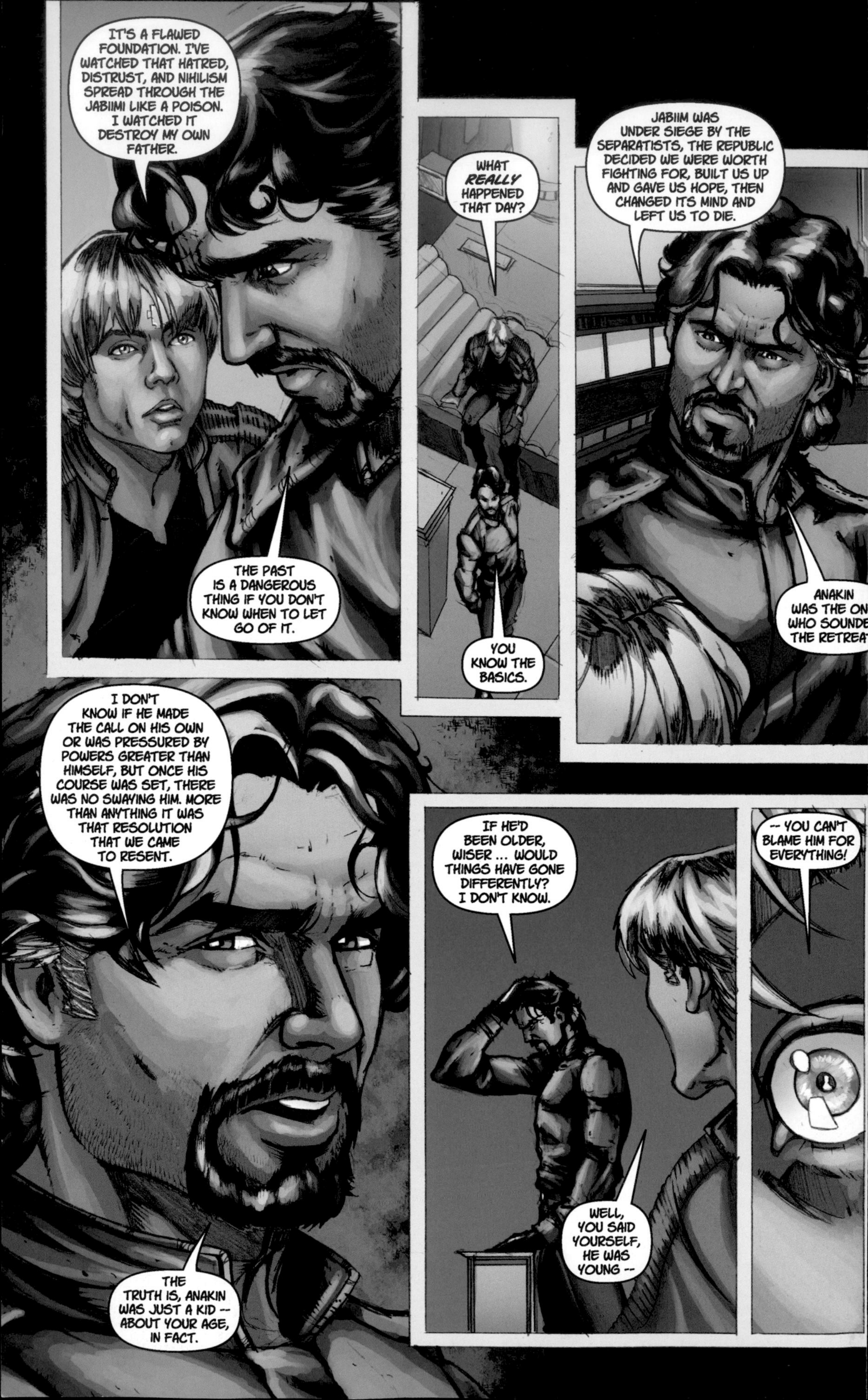
IT'S A FLAWED FOUNDATION. I'VE WATCHED THAT HATRED, DISTRUST, AND NIHILISM SPREAD THROUGH THE JABIIMI LIKE A POISON. I WATCHED IT DESTROY MY OWN FATHER.
THE PAST IS A DANGEROUS THING IF YOU DON'T KNOW WHEN TO LET GO OF IT.
WHAT *REALLY* HAPPENED THAT DAY?
YOU KNOW THE BASICS.
JABIIM WAS UNDER SIEGE BY THE SEPARATISTS, THE REPUBLIC DECIDED WE WERE WORTH FIGHTING FOR, BUILT US UP AND GAVE US HOPE, THEN CHANGED ITS MIND AND LEFT US TO DIE.
ANAKIN WAS THE ON WHO SOUNDE THE RETREA
I DON'T KNOW IF HE MADE THE CALL ON HIS OWN OR WAS PRESSURED BY POWERS GREATER THAN HIMSELF, BUT ONCE HIS COURSE WAS SET, THERE WAS NO SWAYING HIM. MORE THAN ANYTHING IT WAS THAT RESOLUTION THAT WE CAME TO RESENT.
THE TRUTH IS, ANAKIN WAS JUST A KID -- ABOUT YOUR AGE, IN FACT.
IF HE'D BEEN OLDER, WISER ... WOULD THINGS HAVE GONE DIFFERENTLY? I DON'T KNOW.
WELL, YOU SAID YOURSELF, HE WAS YOUNG --
-- YOU CAN'T BLAME HIM FOR EVERYTHING!

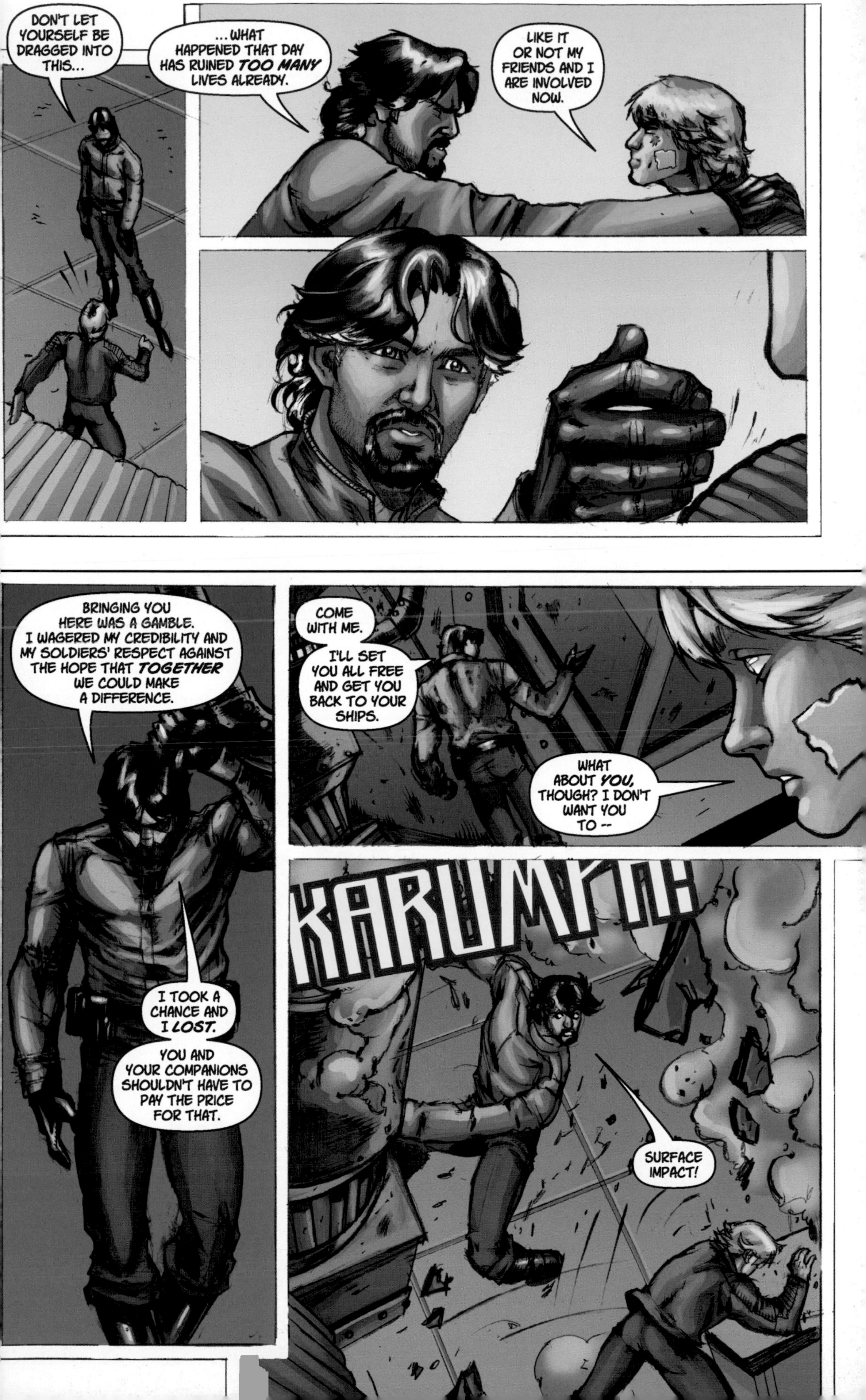
DON'T LET YOURSELF BE DRAGGED INTO THIS...
...WHAT HAPPENED THAT DAY HAS RUINED TOO MANY LIVES ALREADY.
LIKE IT OR NOT MY FRIENDS AND I ARE INVOLVED NOW.
BRINGING YOU HERE WAS A GAMBLE. I WAGERED MY CREDIBILITY AND MY SOLDIERS' RESPECT AGAINST THE HOPE THAT TOGETHER WE COULD MAKE A DIFFERENCE.
I TOOK A CHANCE AND I LOST.
YOU AND YOUR COMPANIONS SHOULDN'T HAVE TO PAY THE PRICE FOR THAT.
COME WITH ME.
I'LL SET YOU ALL FREE AND GET YOU BACK TO YOUR SHIPS.
WHAT ABOUT YOU, THOUGH? I DON'T WANT YOU TO --
KARUMPH!
SURFACE IMPACT!

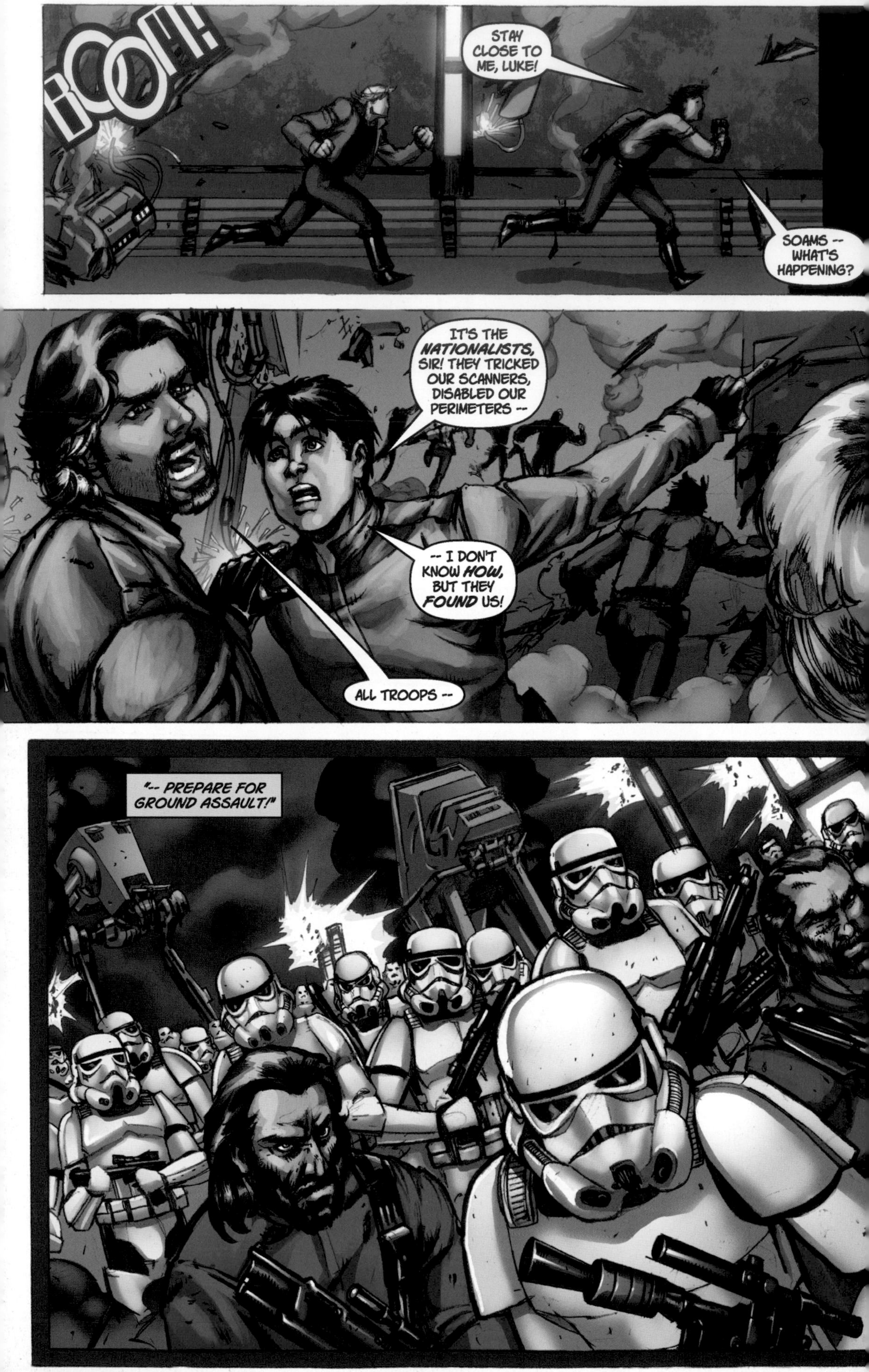
BOOM!
STAY CLOSE TO ME, LUKE!
SOAMS -- WHAT'S HAPPENING?
IT'S THE NATIONALISTS, SIR! THEY TRICKED OUR SCANNERS, DISABLED OUR PERIMETERS --
-- I DON'T KNOW HOW, BUT THEY FOUND US!
ALL TROOPS --
"-- PREPARE FOR GROUND ASSAULT!"

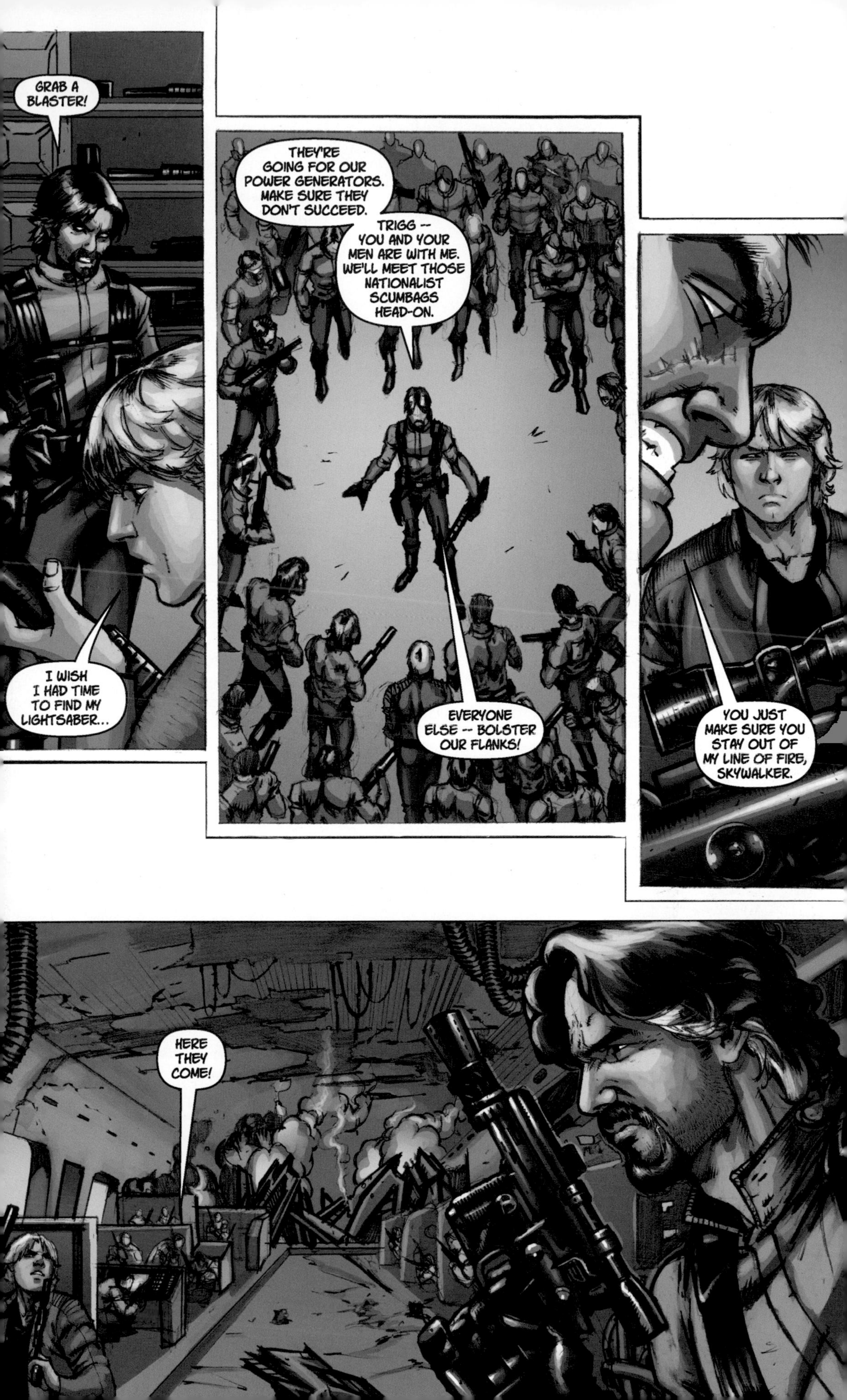
GRAB A BLASTER!
I WISH I HAD TIME TO FIND MY LIGHTSABER...
THEY'RE GOING FOR OUR POWER GENERATORS. MAKE SURE THEY DON'T SUCCEED.
TRIGG -- YOU AND YOUR MEN ARE WITH ME. WE'LL MEET THOSE NATIONALIST SCUMBAGS HEAD-ON.
EVERYONE ELSE -- BOLSTER OUR FLANKS!
YOU JUST MAKE SURE YOU STAY OUT OF MY LINE OF FIRE, SKYWALKER.
HERE THEY COME!

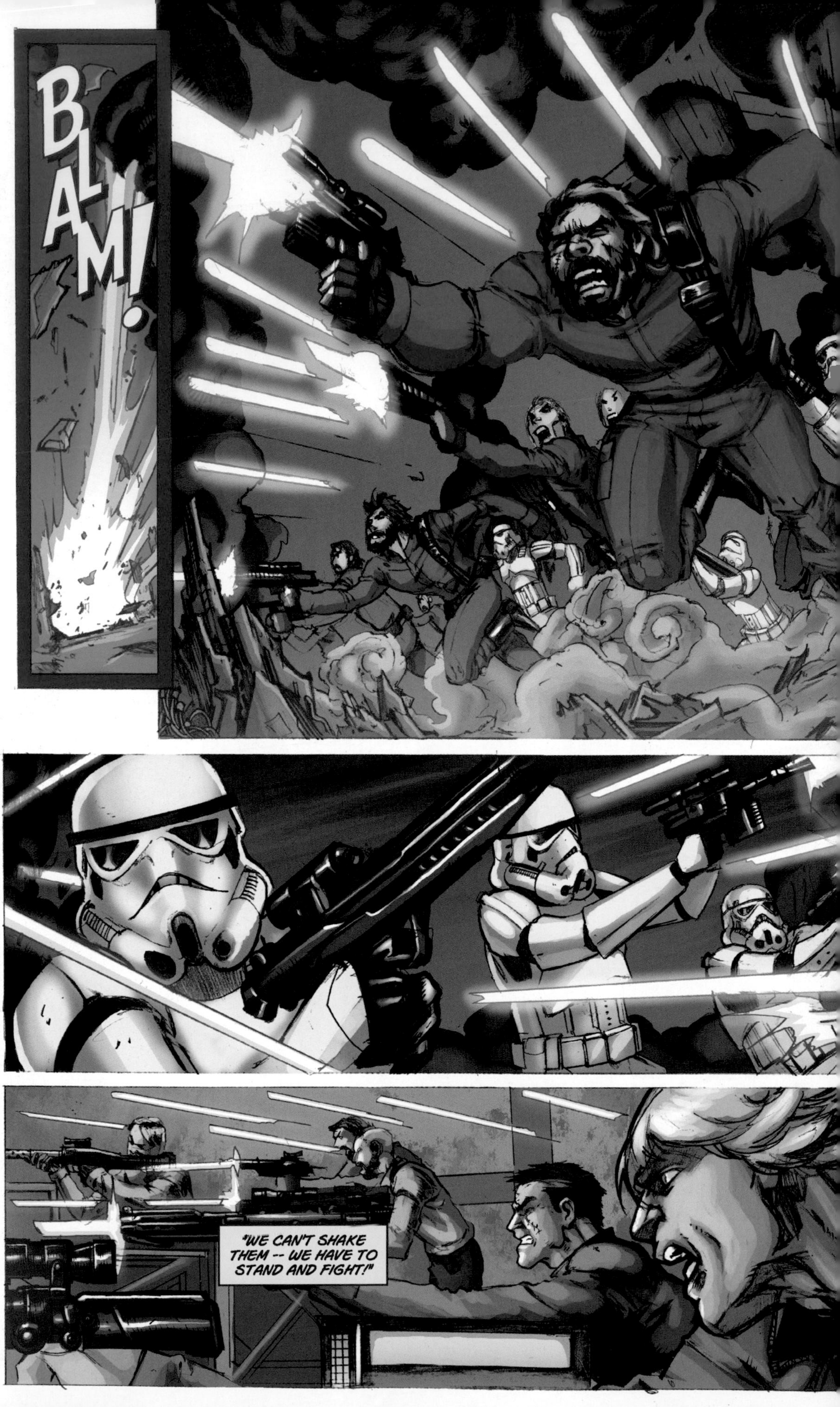
BLAM!
"WE CAN'T SHAKE THEM -- WE HAVE TO STAND AND FIGHT!"

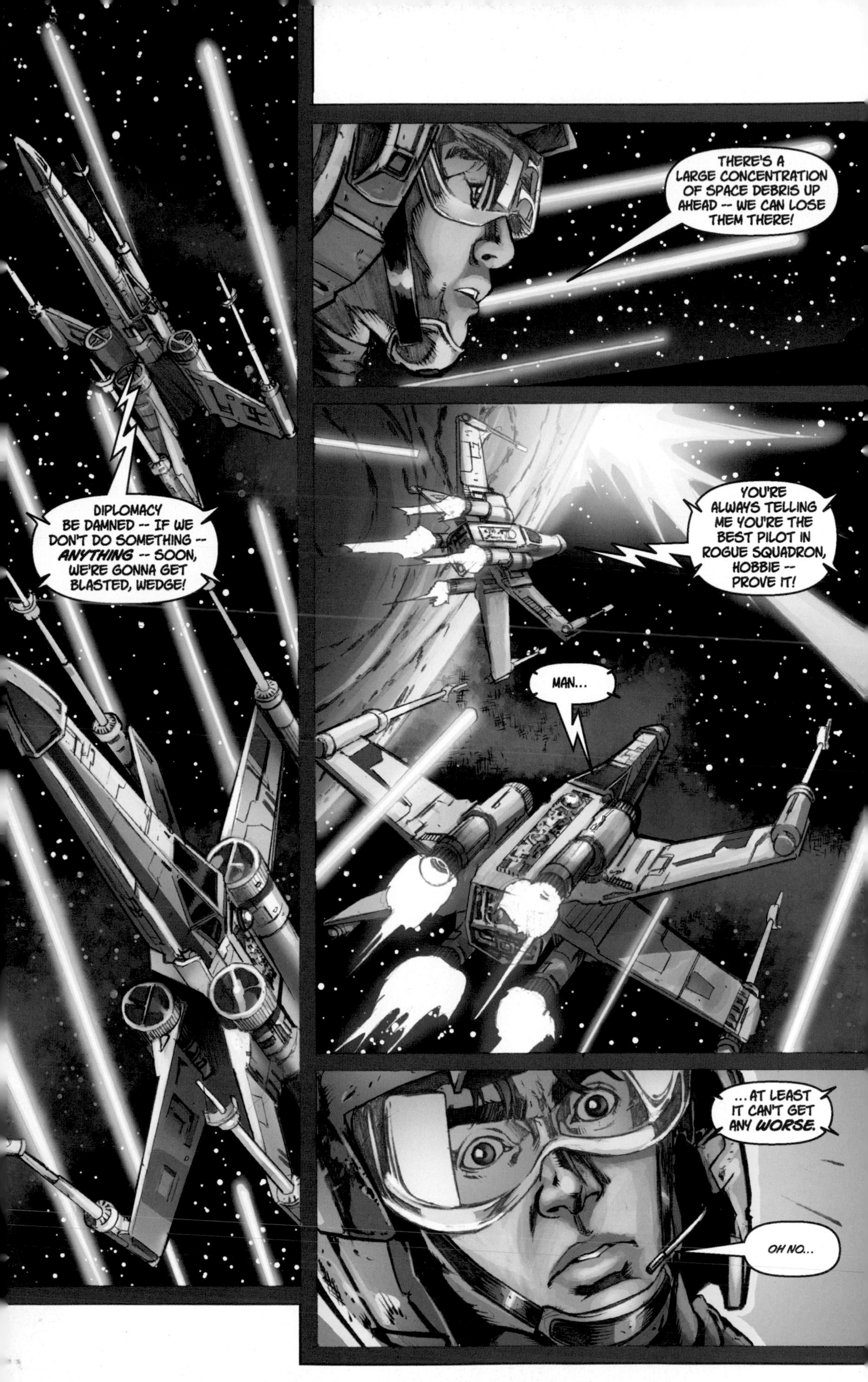
DIPLOMACY BE DAMNED -- IF WE DON'T DO SOMETHING -- *ANYTHING* -- SOON, WE'RE GONNA GET BLASTED, WEDGE!
THERE'S A LARGE CONCENTRATION OF SPACE DEBRIS UP AHEAD -- WE CAN LOSE THEM THERE!
YOU'RE ALWAYS TELLING ME YOU'RE THE BEST PILOT IN ROGUE SQUADRON, HOBBIE -- PROVE IT!
MAN...
...AT LEAST IT CAN'T GET ANY *WORSE*.
OH NO...

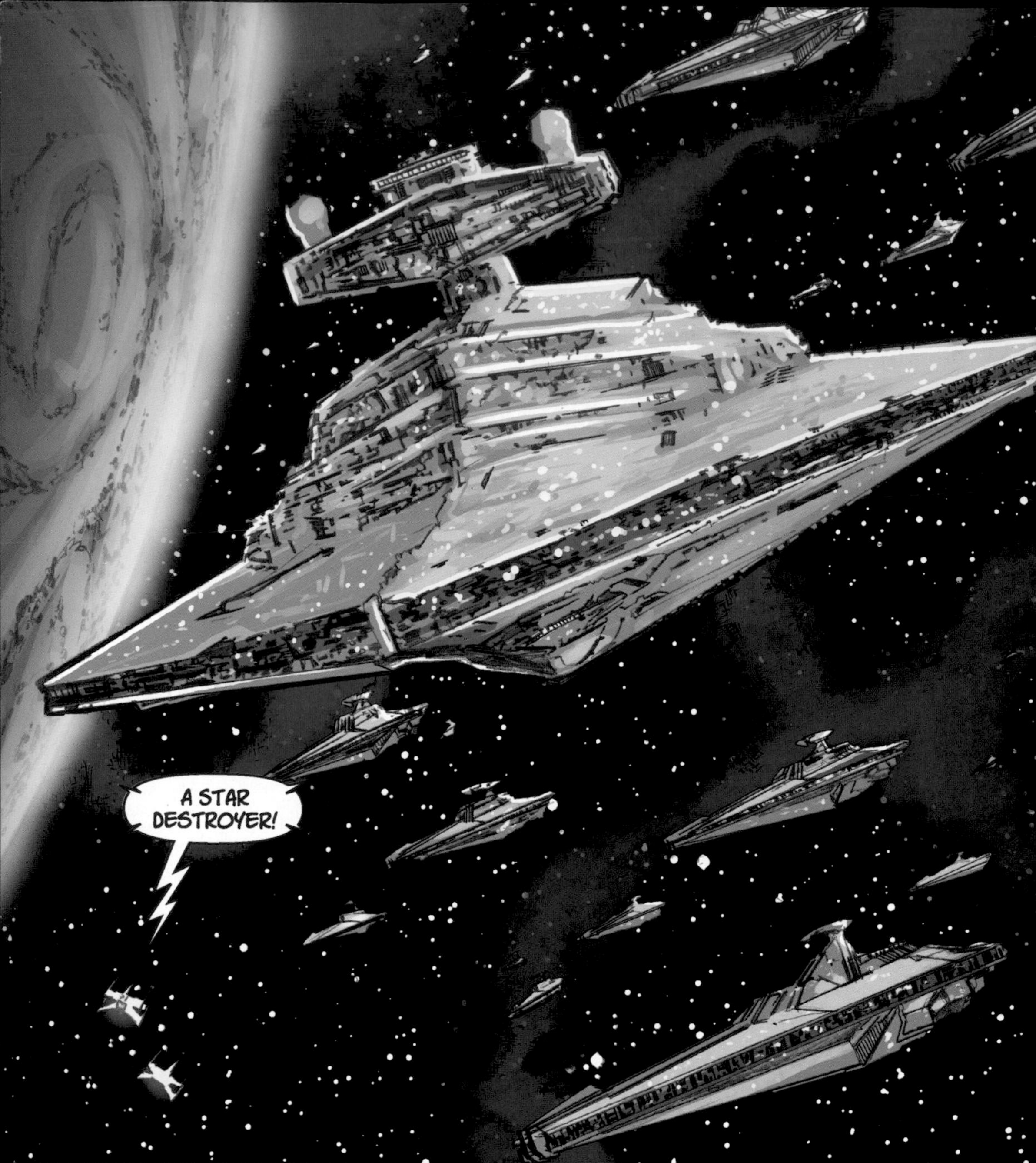
A STAR DESTROYER!

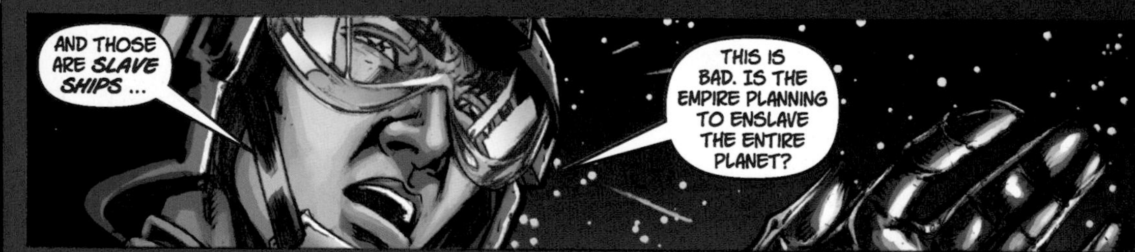
AND THOSE ARE *SLAVE SHIPS* ...
THIS IS BAD. IS THE EMPIRE PLANNING TO ENSLAVE THE ENTIRE PLANET?

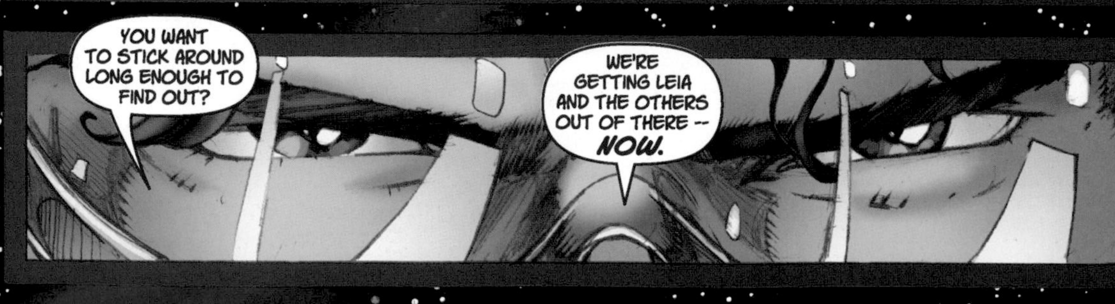
YOU WANT TO STICK AROUND LONG ENOUGH TO FIND OUT?
WE'RE GETTING LEIA AND THE OTHERS OUT OF THERE -- ***NOW.***

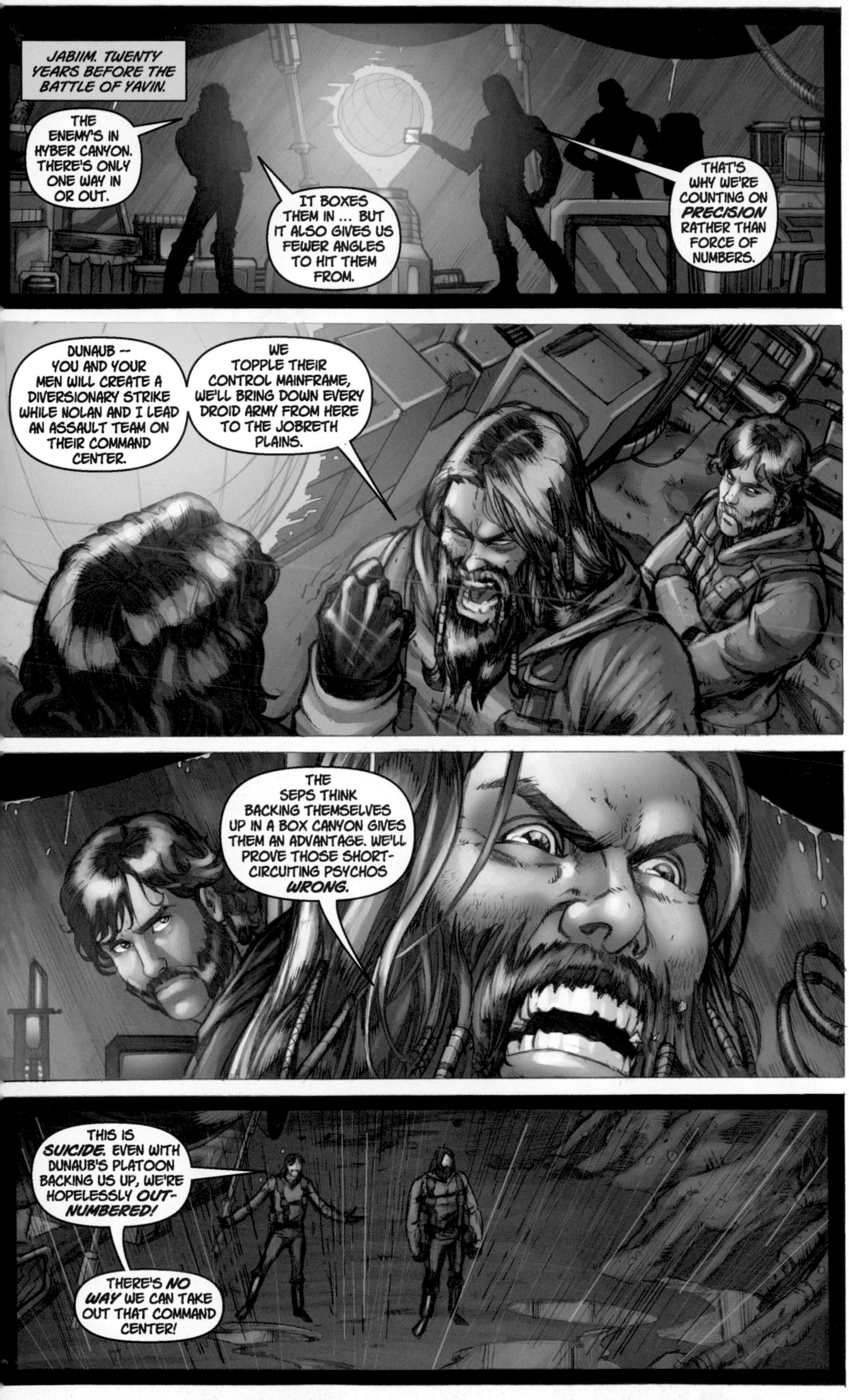
JABIIM. TWENTY YEARS BEFORE THE BATTLE OF YAVIN.
THE ENEMY'S IN HYBER CANYON. THERE'S ONLY ONE WAY IN OR OUT.
IT BOXES THEM IN ... BUT IT ALSO GIVES US FEWER ANGLES TO HIT THEM FROM.
THAT'S WHY WE'RE COUNTING ON PRECISION RATHER THAN FORCE OF NUMBERS.
DUNAUB -- YOU AND YOUR MEN WILL CREATE A DIVERSIONARY STRIKE WHILE NOLAN AND I LEAD AN ASSAULT TEAM ON THEIR COMMAND CENTER.
WE TOPPLE THEIR CONTROL MAINFRAME, WE'LL BRING DOWN EVERY DROID ARMY FROM HERE TO THE JOBRETH PLAINS.
THE SEPS THINK BACKING THEMSELVES UP IN A BOX CANYON GIVES THEM AN ADVANTAGE. WE'LL PROVE THOSE SHORT-CIRCUITING PSYCHOS WRONG.
THIS IS SUICIDE. EVEN WITH DUNAUB'S PLATOON BACKING US UP, WE'RE HOPELESSLY OUT-NUMBERED!
THERE'S NO WAY WE CAN TAKE OUT THAT COMMAND CENTER!

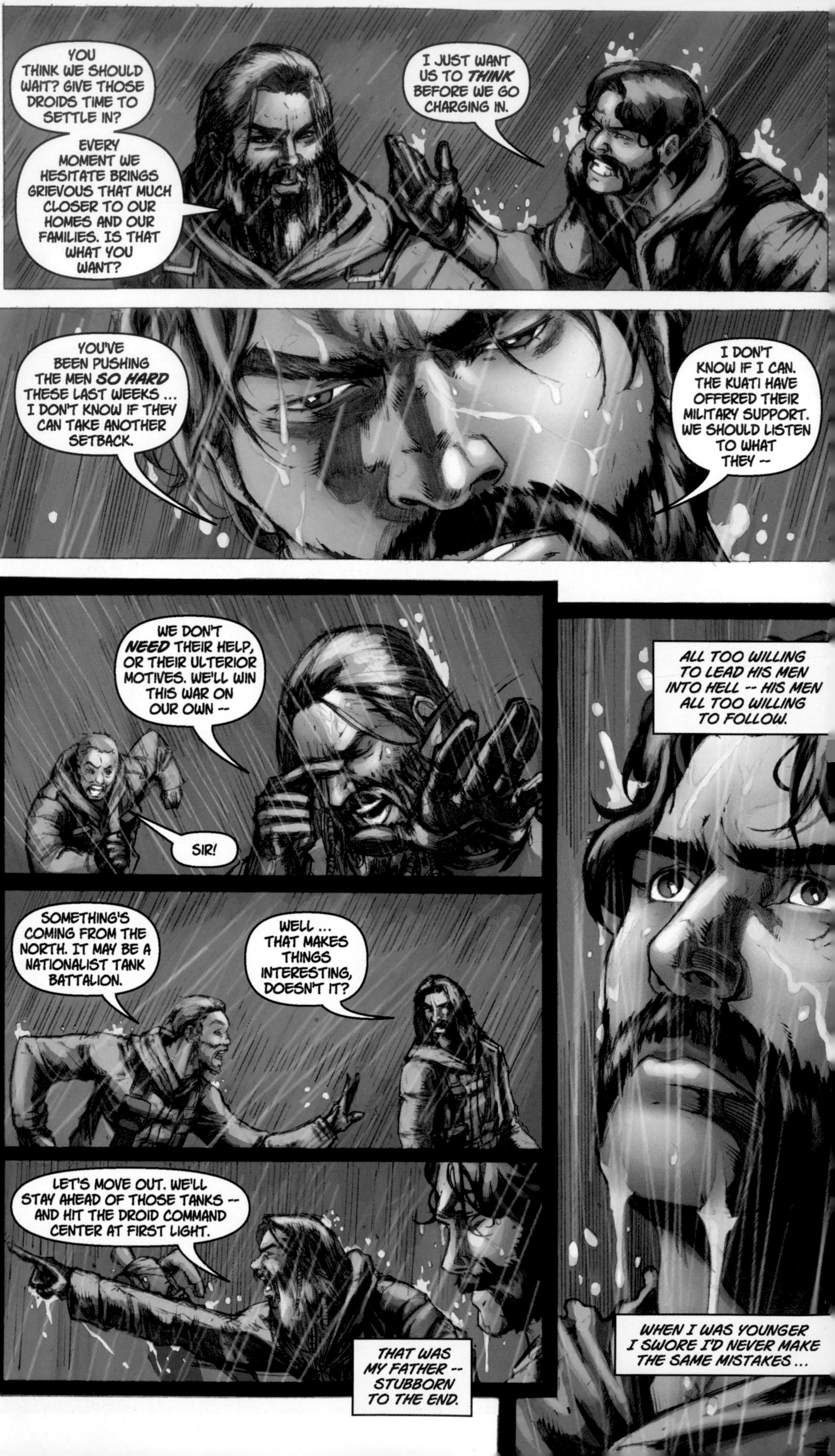
YOU THINK WE SHOULD WAIT? GIVE THOSE DROIDS TIME TO SETTLE IN?
EVERY MOMENT WE HESITATE BRINGS GRIEVOUS THAT MUCH CLOSER TO OUR HOMES AND OUR FAMILIES. IS THAT WHAT YOU WANT?
I JUST WANT US TO *THINK* BEFORE WE GO CHARGING IN.
YOU'VE BEEN PUSHING THE MEN *SO HARD* THESE LAST WEEKS ... I DON'T KNOW IF THEY CAN TAKE ANOTHER SETBACK.
I DON'T KNOW IF I CAN. THE KUATI HAVE OFFERED THEIR MILITARY SUPPORT. WE SHOULD LISTEN TO WHAT THEY --
WE DON'T *NEED* THEIR HELP, OR THEIR ULTERIOR MOTIVES. WE'LL WIN THIS WAR ON OUR OWN --
SIR!
SOMETHING'S COMING FROM THE NORTH. IT MAY BE A NATIONALIST TANK BATTALION.
WELL ... THAT MAKES THINGS INTERESTING, DOESN'T IT?
LET'S MOVE OUT. WE'LL STAY AHEAD OF THOSE TANKS -- AND HIT THE DROID COMMAND CENTER AT FIRST LIGHT.
THAT WAS MY FATHER -- STUBBORN TO THE END.
ALL TOO WILLING TO LEAD HIS MEN INTO HELL -- HIS MEN ALL TOO WILLING TO FOLLOW.
WHEN I WAS YOUNGER I SWORE I'D NEVER MAKE THE SAME MISTAKES ...

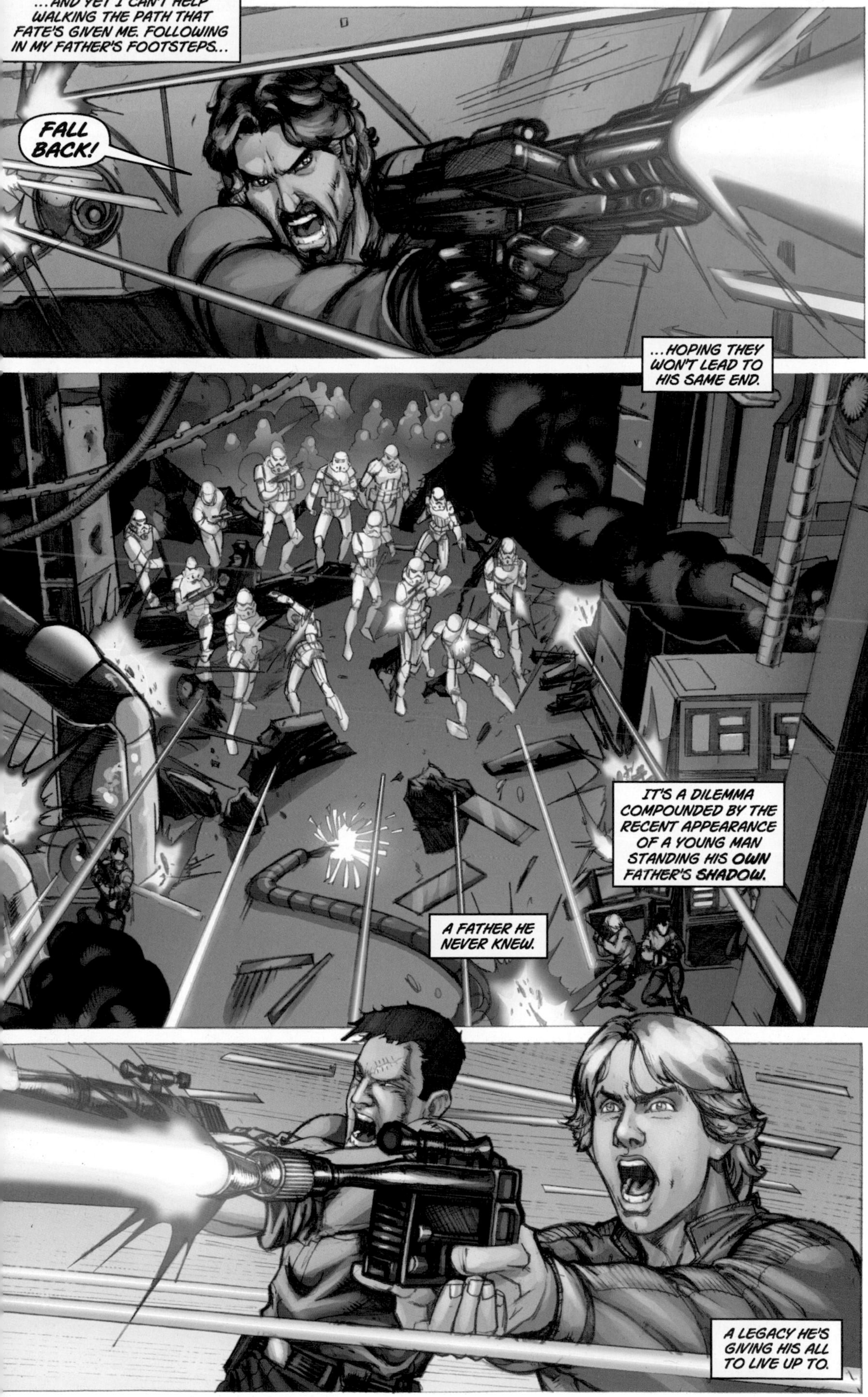

...AND YET I CAN'T HELP WALKING THE PATH THAT FATE'S GIVEN ME. FOLLOWING IN MY FATHER'S FOOTSTEPS...
FALL BACK!
...HOPING THEY WON'T LEAD TO HIS SAME END.
IT'S A DILEMMA COMPOUNDED BY THE RECENT APPEARANCE OF A YOUNG MAN STANDING HIS OWN FATHER'S SHADOW.
A FATHER HE NEVER KNEW.
A LEGACY HE'S GIVING HIS ALL TO LIVE UP TO.

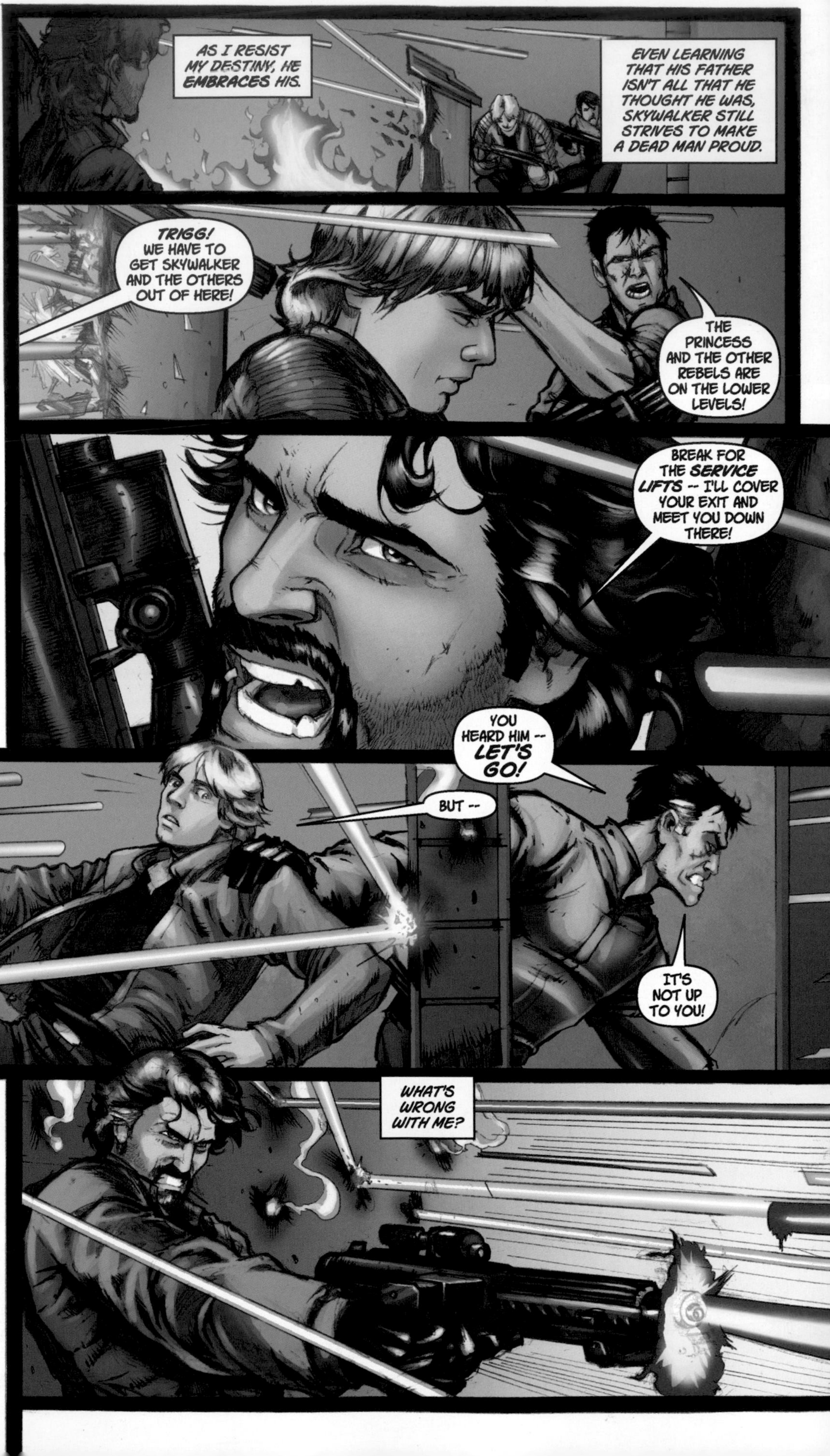
AS I RESIST MY DESTINY, HE EMBRACES HIS.
EVEN LEARNING THAT HIS FATHER ISN'T ALL THAT HE THOUGHT HE WAS, SKYWALKER STILL STRIVES TO MAKE A DEAD MAN PROUD.
TRIGG! WE HAVE TO GET SKYWALKER AND THE OTHERS OUT OF HERE!
THE PRINCESS AND THE OTHER REBELS ARE ON THE LOWER LEVELS!
BREAK FOR THE SERVICE LIFTS -- I'LL COVER YOUR EXIT AND MEET YOU DOWN THERE!
YOU HEARD HIM -- LET'S GO!
BUT --
IT'S NOT UP TO YOU!
WHAT'S WRONG WITH ME?

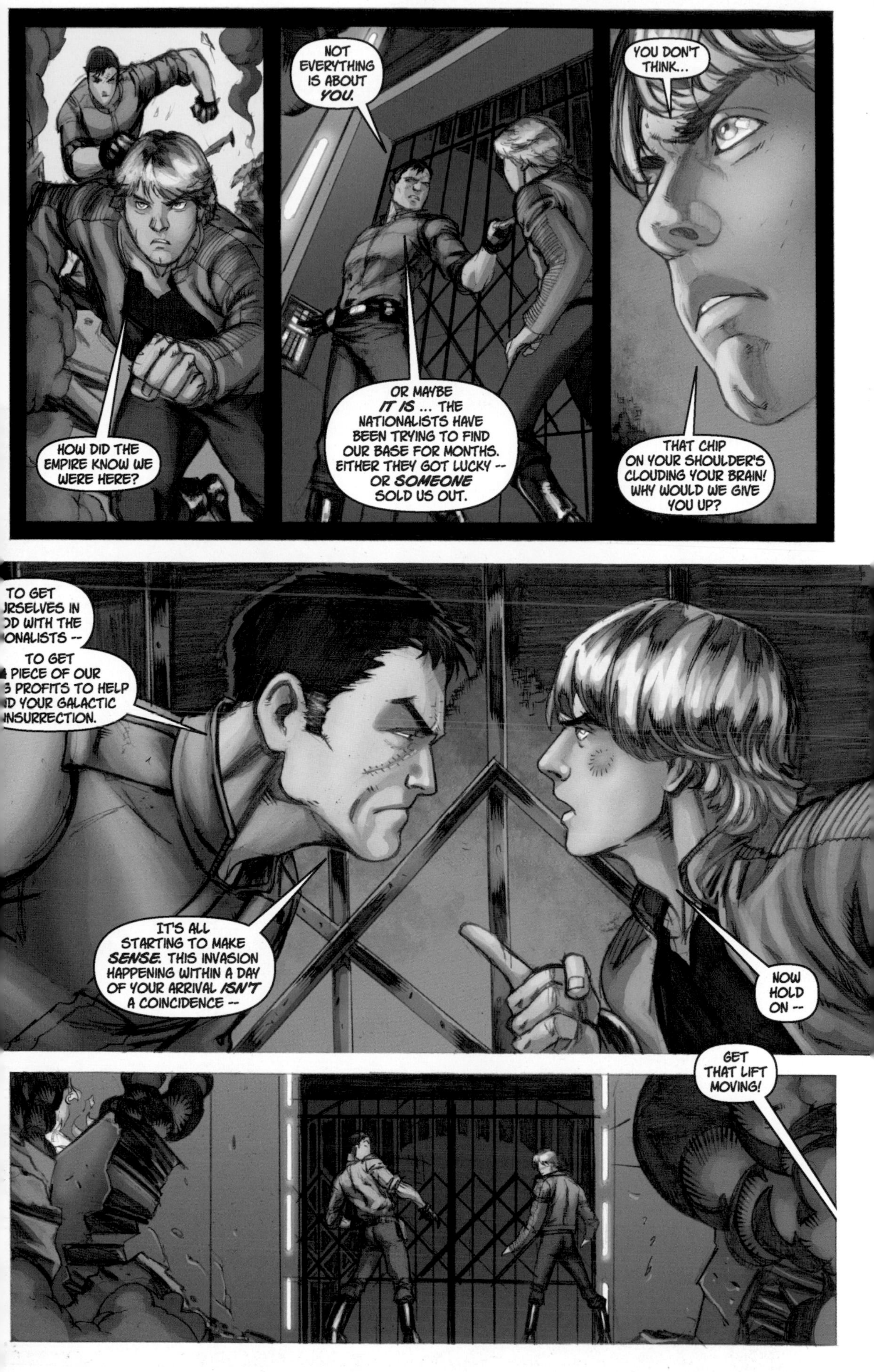
HOW DID THE EMPIRE KNOW WE WERE HERE?
NOT EVERYTHING IS ABOUT *YOU.*
OR MAYBE *IT IS* ... THE NATIONALISTS HAVE BEEN TRYING TO FIND OUR BASE FOR MONTHS. EITHER THEY GOT LUCKY -- OR *SOMEONE* SOLD US OUT.
YOU DON'T THINK...
THAT CHIP ON YOUR SHOULDER'S CLOUDING YOUR BRAIN! WHY WOULD WE GIVE YOU UP?
TO GET URSELVES IN OD WITH THE ONALISTS --
TO GET PIECE OF OUR PROFITS TO HELP D YOUR GALACTIC NSURRECTION.
IT'S ALL STARTING TO MAKE *SENSE.* THIS INVASION HAPPENING WITHIN A DAY OF YOUR ARRIVAL *ISN'T* A COINCIDENCE --
NOW HOLD ON --
GET THAT LIFT MOVING!

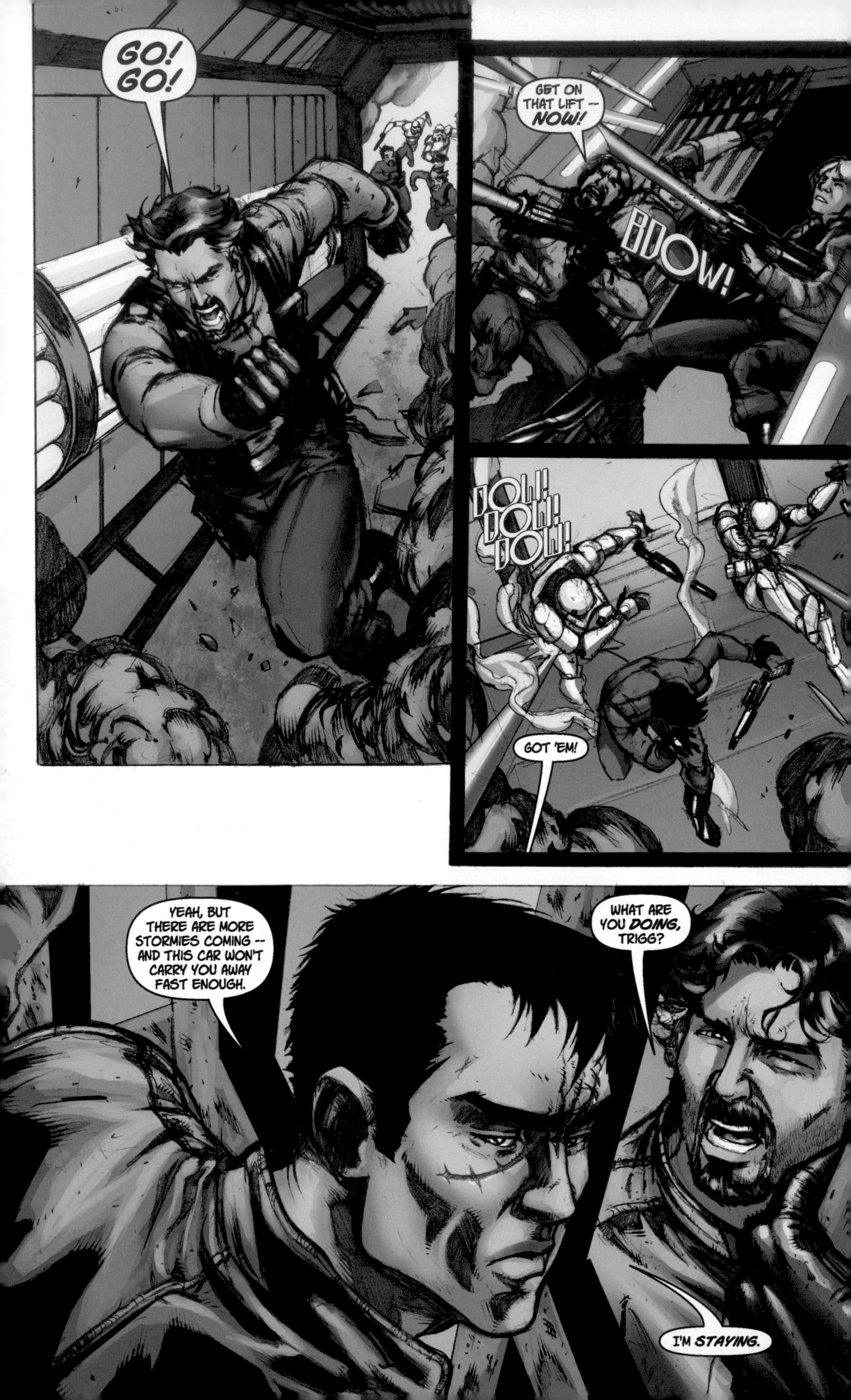
GO! GO!
GET ON THAT LIFT -- NOW!
BDOW!
DOW! DOW! DOW!
GOT 'EM!
YEAH, BUT THERE ARE MORE STORMIES COMING -- AND THIS CAR WON'T CARRY YOU AWAY FAST ENOUGH.
WHAT ARE YOU DOING, TRIGG?
I'M STAYING.

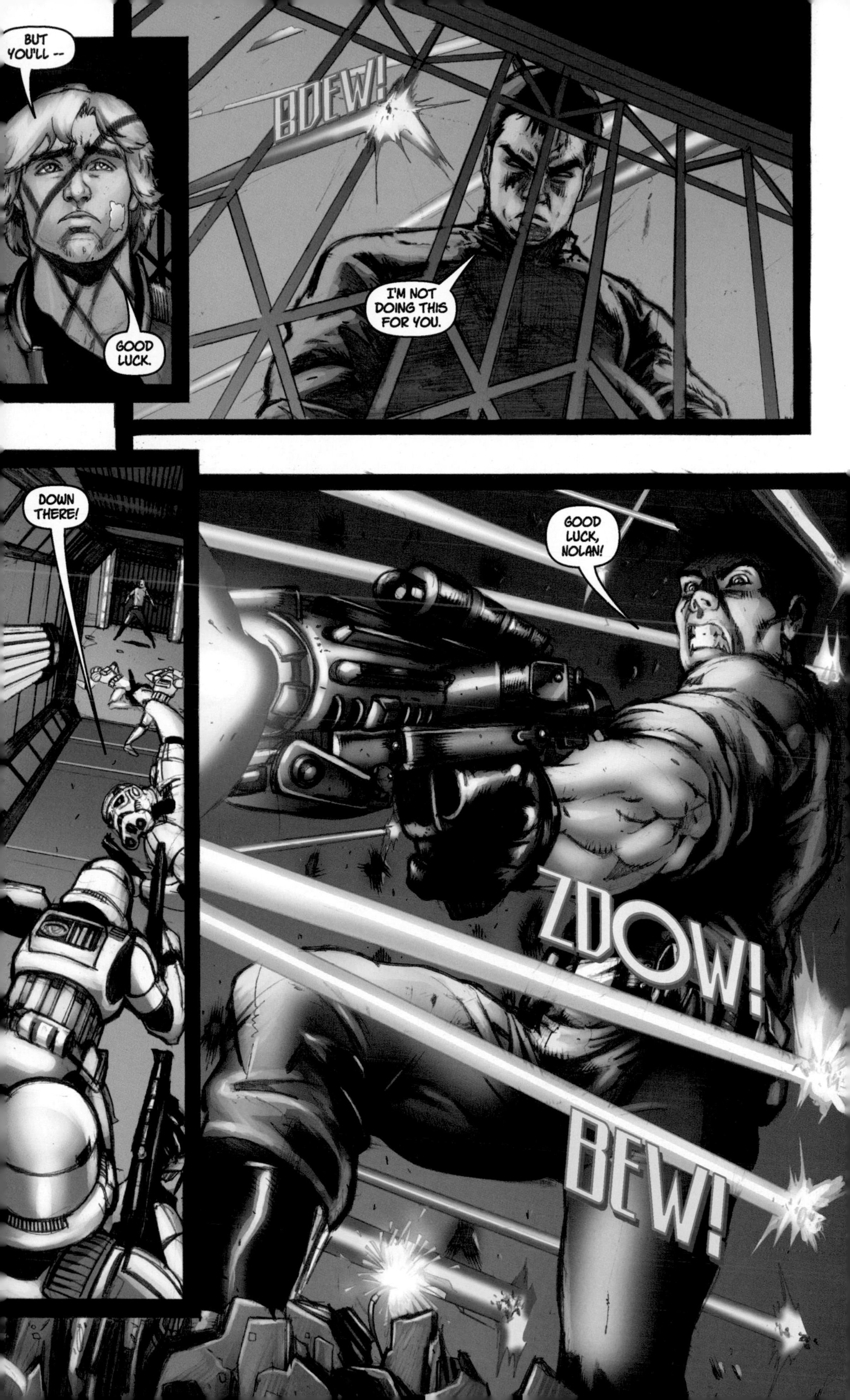
BUT YOU'LL --
GOOD LUCK.
BDEW!
I'M NOT DOING THIS FOR YOU.
DOWN THERE!
GOOD LUCK, NOLAN!
ZDOW!
BEW!

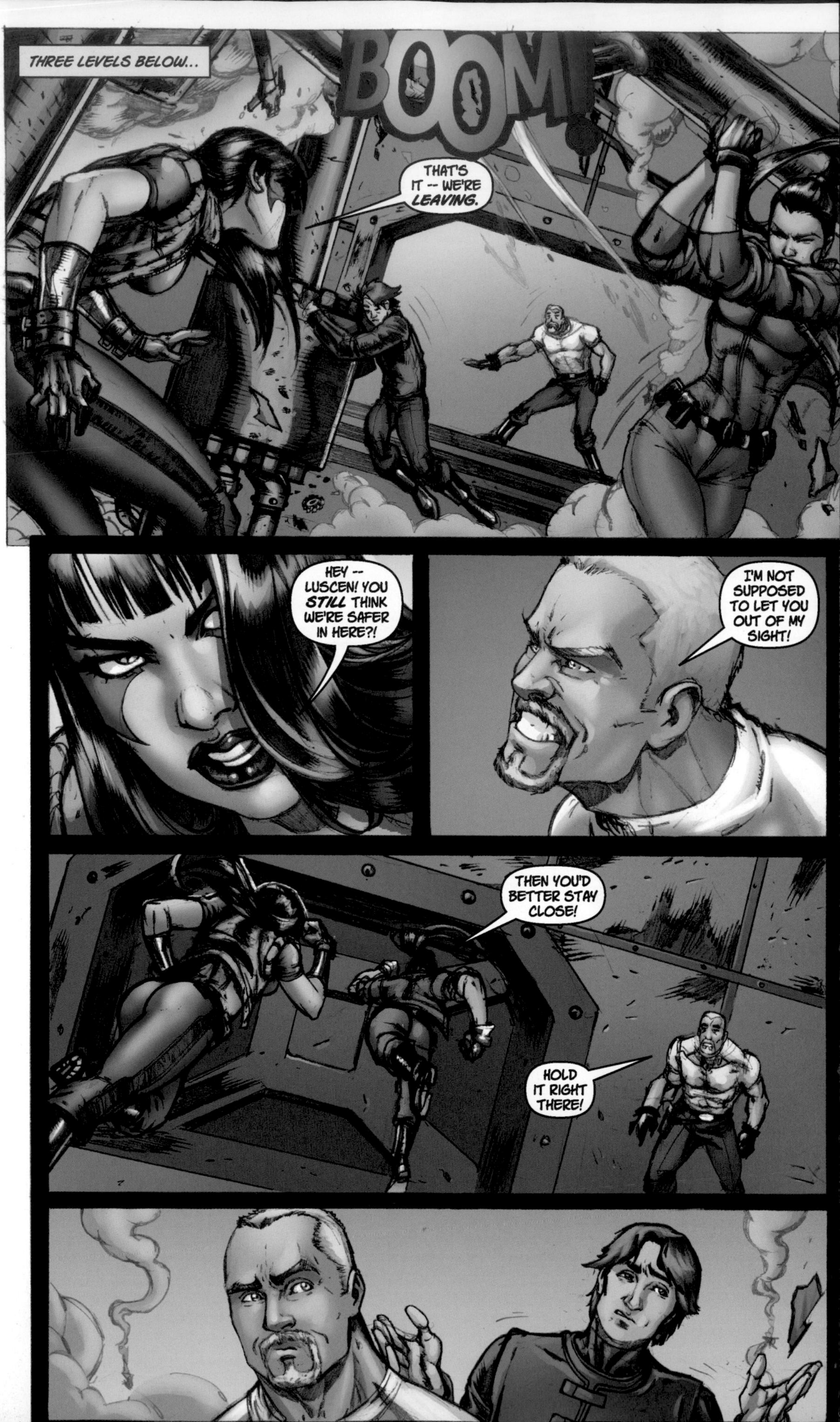
THREE LEVELS BELOW...
BOOM!
THAT'S IT -- WE'RE LEAVING.
HEY -- LUSCEN! YOU STILL THINK WE'RE SAFER IN HERE?!
I'M NOT SUPPOSED TO LET YOU OUT OF MY SIGHT!
THEN YOU'D BETTER STAY CLOSE!
HOLD IT RIGHT THERE!

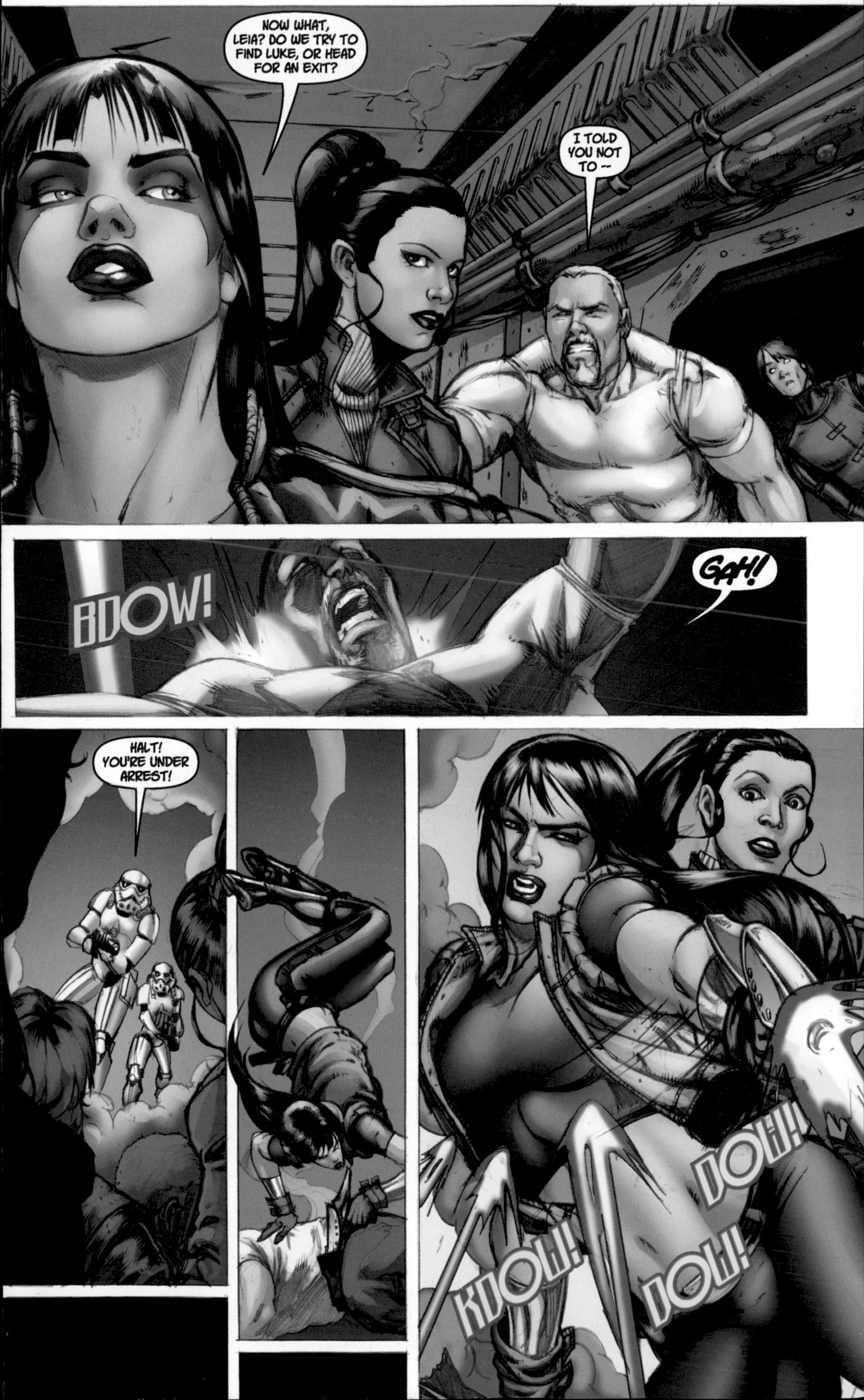
NOW WHAT, LEIA? DO WE TRY TO FIND LUKE, OR HEAD FOR AN EXIT?
I TOLD YOU NOT TO --
BDOW!
GAH!
HALT! YOU'RE UNDER ARREST!
KDOW!
DOW!
DOW!

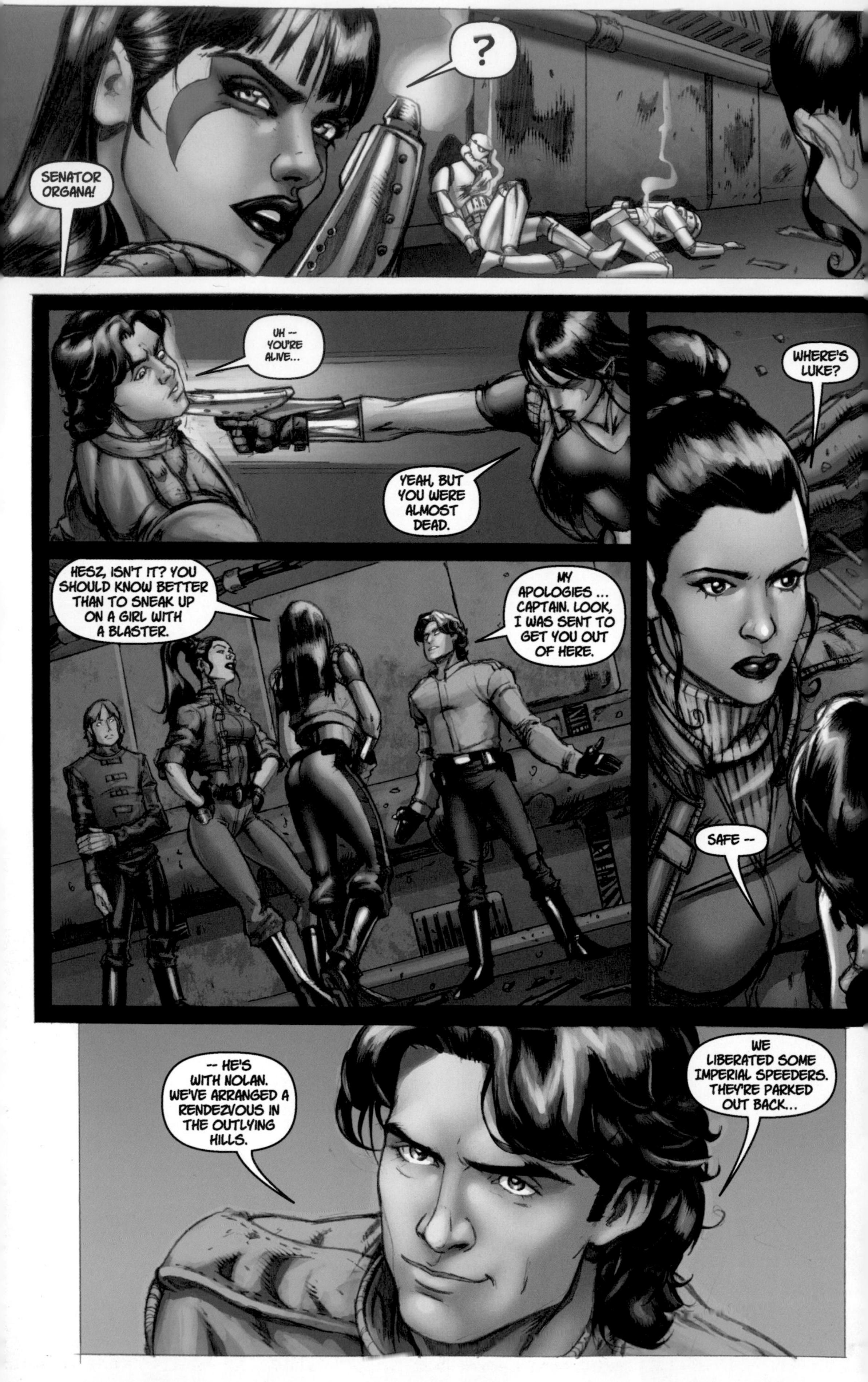
?
SENATOR ORGANA!
UH -- YOU'RE ALIVE...
YEAH, BUT YOU WERE ALMOST DEAD.
WHERE'S LUKE?
HESZ, ISN'T IT? YOU SHOULD KNOW BETTER THAN TO SNEAK UP ON A GIRL WITH A BLASTER.
MY APOLOGIES ... CAPTAIN. LOOK, I WAS SENT TO GET YOU OUT OF HERE.
SAFE --
-- HE'S WITH NOLAN. WE'VE ARRANGED A RENDEZVOUS IN THE OUTLYING HILLS.
WE LIBERATED SOME IMPERIAL SPEEDERS. THEY'RE PARKED OUT BACK...

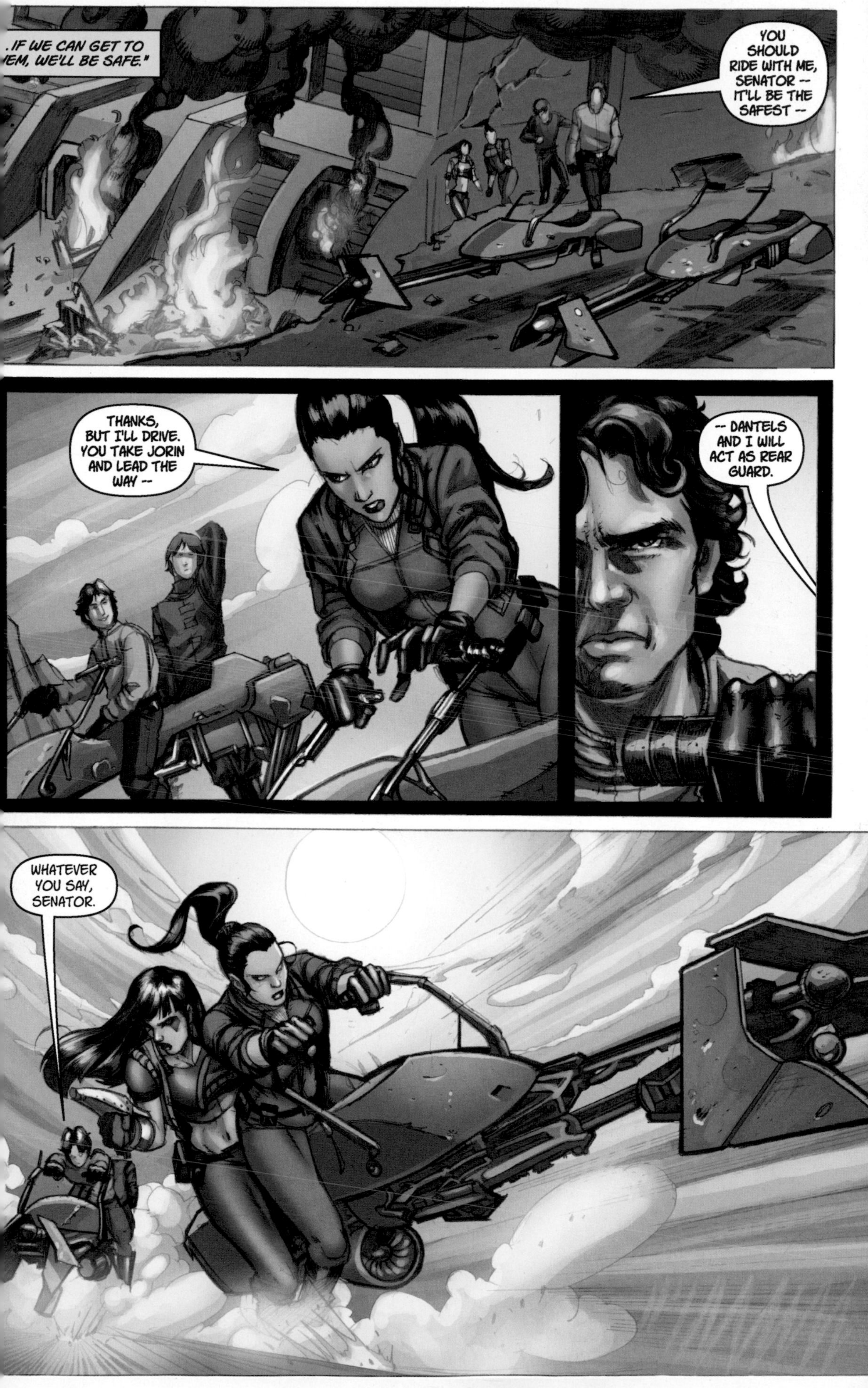

.IF WE CAN GET TO
'EM, WE'LL BE SAFE."
YOU SHOULD RIDE WITH ME, SENATOR -- IT'LL BE THE SAFEST --
THANKS, BUT I'LL DRIVE. YOU TAKE JORIN AND LEAD THE WAY --
-- DANTELS AND I WILL ACT AS REAR GUARD.
WHATEVER YOU SAY, SENATOR.

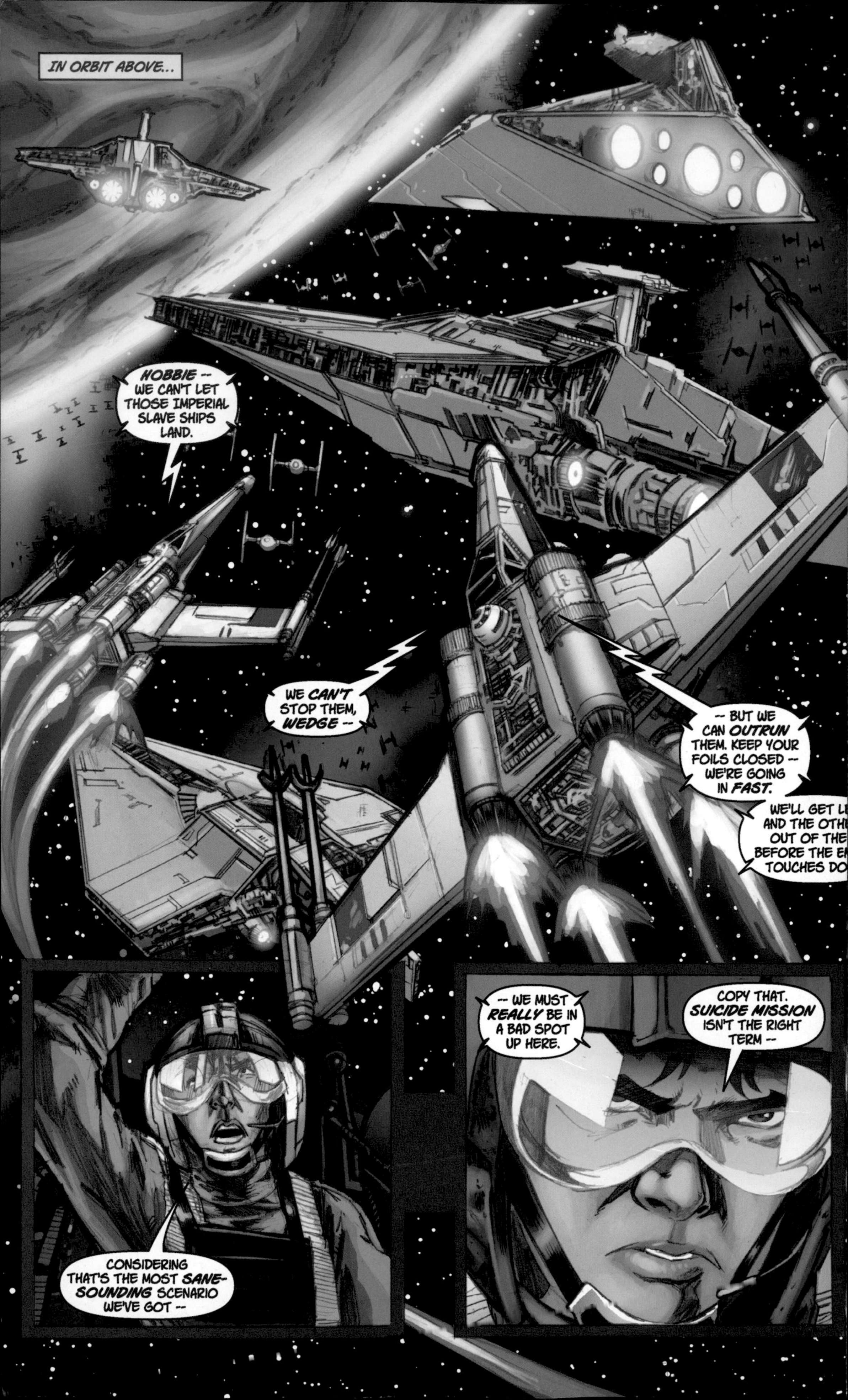
IN ORBIT ABOVE...
HOBBIE -- WE CAN'T LET THOSE IMPERIAL SLAVE SHIPS LAND.
WE CAN'T STOP THEM, WEDGE --
-- BUT WE CAN OUTRUN THEM. KEEP YOUR FOILS CLOSED -- WE'RE GOING IN FAST.
WE'LL GET L
AND THE OTH
OUT OF THE
BEFORE THE E
TOUCHES DO
CONSIDERING THAT'S THE MOST SANE-SOUNDING SCENARIO WE'VE GOT --
-- WE MUST REALLY BE IN A BAD SPOT UP HERE.
COPY THAT. SUICIDE MISSION ISN'T THE RIGHT TERM --

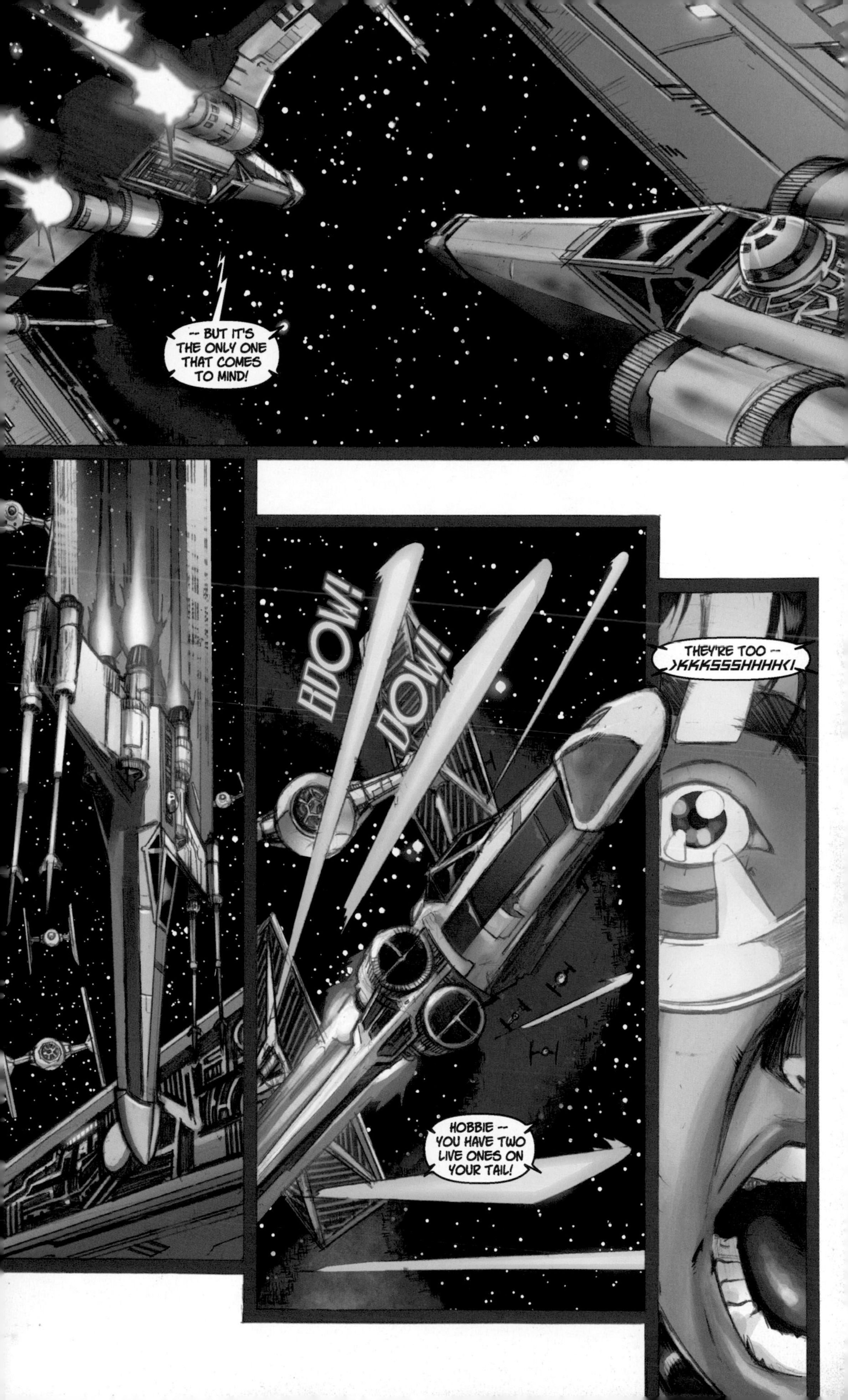
-- BUT IT'S THE ONLY ONE THAT COMES TO MIND!
BDOW!
DOW!
HOBBIE -- YOU HAVE TWO LIVE ONES ON YOUR TAIL!
THEY'RE TOO -- >KKKSSSHHHH<!

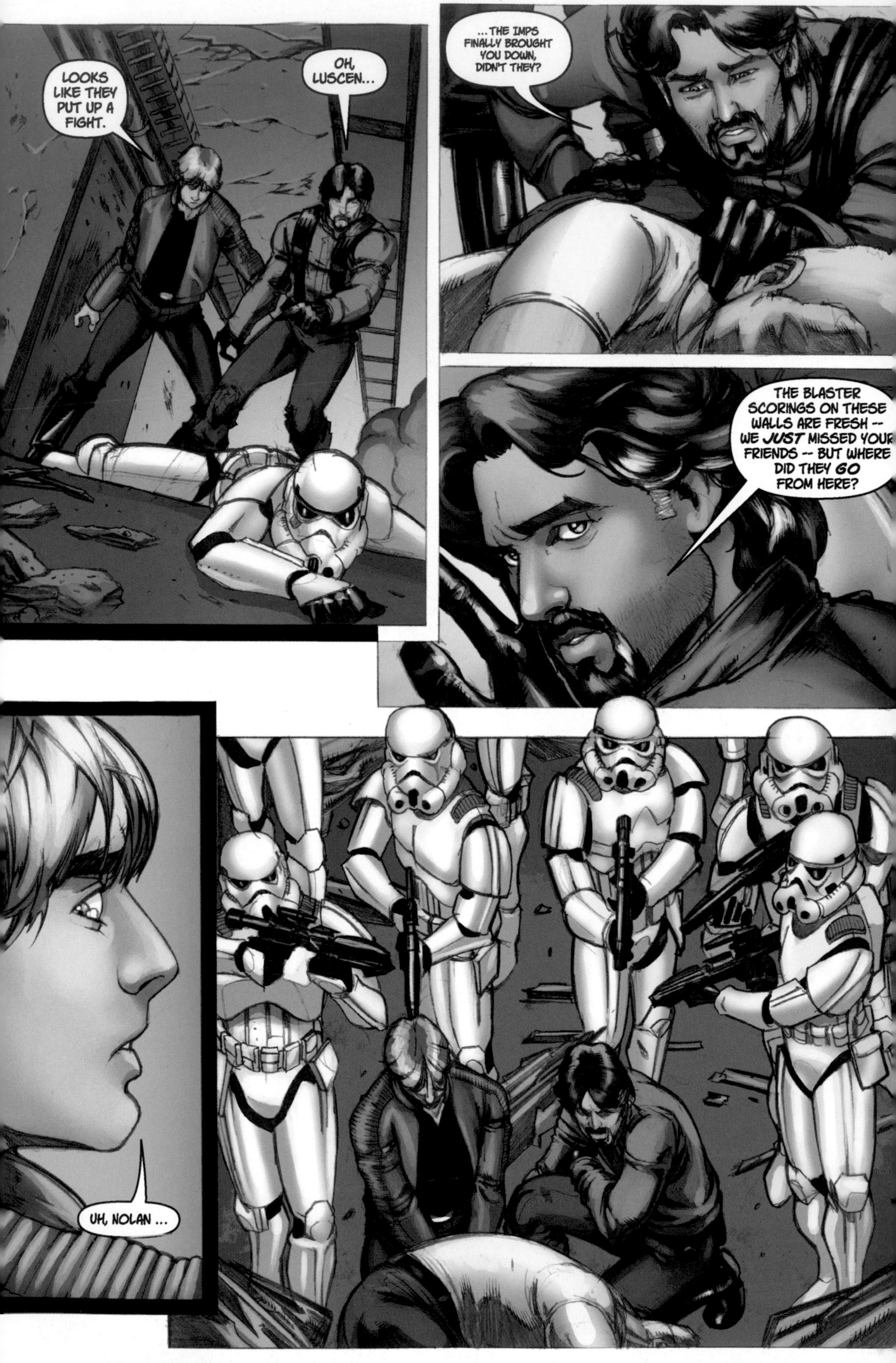
LOOKS LIKE THEY PUT UP A FIGHT.
OH, LUSCEN...
...THE IMPS FINALLY BROUGHT YOU DOWN, DIDN'T THEY?
THE BLASTER SCORINGS ON THESE WALLS ARE FRESH -- WE *JUST* MISSED YOUR FRIENDS -- BUT WHERE DID THEY *GO* FROM HERE?
UH, NOLAN ...

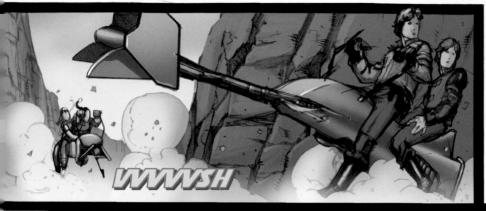

VVVVVSH

WHY'D WE STOP?

HAVE A LOOK.

VROOOOOMM

HEAR THAT? IMPERIALS ARE ON OUR TAIL. WE'RE TRAPPED!

IT'S A MINEFIELD, YOUR HIGHNESS.

A DEAD END.

YIPES!

MAYBE NOT.

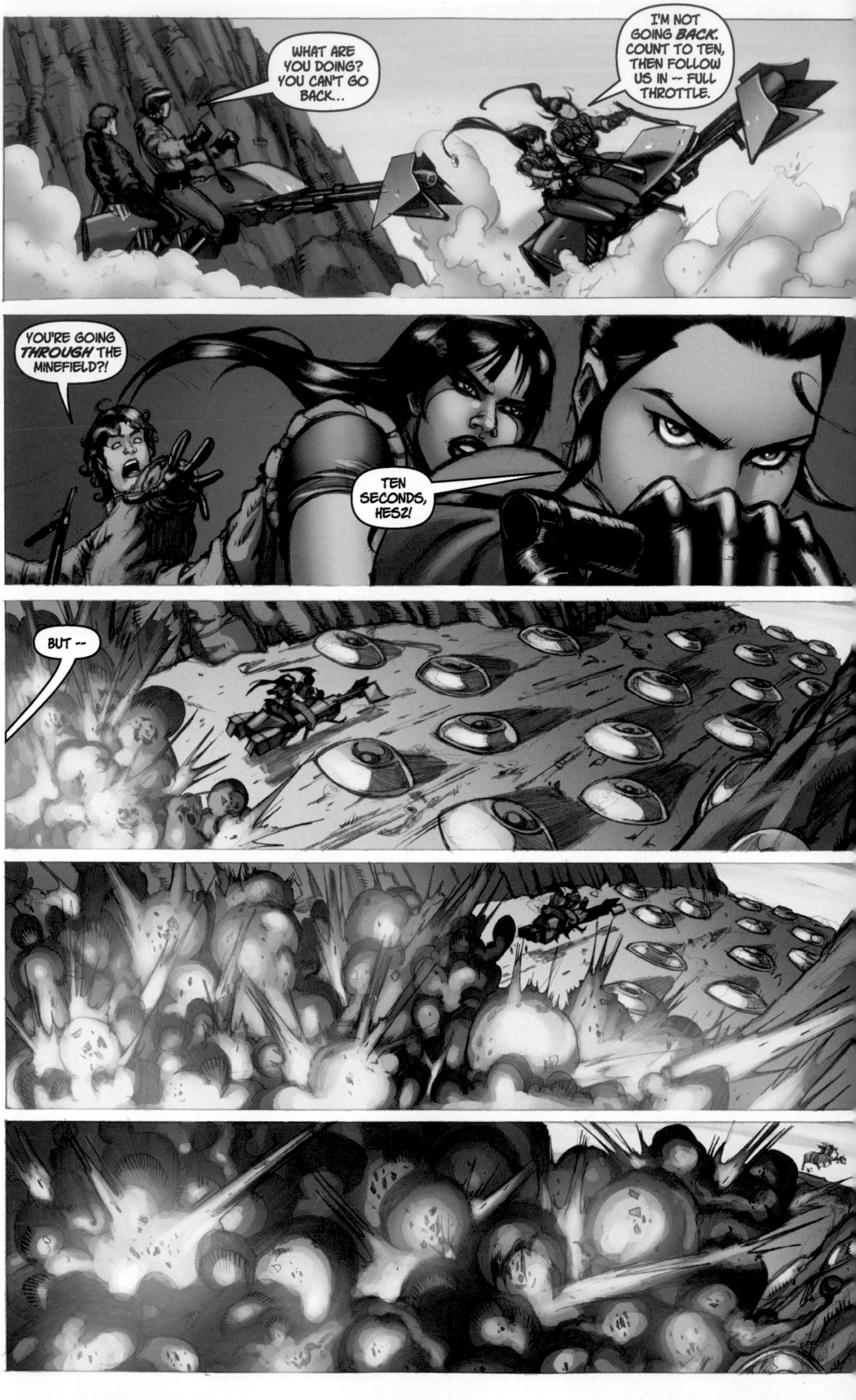
WHAT ARE YOU DOING? YOU CAN'T GO BACK...
I'M NOT GOING *BACK*. COUNT TO TEN, THEN FOLLOW US IN -- FULL THROTTLE.
YOU'RE GOING *THROUGH* THE MINEFIELD?!
TEN SECONDS, HESZ!
BUT --

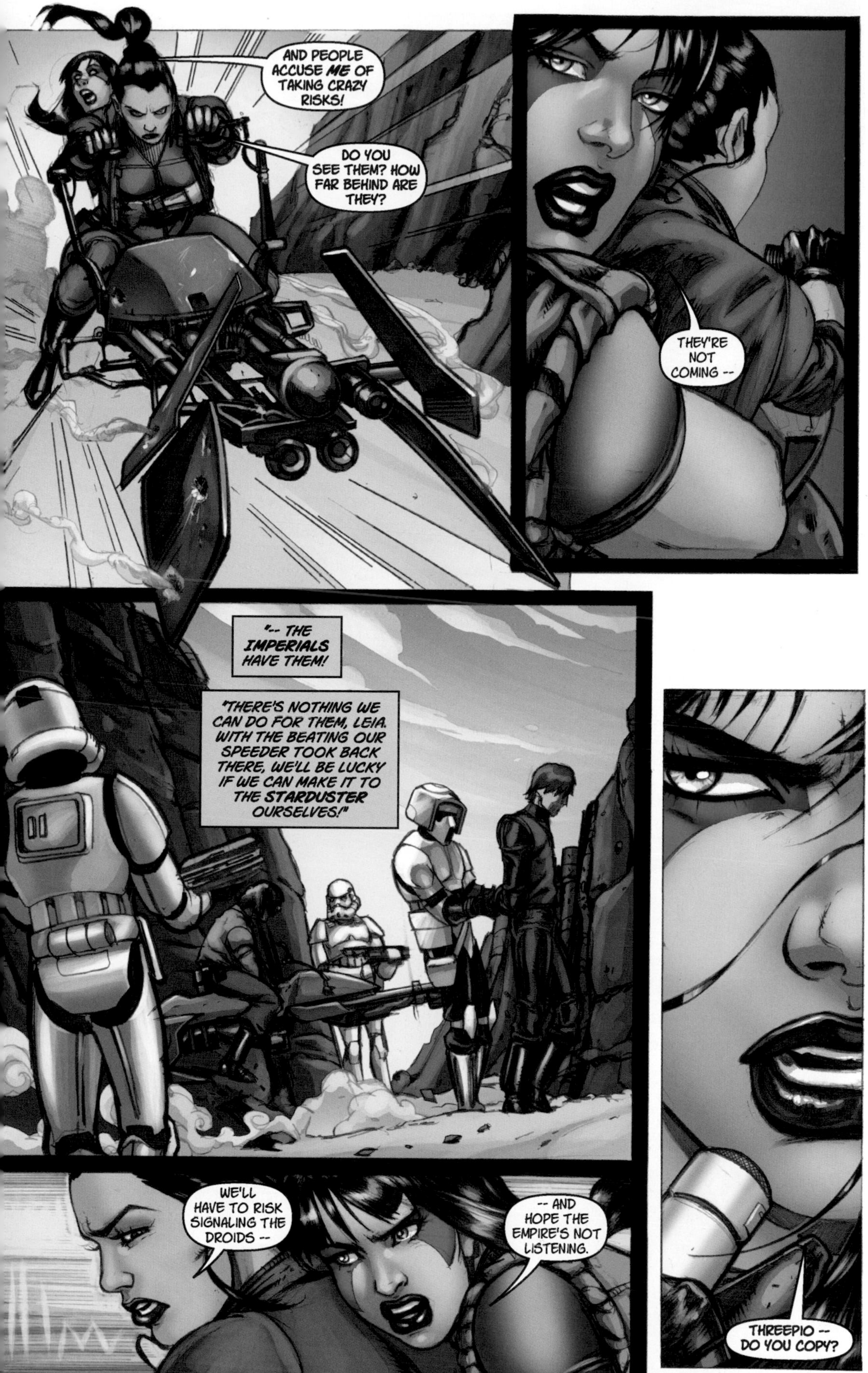
AND PEOPLE ACCUSE ME OF TAKING CRAZY RISKS!
DO YOU SEE THEM? HOW FAR BEHIND ARE THEY?
THEY'RE NOT COMING --
"-- THE IMPERIALS HAVE THEM!
"THERE'S NOTHING WE CAN DO FOR THEM, LEIA. WITH THE BEATING OUR SPEEDER TOOK BACK THERE, WE'LL BE LUCKY IF WE CAN MAKE IT TO THE STARDUSTER OURSELVES!"
WE'LL HAVE TO RISK SIGNALING THE DROIDS --
-- AND HOPE THE EMPIRE'S NOT LISTENING.
THREEPIO -- DO YOU COPY?

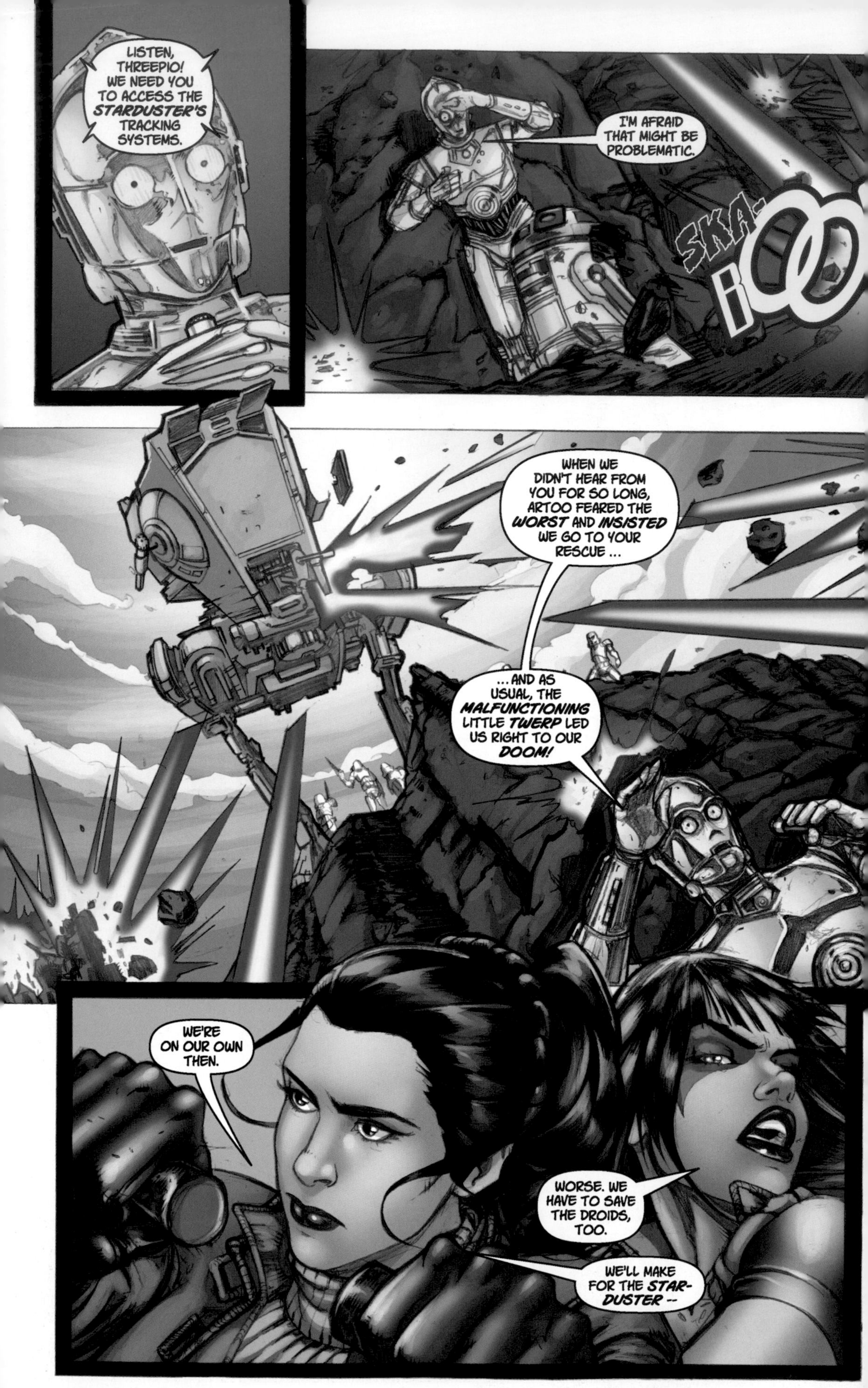
LISTEN, THREEPIO! WE NEED YOU TO ACCESS THE STARDUSTER'S TRACKING SYSTEMS.
I'M AFRAID THAT MIGHT BE PROBLEMATIC.
SKA-BOOM
WHEN WE DIDN'T HEAR FROM YOU FOR SO LONG, ARTOO FEARED THE WORST AND INSISTED WE GO TO YOUR RESCUE ...
... AND AS USUAL, THE MALFUNCTIONING LITTLE TWERP LED US RIGHT TO OUR DOOM!
WE'RE ON OUR OWN THEN.
WORSE. WE HAVE TO SAVE THE DROIDS, TOO.
WE'LL MAKE FOR THE STAR-DUSTER --

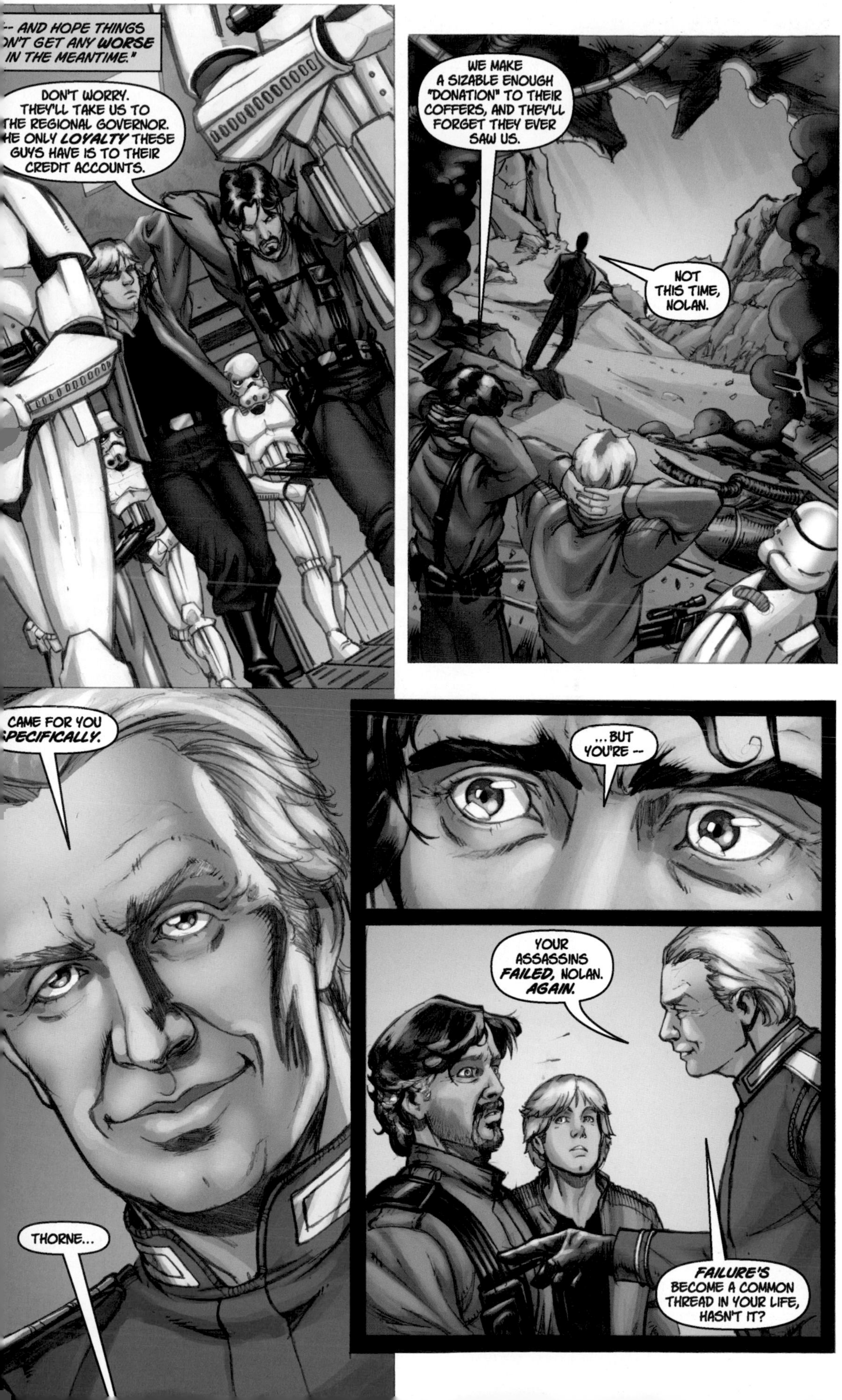

-- AND HOPE THINGS
ON'T GET ANY WORSE
IN THE MEANTIME."
DON'T WORRY. THEY'LL TAKE US TO THE REGIONAL GOVERNOR. HE ONLY LOYALTY THESE GUYS HAVE IS TO THEIR CREDIT ACCOUNTS.
WE MAKE A SIZABLE ENOUGH "DONATION" TO THEIR COFFERS, AND THEY'LL FORGET THEY EVER SAW US.
NOT THIS TIME, NOLAN.
CAME FOR YOU
PECIFICALLY.
THORNE...
...BUT YOU'RE --
YOUR ASSASSINS FAILED, NOLAN. AGAIN.
FAILURE'S BECOME A COMMON THREAD IN YOUR LIFE, HASN'T IT?

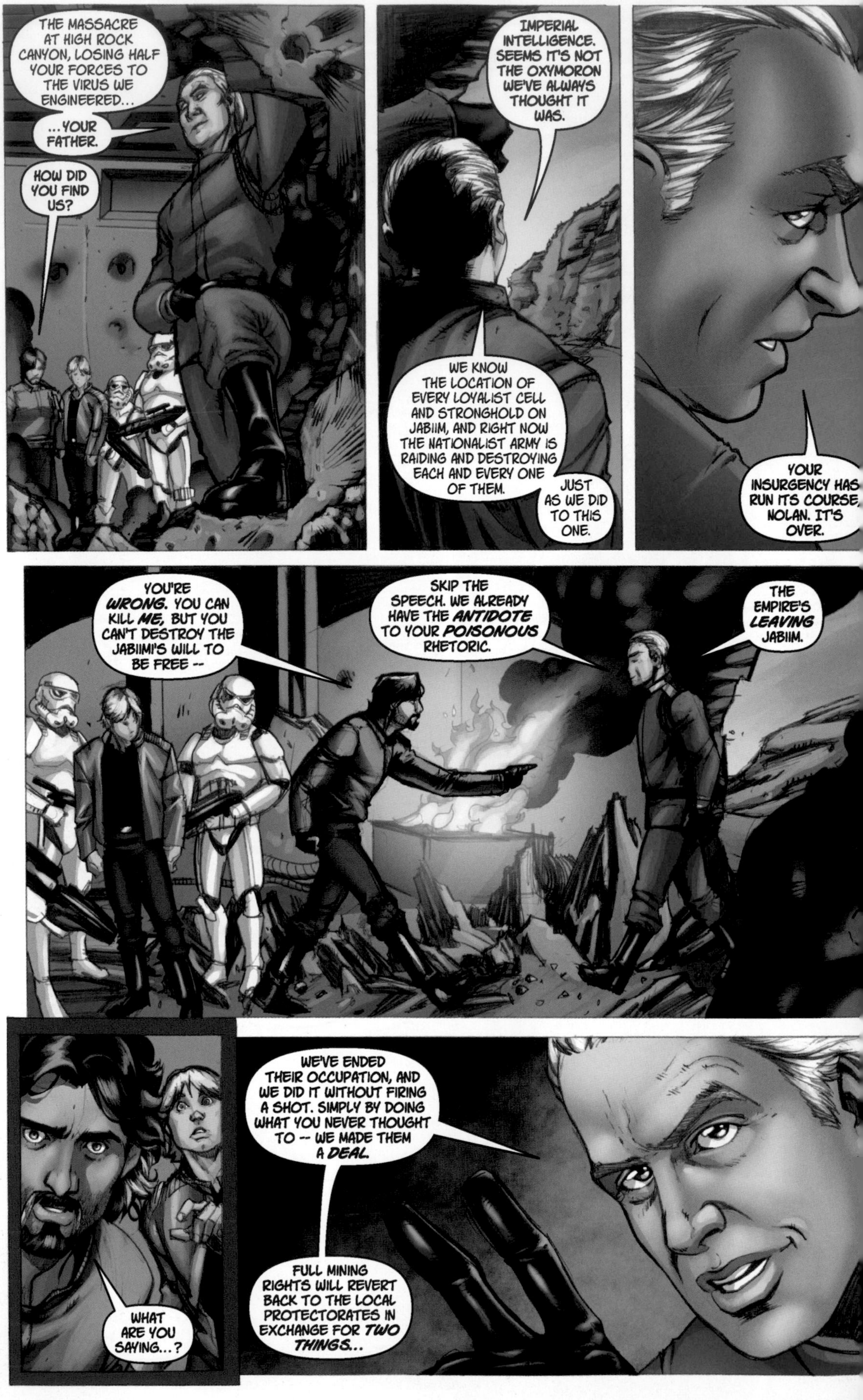
THE MASSACRE AT HIGH ROCK CANYON, LOSING HALF YOUR FORCES TO THE VIRUS WE ENGINEERED...
...YOUR FATHER.
HOW DID YOU FIND US?
IMPERIAL INTELLIGENCE. SEEMS IT'S NOT THE OXYMORON WE'VE ALWAYS THOUGHT IT WAS.
WE KNOW THE LOCATION OF EVERY LOYALIST CELL AND STRONGHOLD ON JABIIM, AND RIGHT NOW THE NATIONALIST ARMY IS RAIDING AND DESTROYING EACH AND EVERY ONE OF THEM.
JUST AS WE DID TO THIS ONE.
YOUR INSURGENCY HAS RUN ITS COURSE, NOLAN. IT'S OVER.
YOU'RE *WRONG.* YOU CAN KILL *ME,* BUT YOU CAN'T DESTROY THE JABIIMI'S WILL TO BE FREE --
SKIP THE SPEECH. WE ALREADY HAVE THE *ANTIDOTE* TO YOUR *POISONOUS* RHETORIC.
THE EMPIRE'S *LEAVING* JABIIM.
WE'VE ENDED THEIR OCCUPATION, AND WE DID IT WITHOUT FIRING A SHOT. SIMPLY BY DOING WHAT YOU NEVER THOUGHT TO -- WE MADE THEM A *DEAL.*
FULL MINING RIGHTS WILL REVERT BACK TO THE LOCAL PROTECTORATES IN EXCHANGE FOR *TWO THINGS...*
WHAT ARE YOU SAYING...?

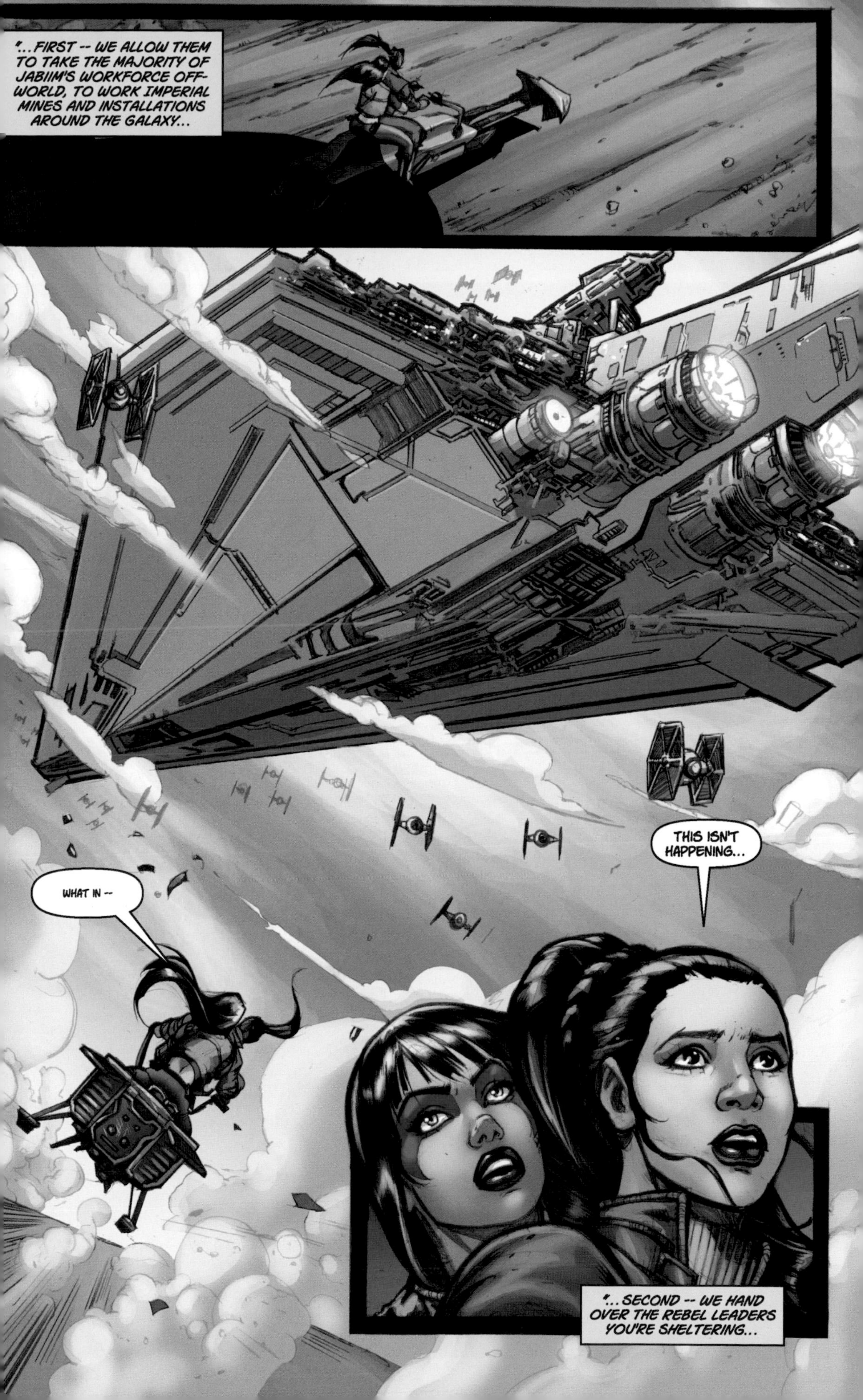
"...FIRST -- WE ALLOW THEM TO TAKE THE MAJORITY OF JABIIM'S WORKFORCE OFF-WORLD, TO WORK IMPERIAL MINES AND INSTALLATIONS AROUND THE GALAXY...
WHAT IN --
THIS ISN'T HAPPENING...
"...SECOND -- WE HAND OVER THE REBEL LEADERS YOU'RE SHELTERING...

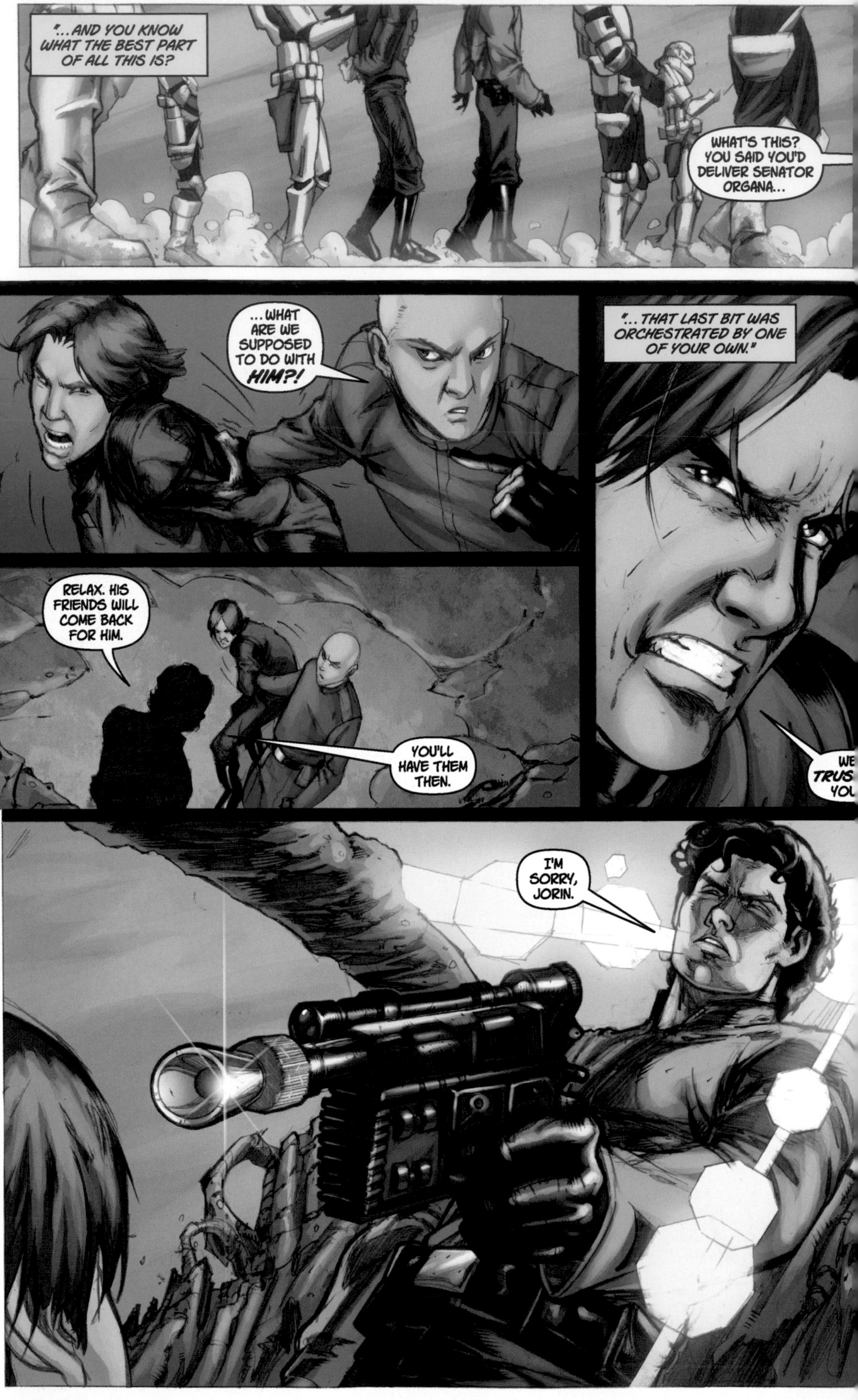
"...AND YOU KNOW WHAT THE BEST PART OF ALL THIS IS?
WHAT'S THIS? YOU SAID YOU'D DELIVER SENATOR ORGANA...
...WHAT ARE WE SUPPOSED TO DO WITH HIM?!
"...THAT LAST BIT WAS ORCHESTRATED BY ONE OF YOUR OWN."
RELAX. HIS FRIENDS WILL COME BACK FOR HIM.
YOU'LL HAVE THEM THEN.
WE TRUS YOU
I'M SORRY, JORIN.

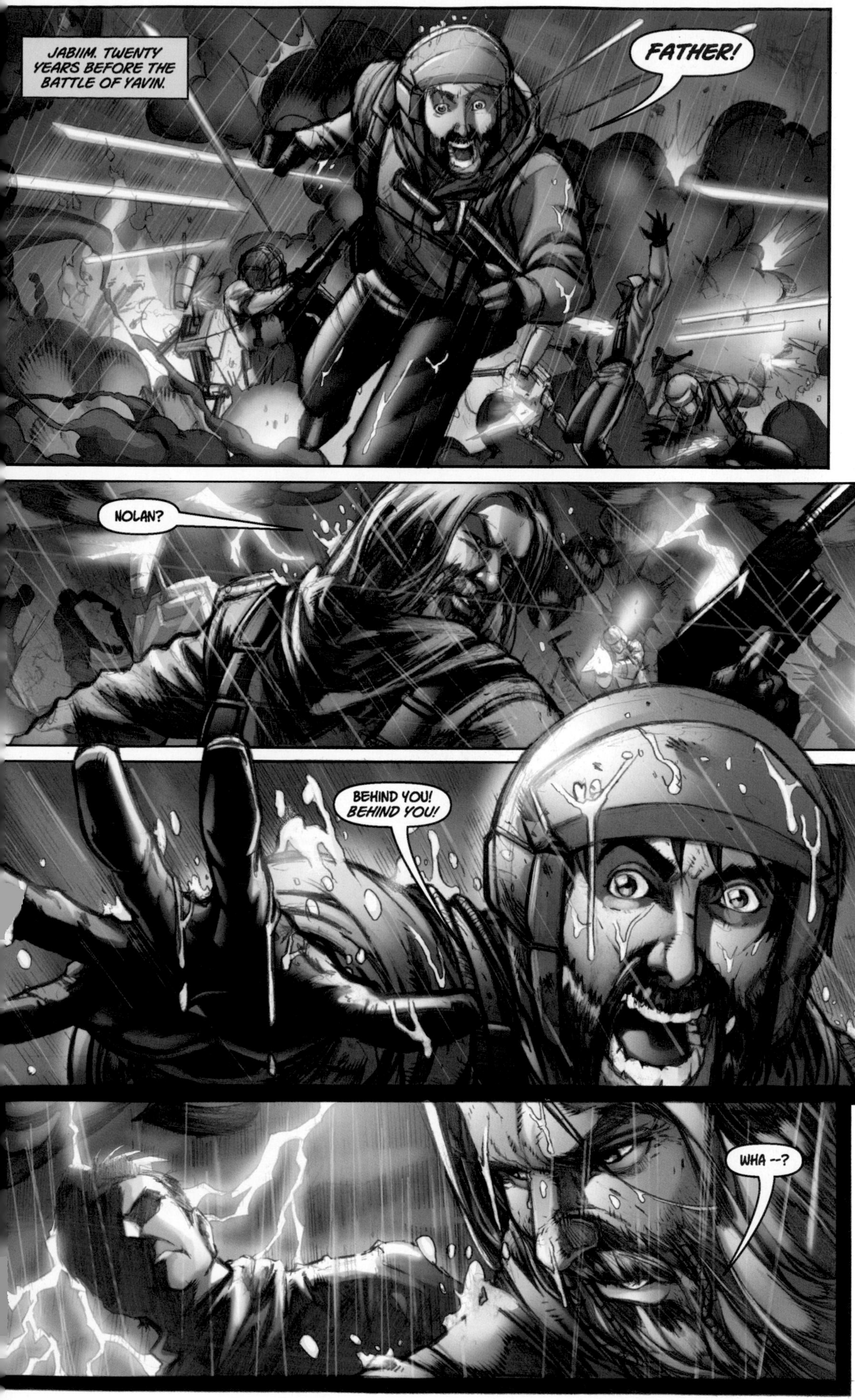
JABIIM. TWENTY YEARS BEFORE THE BATTLE OF YAVIN.
FATHER!
NOLAN?
BEHIND YOU! BEHIND YOU!
WHA --?

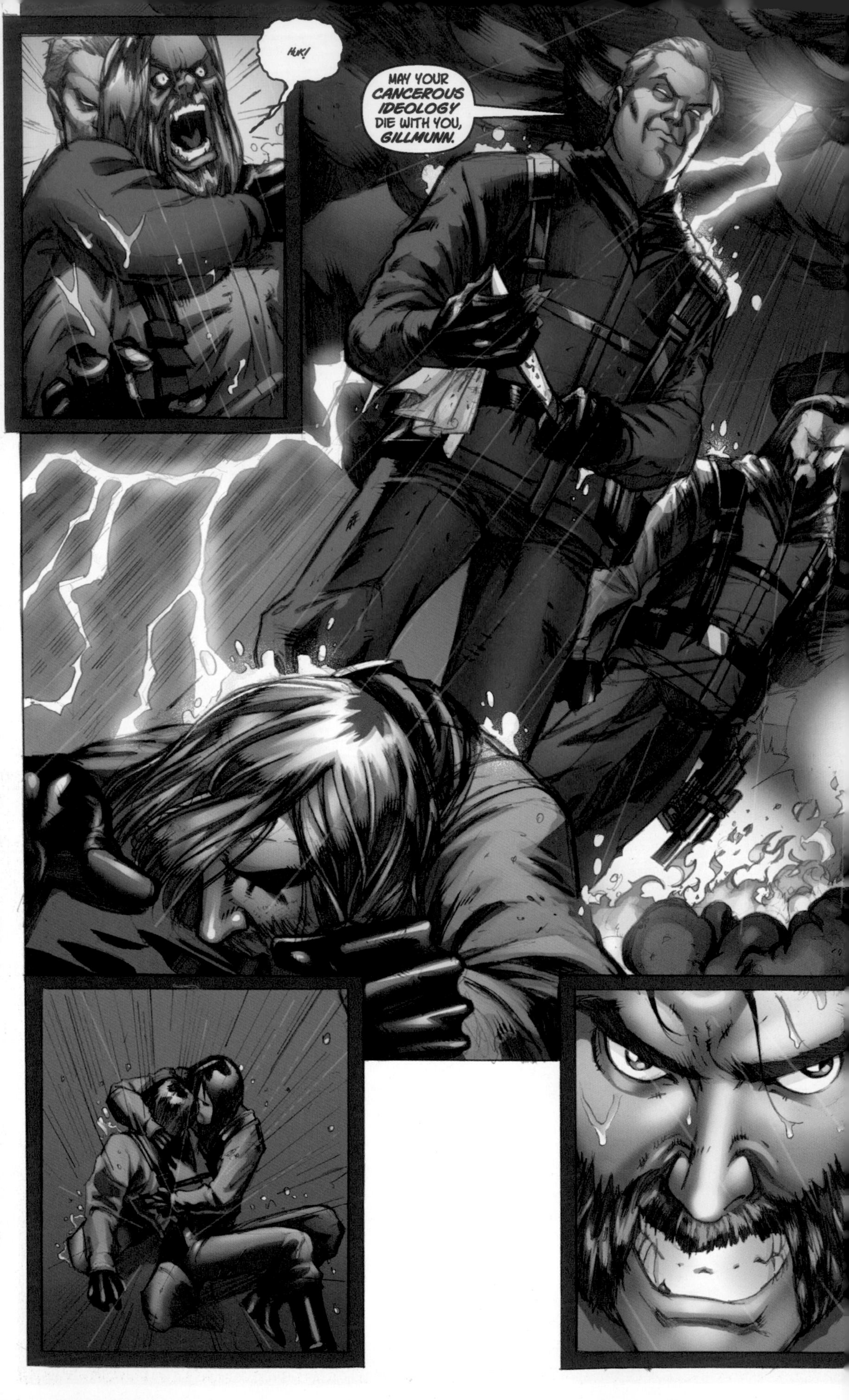
HUK!
MAY YOUR CANCEROUS IDEOLOGY DIE WITH YOU, GILLMUNN.

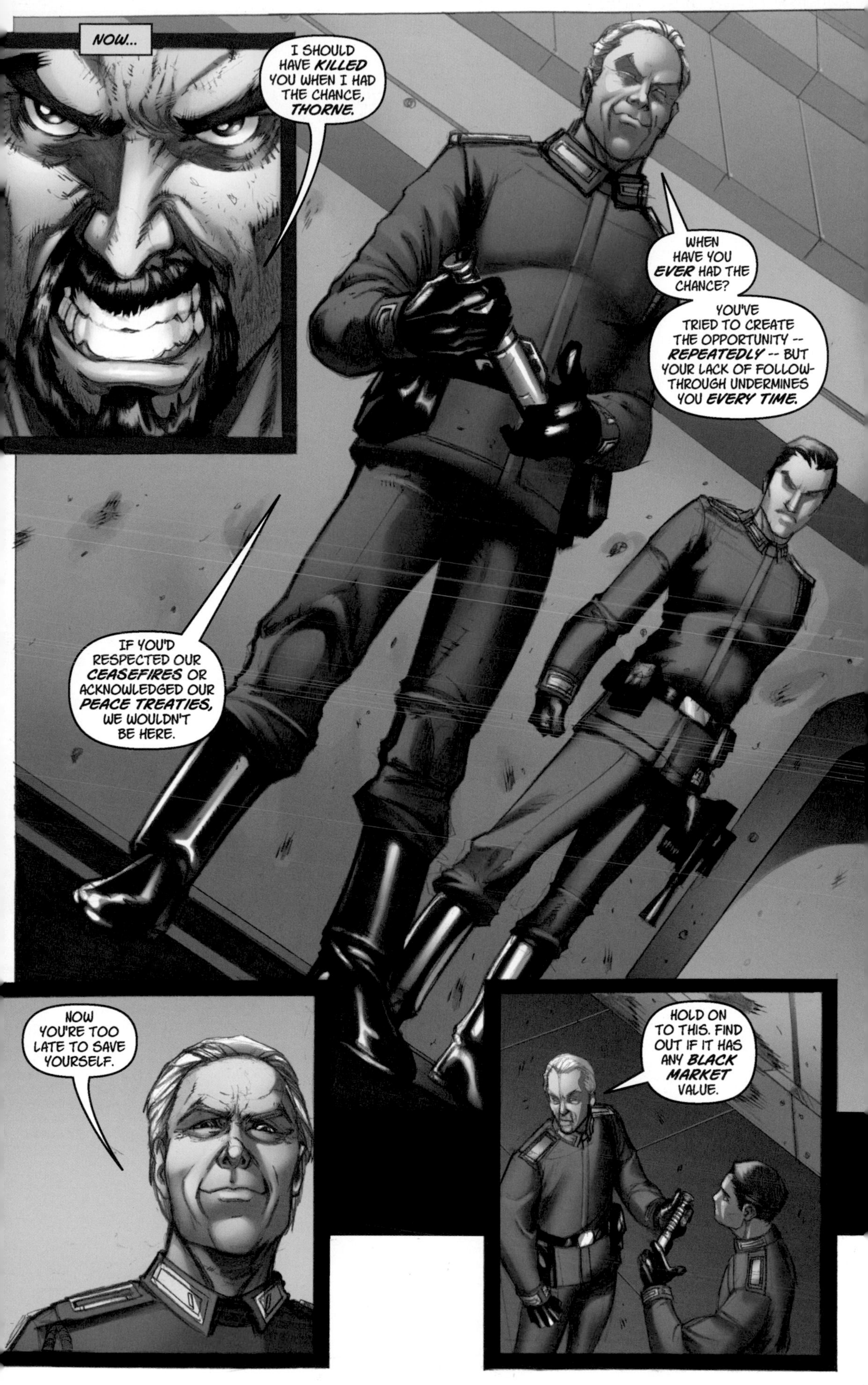
NOW...
I SHOULD HAVE KILLED YOU WHEN I HAD THE CHANCE, THORNE.
WHEN HAVE YOU EVER HAD THE CHANCE?
YOU'VE TRIED TO CREATE THE OPPORTUNITY -- REPEATEDLY -- BUT YOUR LACK OF FOLLOW-THROUGH UNDERMINES YOU EVERY TIME.
IF YOU'D RESPECTED OUR CEASEFIRES OR ACKNOWLEDGED OUR PEACE TREATIES, WE WOULDN'T BE HERE.
NOW YOU'RE TOO LATE TO SAVE YOURSELF.
HOLD ON TO THIS. FIND OUT IF IT HAS ANY BLACK MARKET VALUE.

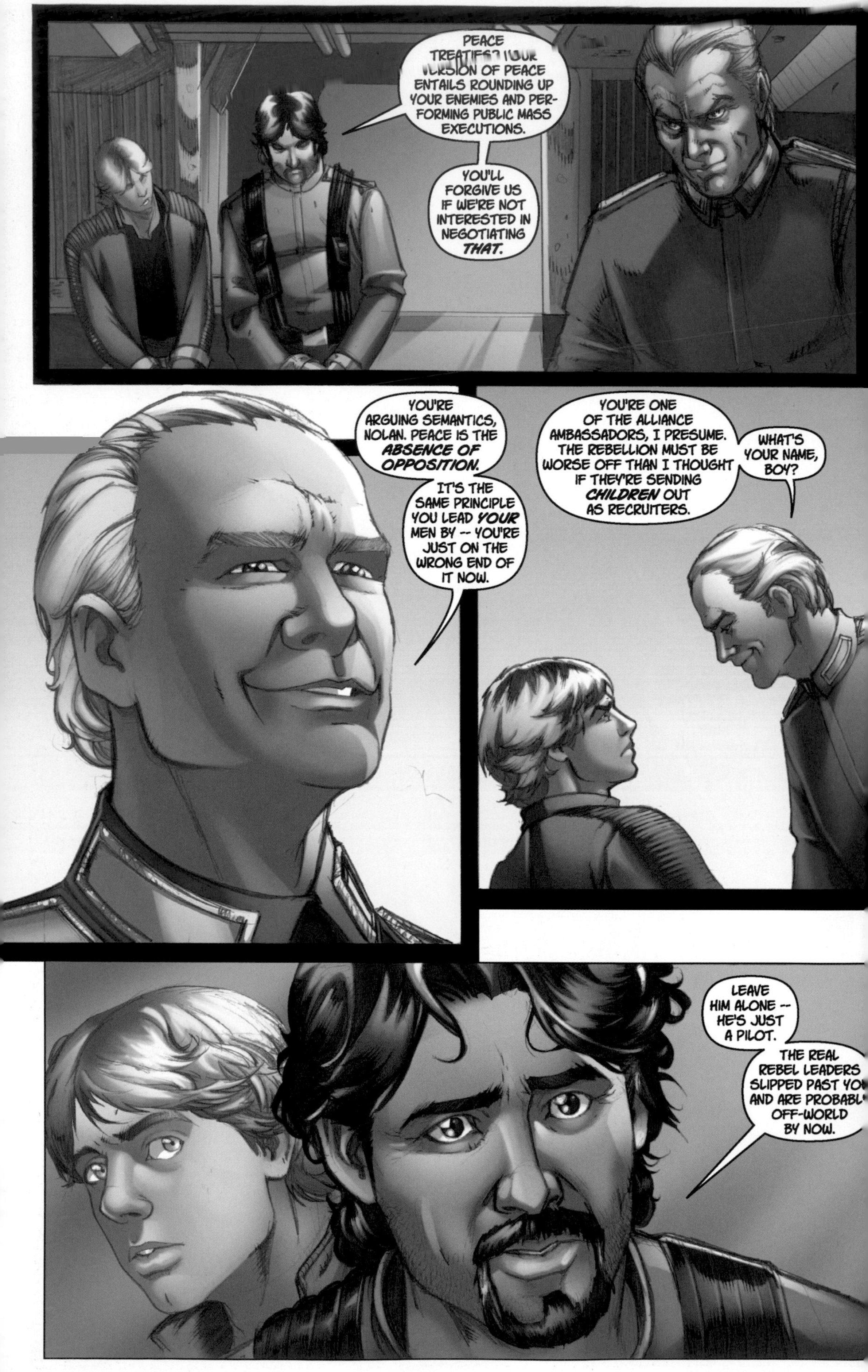
PEACE TREATIES? YOUR VERSION OF PEACE ENTAILS ROUNDING UP YOUR ENEMIES AND PER-FORMING PUBLIC MASS EXECUTIONS.
YOU'LL FORGIVE US IF WE'RE NOT INTERESTED IN NEGOTIATING *THAT*.
YOU'RE ARGUING SEMANTICS, NOLAN. PEACE IS THE *ABSENCE OF OPPOSITION*.
IT'S THE SAME PRINCIPLE YOU LEAD *YOUR* MEN BY -- YOU'RE JUST ON THE WRONG END OF IT NOW.
YOU'RE ONE OF THE ALLIANCE AMBASSADORS, I PRESUME. THE REBELLION MUST BE WORSE OFF THAN I THOUGHT IF THEY'RE SENDING *CHILDREN* OUT AS RECRUITERS.
WHAT'S YOUR NAME, BOY?
LEAVE HIM ALONE -- HE'S JUST A PILOT.
THE REAL REBEL LEADERS SLIPPED PAST YO AND ARE PROBABL OFF-WORLD BY NOW.

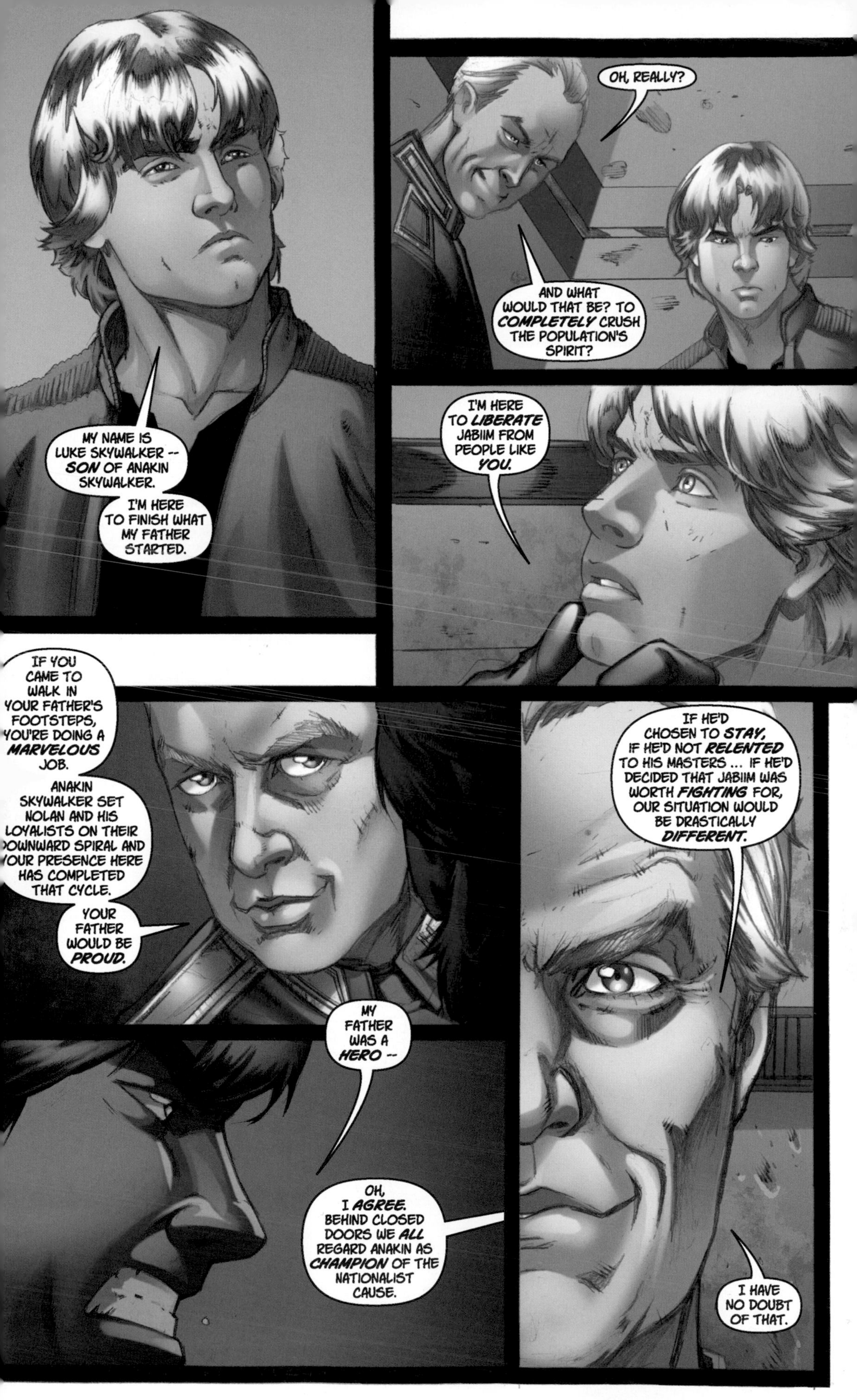
MY NAME IS LUKE SKYWALKER -- SON OF ANAKIN SKYWALKER.
I'M HERE TO FINISH WHAT MY FATHER STARTED.
OH, REALLY?
AND WHAT WOULD THAT BE? TO COMPLETELY CRUSH THE POPULATION'S SPIRIT?
I'M HERE TO LIBERATE JABIIM FROM PEOPLE LIKE YOU.
IF YOU CAME TO WALK IN YOUR FATHER'S FOOTSTEPS, YOU'RE DOING A MARVELOUS JOB.
ANAKIN SKYWALKER SET NOLAN AND HIS LOYALISTS ON THEIR DOWNWARD SPIRAL AND YOUR PRESENCE HERE HAS COMPLETED THAT CYCLE.
YOUR FATHER WOULD BE PROUD.
IF HE'D CHOSEN TO STAY, IF HE'D NOT RELENTED TO HIS MASTERS ... IF HE'D DECIDED THAT JABIIM WAS WORTH FIGHTING FOR, OUR SITUATION WOULD BE DRASTICALLY DIFFERENT.
MY FATHER WAS A HERO --
OH, I AGREE. BEHIND CLOSED DOORS WE ALL REGARD ANAKIN AS CHAMPION OF THE NATIONALIST CAUSE.
I HAVE NO DOUBT OF THAT.

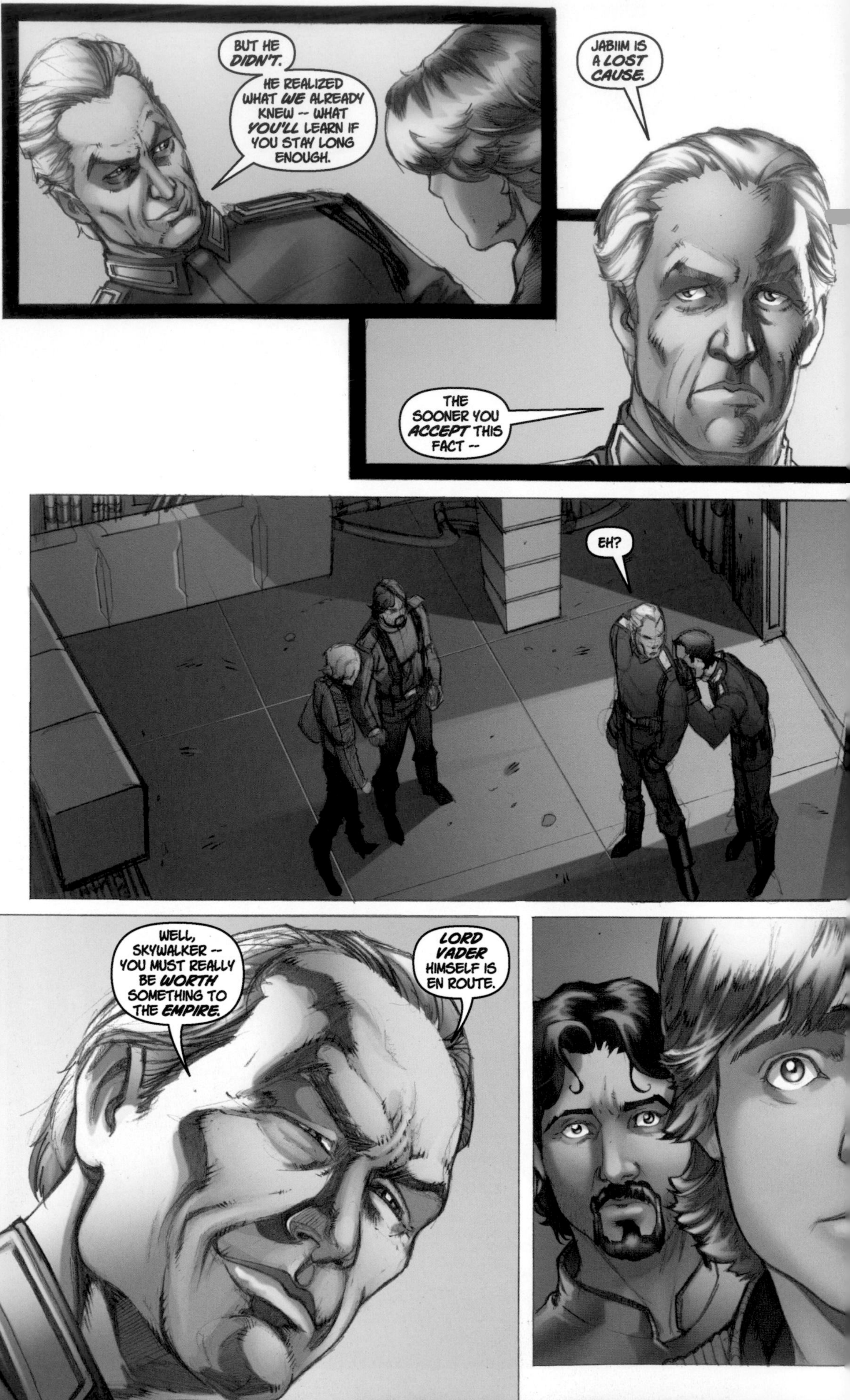
BUT HE DIDN'T.
HE REALIZED WHAT WE ALREADY KNEW -- WHAT YOU'LL LEARN IF YOU STAY LONG ENOUGH.
JABIIM IS A LOST CAUSE.
THE SOONER YOU ACCEPT THIS FACT --
EH?
WELL, SKYWALKER -- YOU MUST REALLY BE WORTH SOMETHING TO THE EMPIRE.
LORD VADER HIMSELF IS EN ROUTE.

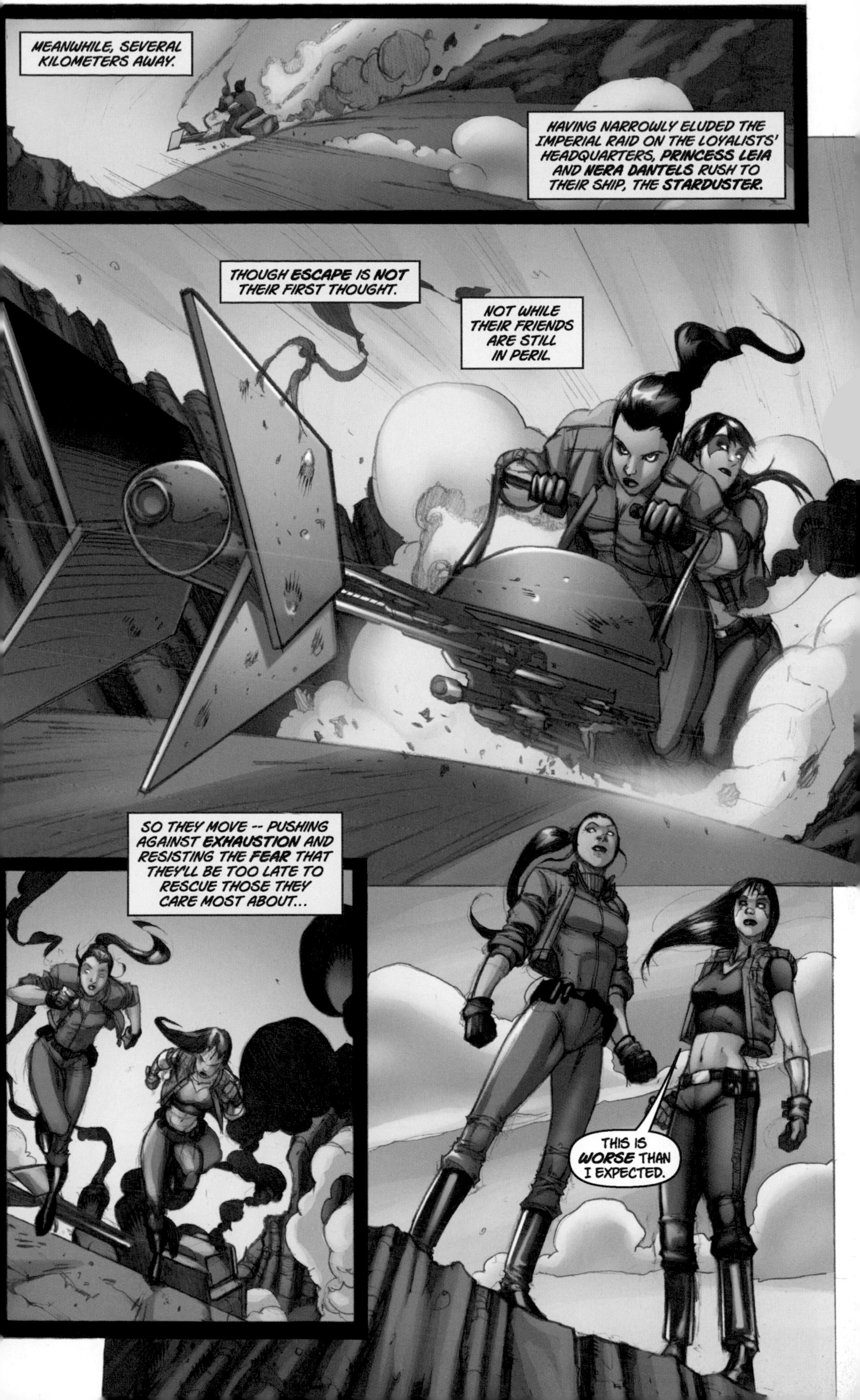
MEANWHILE, SEVERAL KILOMETERS AWAY.
HAVING NARROWLY ELUDED THE IMPERIAL RAID ON THE LOYALISTS' HEADQUARTERS, PRINCESS LEIA AND NERA DANTELS RUSH TO THEIR SHIP, THE STARDUSTER.
THOUGH ESCAPE IS NOT THEIR FIRST THOUGHT.
NOT WHILE THEIR FRIENDS ARE STILL IN PERIL.
SO THEY MOVE -- PUSHING AGAINST EXHAUSTION AND RESISTING THE FEAR THAT THEY'LL BE TOO LATE TO RESCUE THOSE THEY CARE MOST ABOUT...
THIS IS WORSE THAN I EXPECTED.

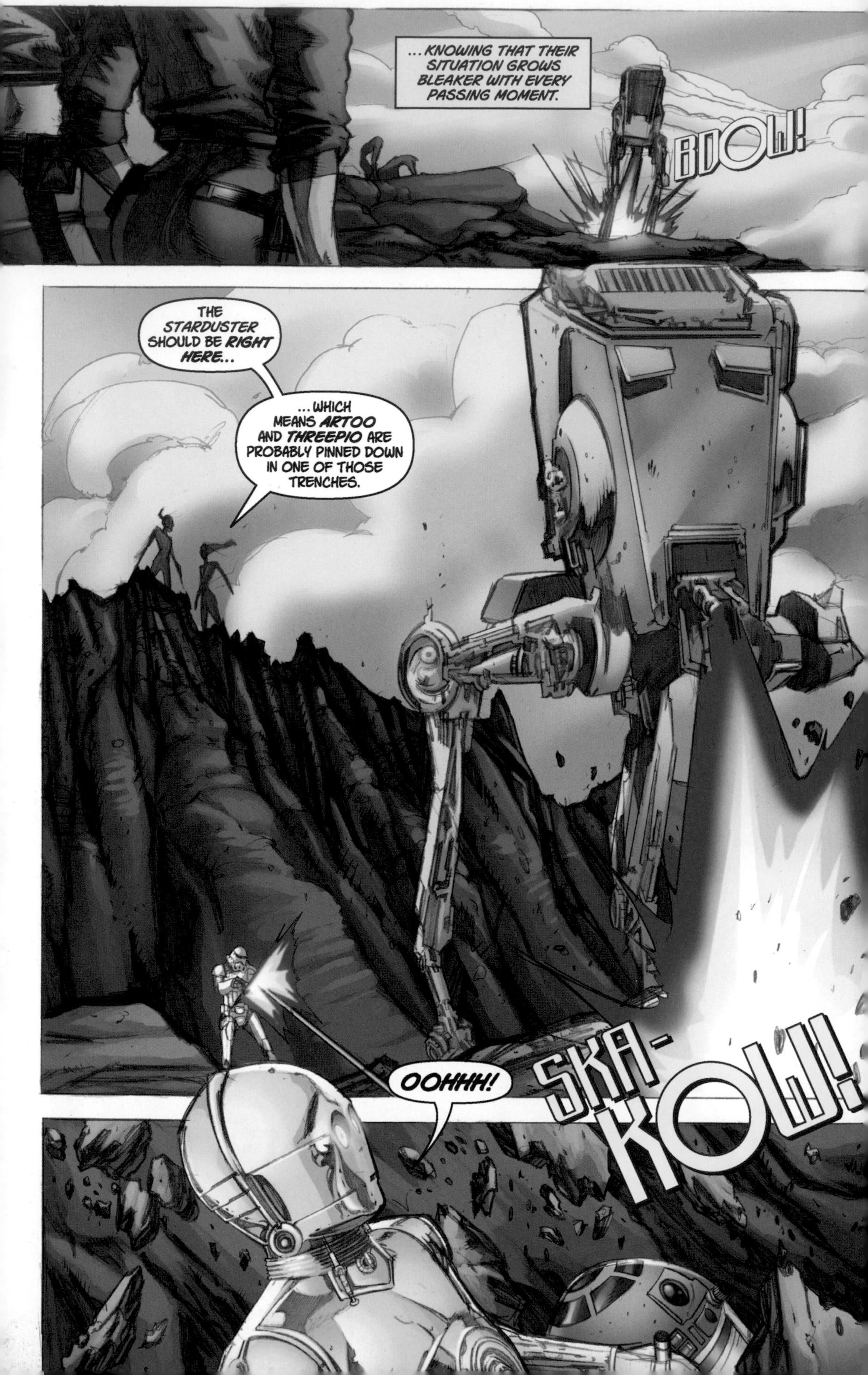
...KNOWING THAT THEIR SITUATION GROWS BLEAKER WITH EVERY PASSING MOMENT.
BDOW!
THE STARDUSTER SHOULD BE RIGHT HERE...
...WHICH MEANS ARTOO AND THREEPIO ARE PROBABLY PINNED DOWN IN ONE OF THOSE TRENCHES.
SKA-KOW!
OOHHH!

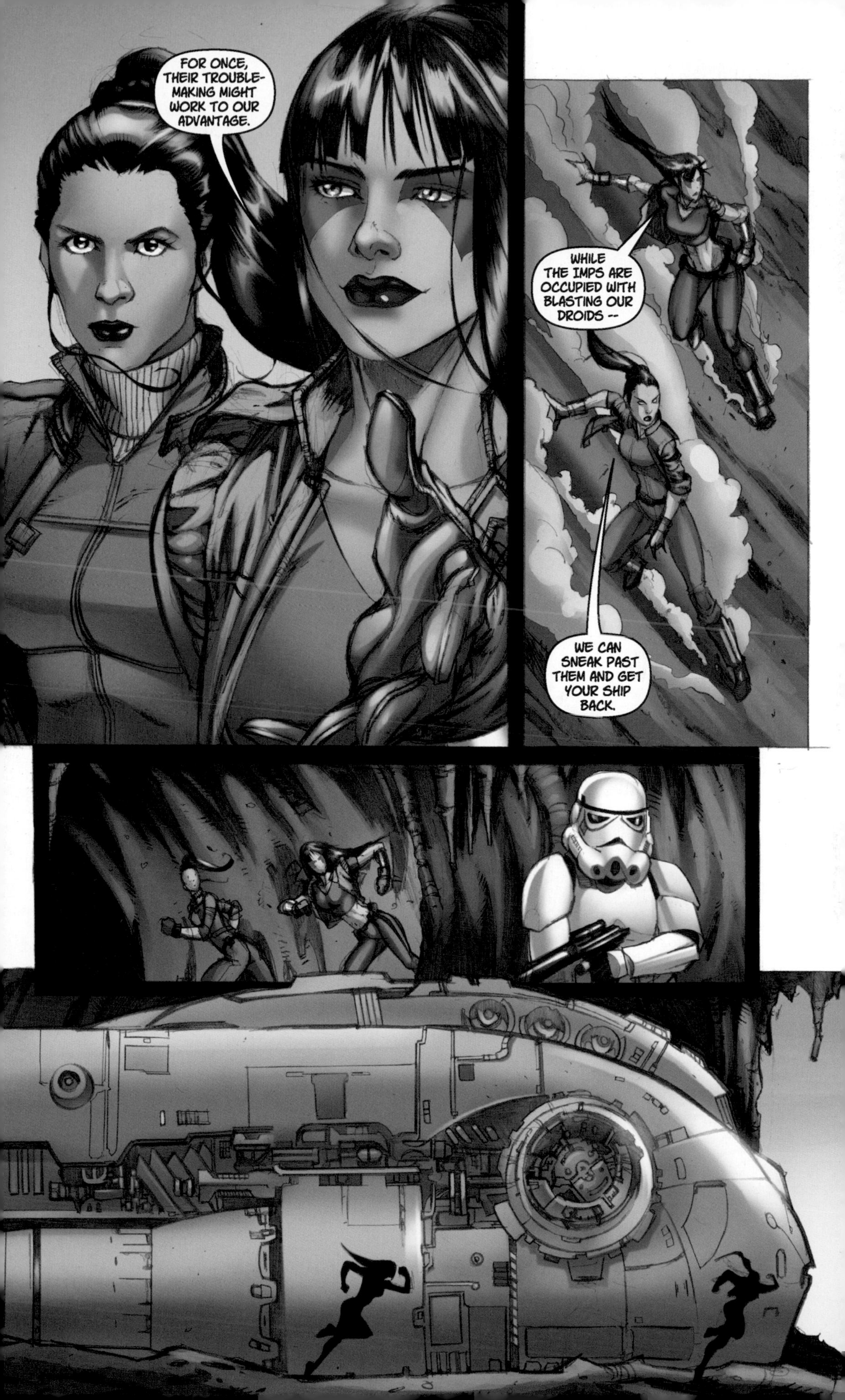
FOR ONCE, THEIR TROUBLE-MAKING MIGHT WORK TO OUR ADVANTAGE.
WHILE THE IMPS ARE OCCUPIED WITH BLASTING OUR DROIDS --
WE CAN SNEAK PAST THEM AND GET YOUR SHIP BACK.

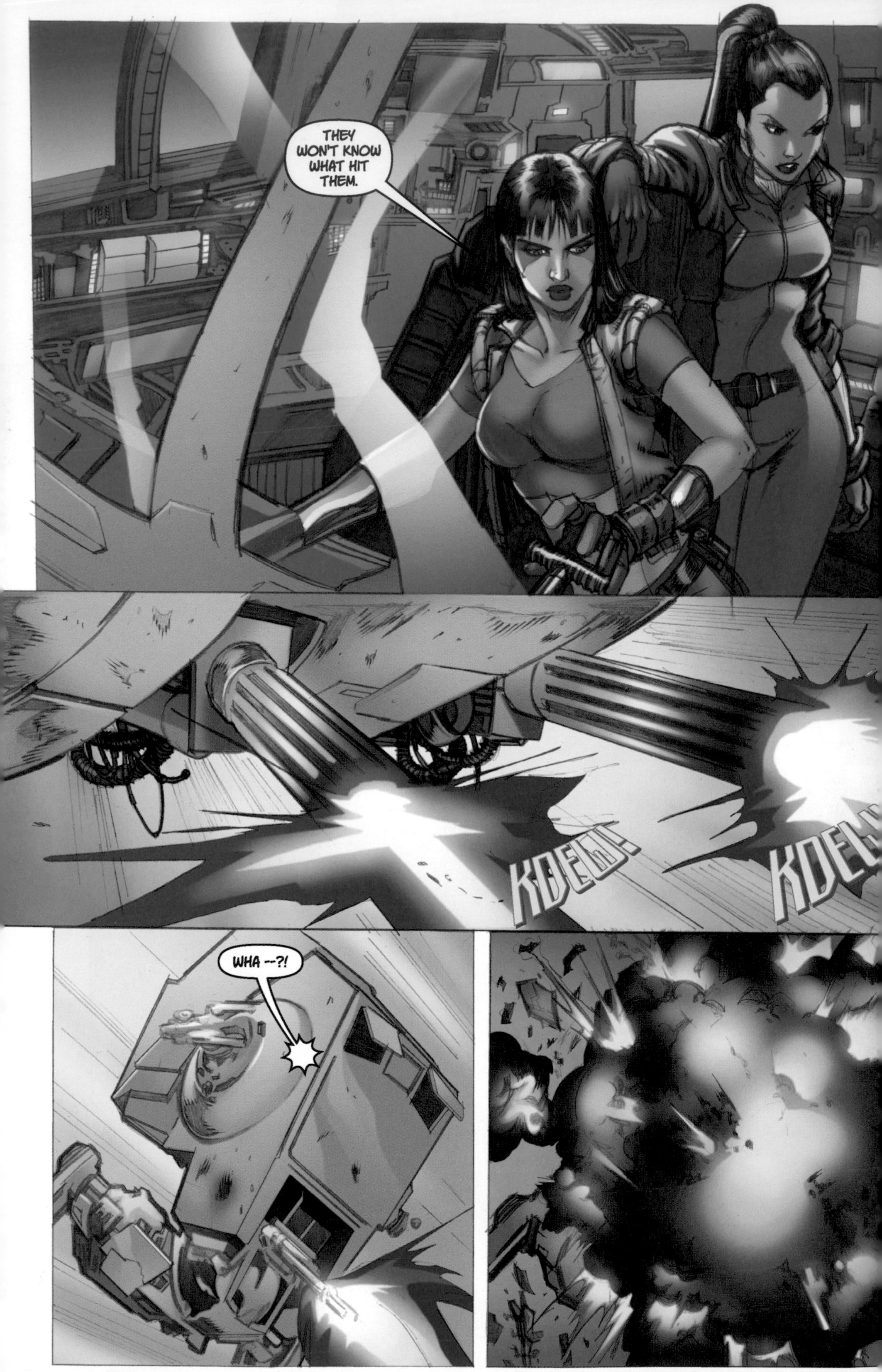
THEY WON'T KNOW WHAT HIT THEM.
KDEW!
WHA --?!

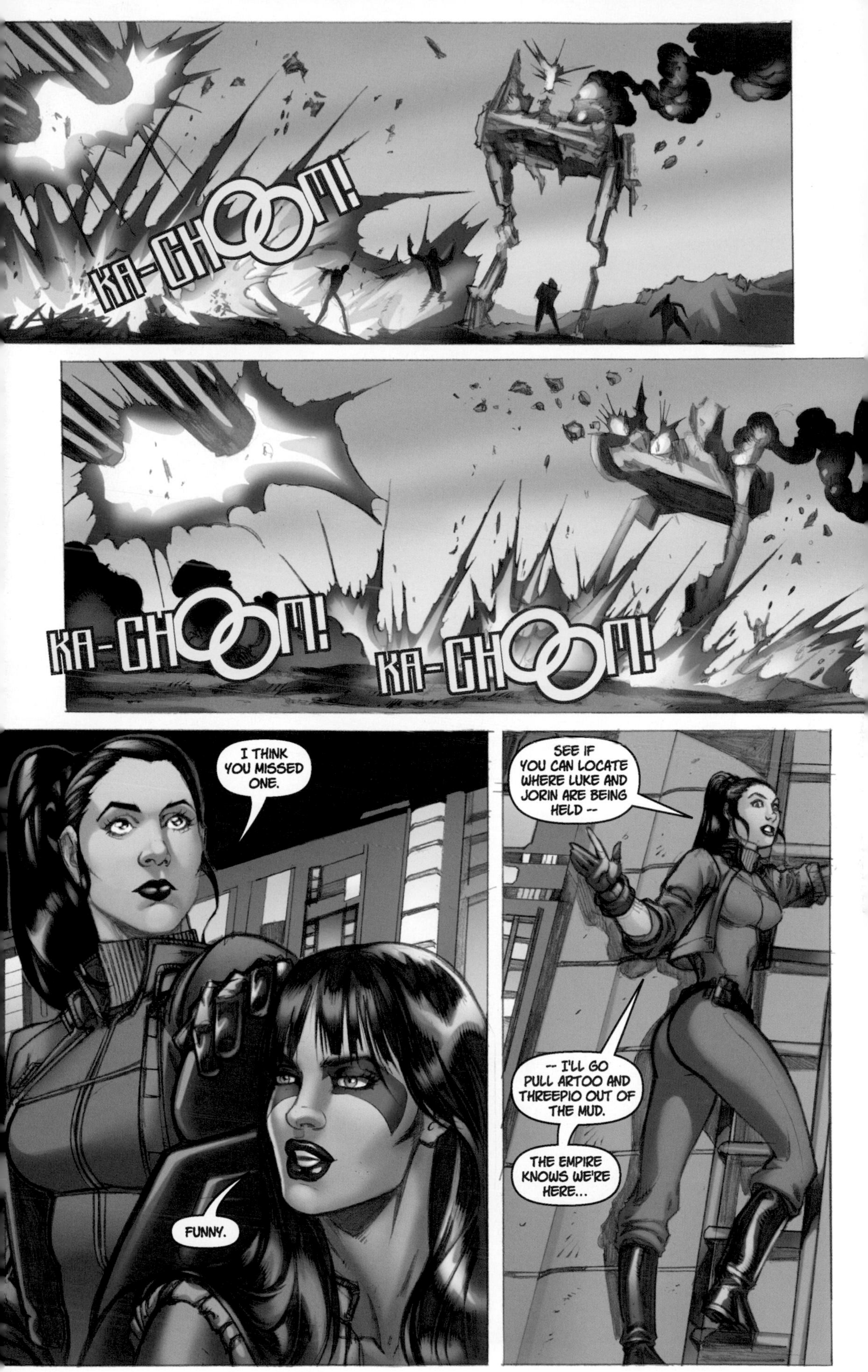
KA-CHOOM!
KA-CHOOM!
KA-CHOOM!
I THINK YOU MISSED ONE.
FUNNY.
SEE IF YOU CAN LOCATE WHERE LUKE AND JORIN ARE BEING HELD --
-- I'LL GO PULL ARTOO AND THREEPIO OUT OF THE MUD.
THE EMPIRE KNOWS WE'RE HERE...

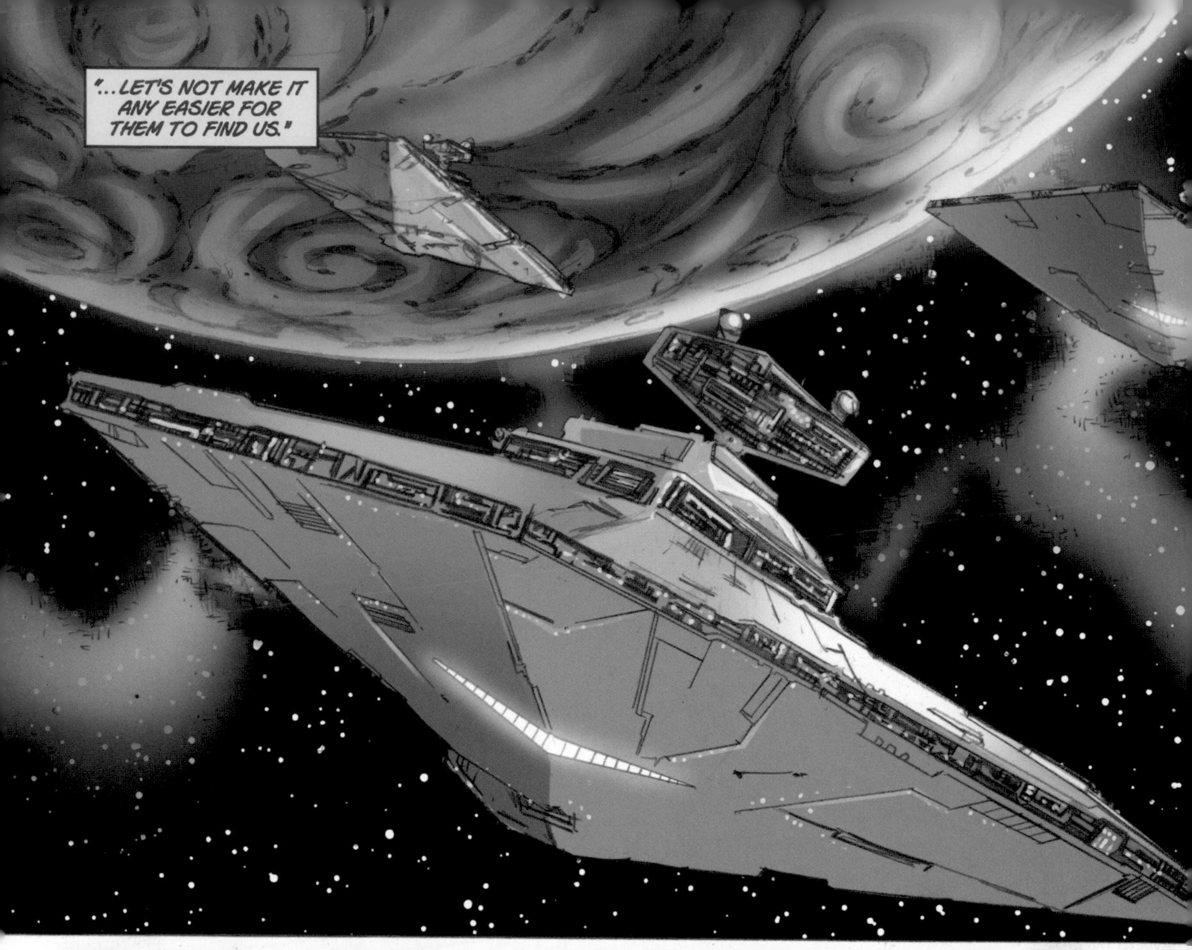
"...LET'S NOT MAKE IT ANY EASIER FOR THEM TO FIND US."

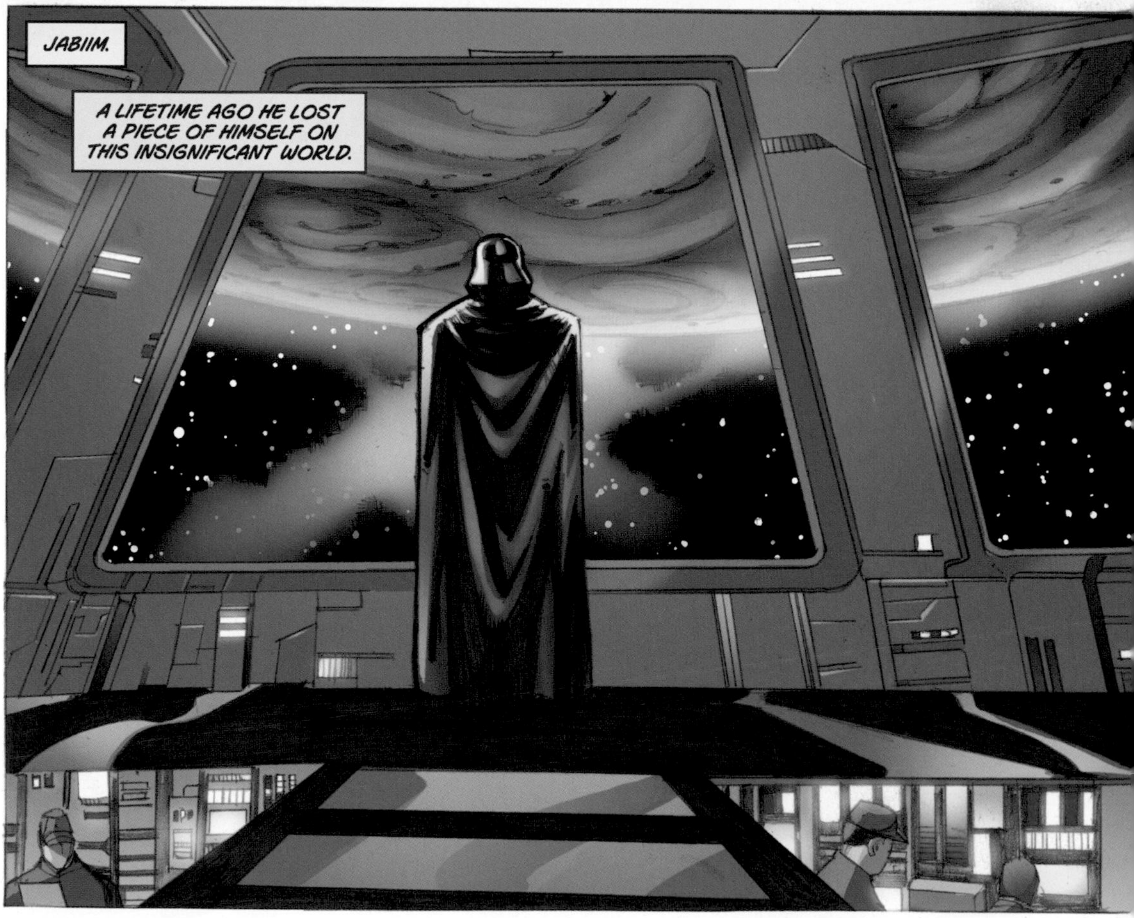
JABIIM.
A LIFETIME AGO HE LOST A PIECE OF HIMSELF ON THIS INSIGNIFICANT WORLD.

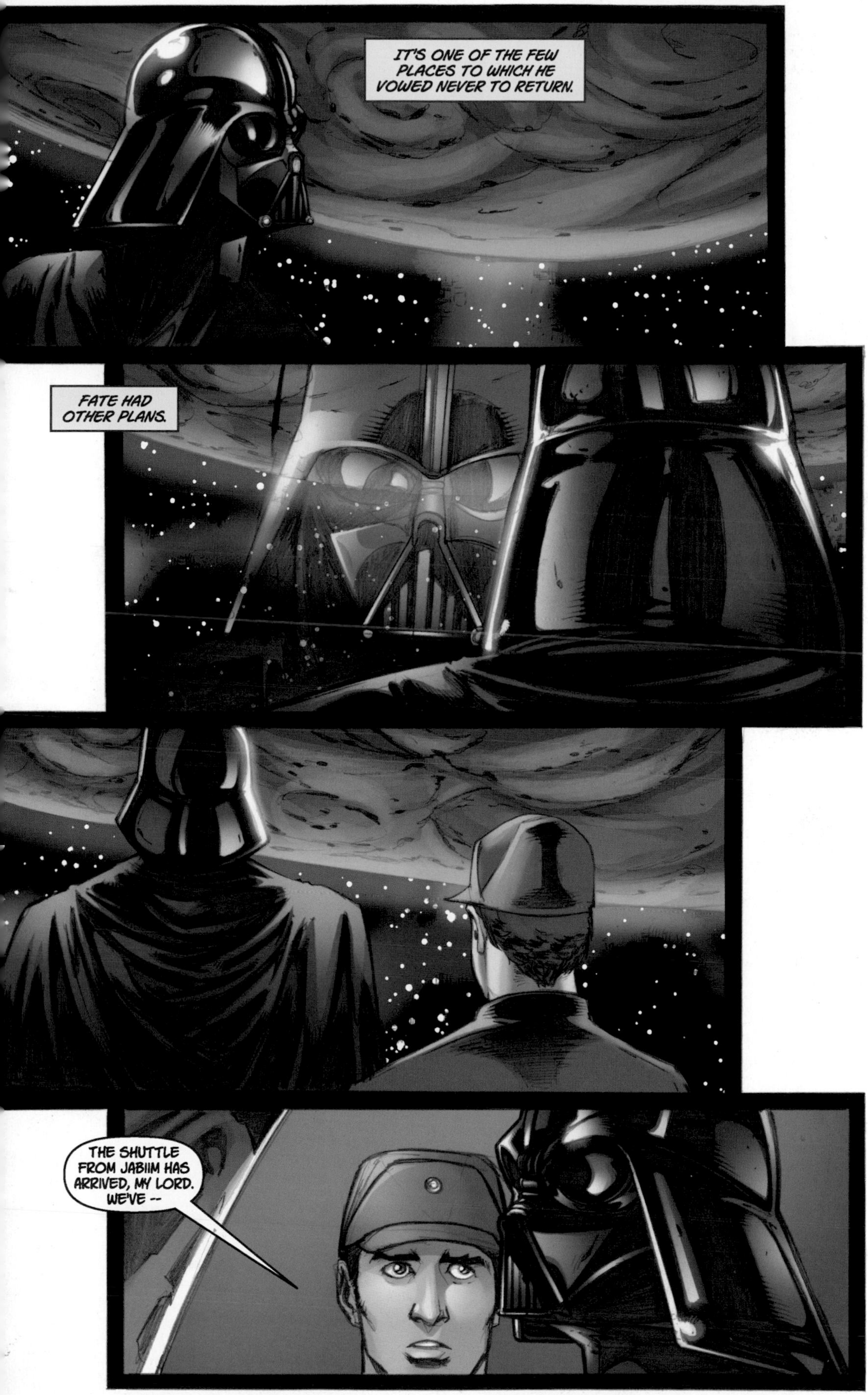
IT'S ONE OF THE FEW PLACES TO WHICH HE VOWED NEVER TO RETURN.
FATE HAD OTHER PLANS.
THE SHUTTLE FROM JABIIM HAS ARRIVED, MY LORD. WE'VE --

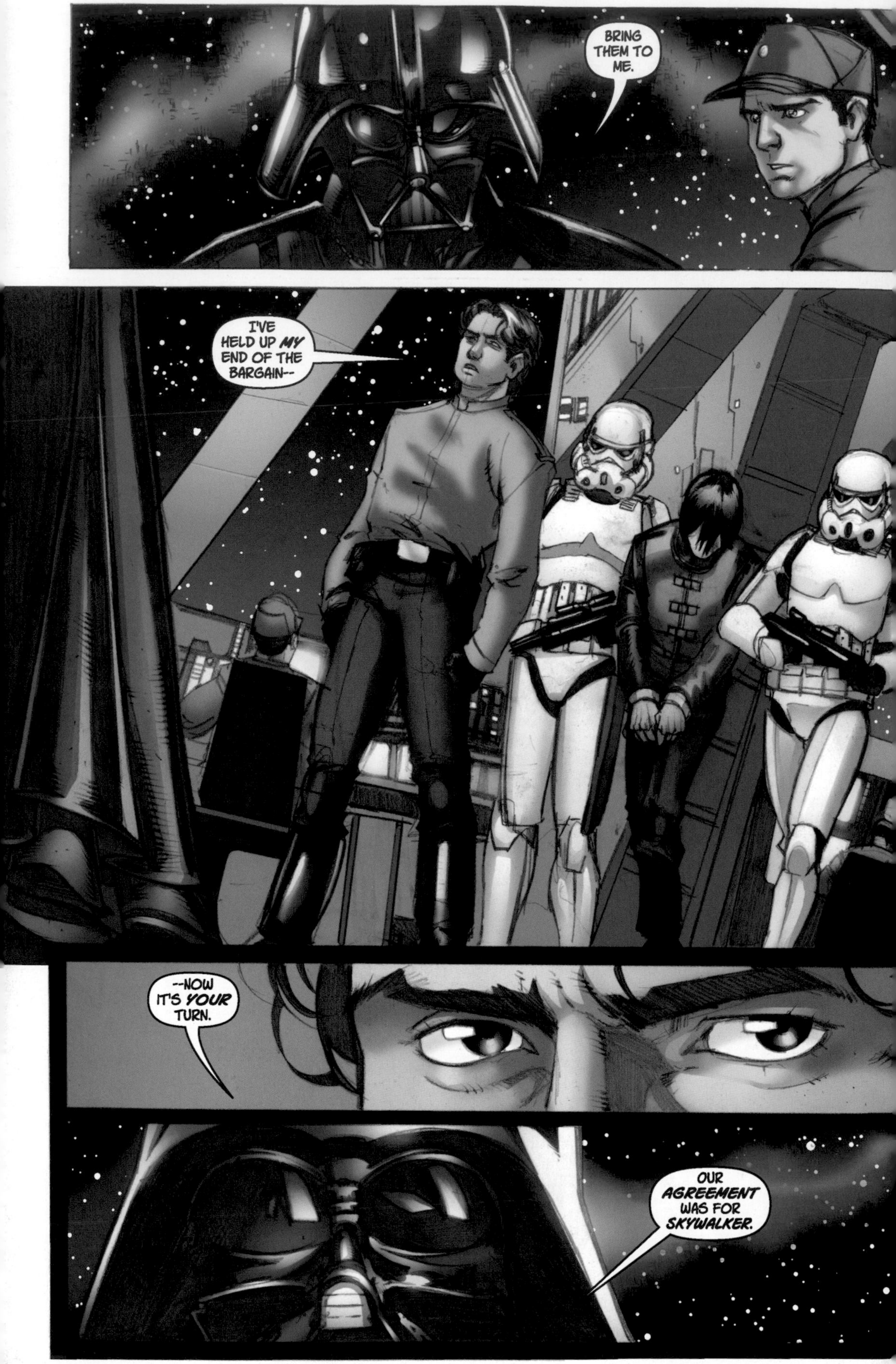
BRING THEM TO ME.
I'VE HELD UP MY END OF THE BARGAIN--
--NOW IT'S YOUR TURN.
OUR AGREEMENT WAS FOR SKYWALKER.

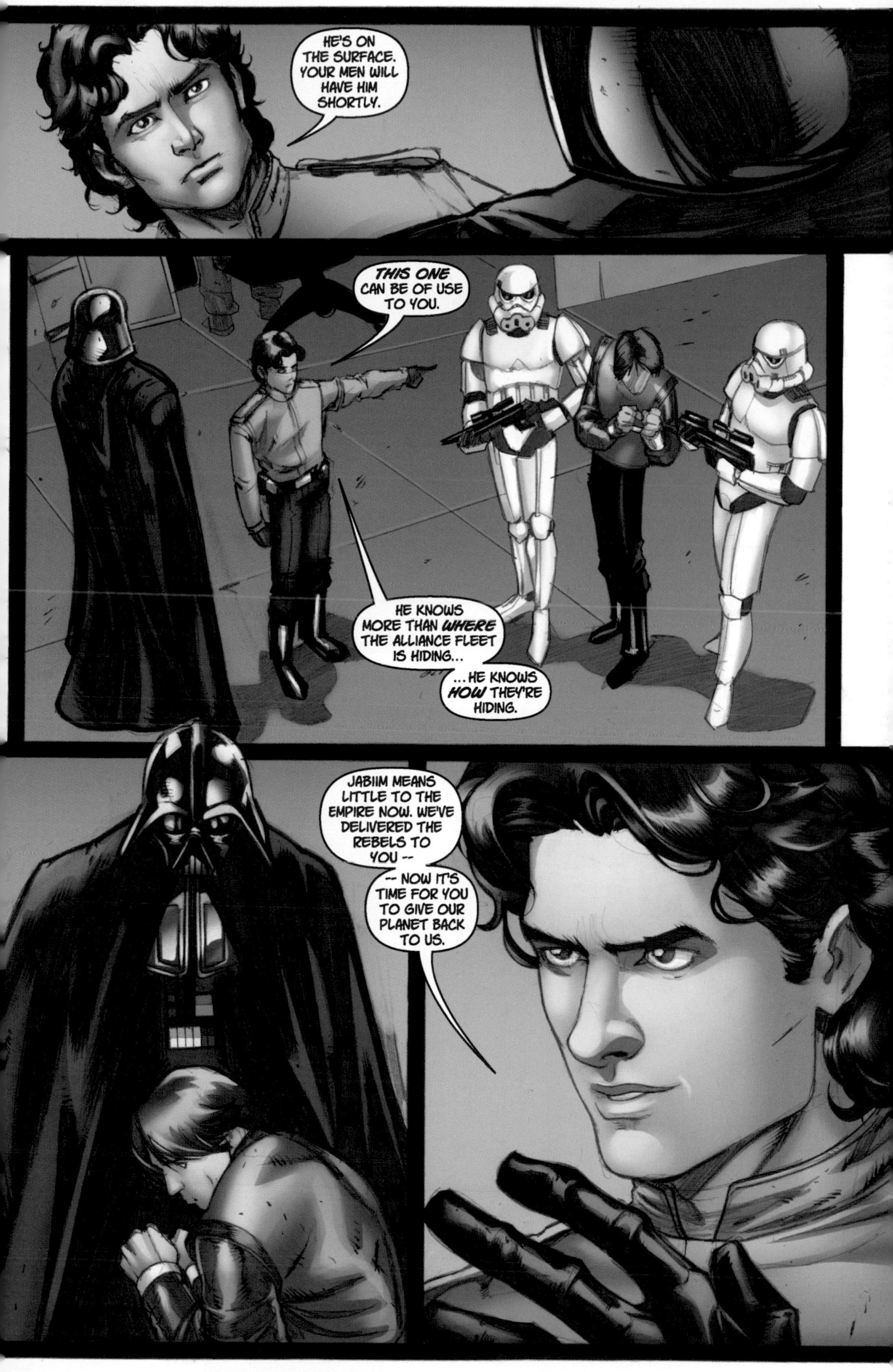
HE'S ON THE SURFACE. YOUR MEN WILL HAVE HIM SHORTLY.
THIS ONE CAN BE OF USE TO YOU.
HE KNOWS MORE THAN WHERE THE ALLIANCE FLEET IS HIDING...
...HE KNOWS HOW THEY'RE HIDING.
JABIIM MEANS LITTLE TO THE EMPIRE NOW. WE'VE DELIVERED THE REBELS TO YOU --
-- NOW IT'S TIME FOR YOU TO GIVE OUR PLANET BACK TO US.

I *TOLD* HIM WE SHOULD'VE STAYED PUT, YOUR HIGHNESS. HIS PROCESSORS NEED OVERHAULING!

WE'LL HAVE HIM CHECKED OUT WHEN WE GET BACK TO THE FLEET, *THREEPIO.*

ARTOO -- THINK YOU CAN GET OUT OF THERE?

FHOOT!

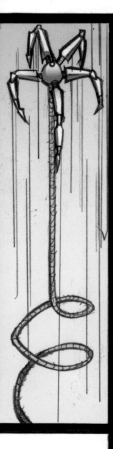

SCHIKK!

HOW *HUMIL ATING*

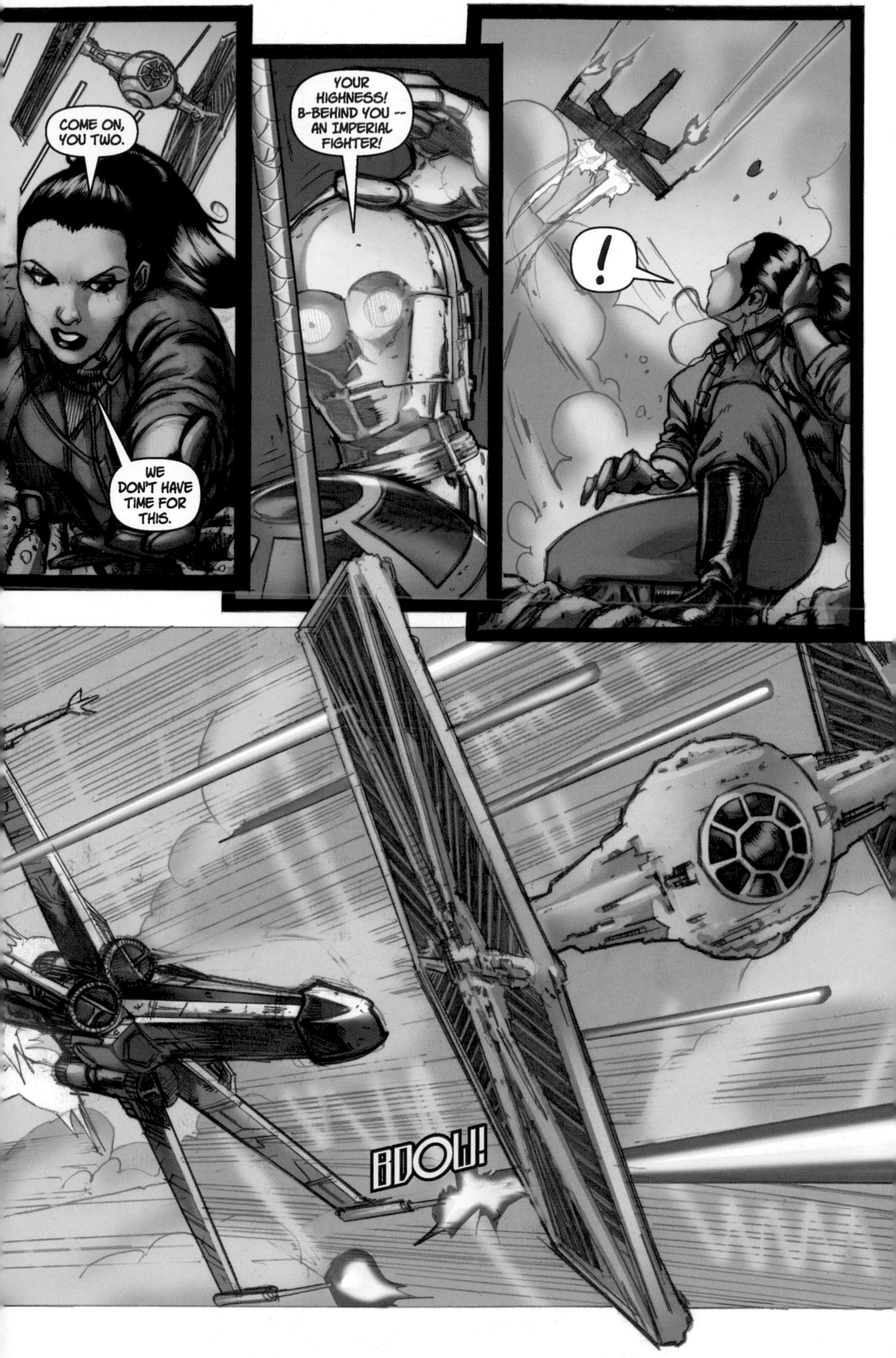
COME ON, YOU TWO.
WE DON'T HAVE TIME FOR THIS.
YOUR HIGHNESS! B-BEHIND YOU -- AN IMPERIAL FIGHTER!
!
BDOW!

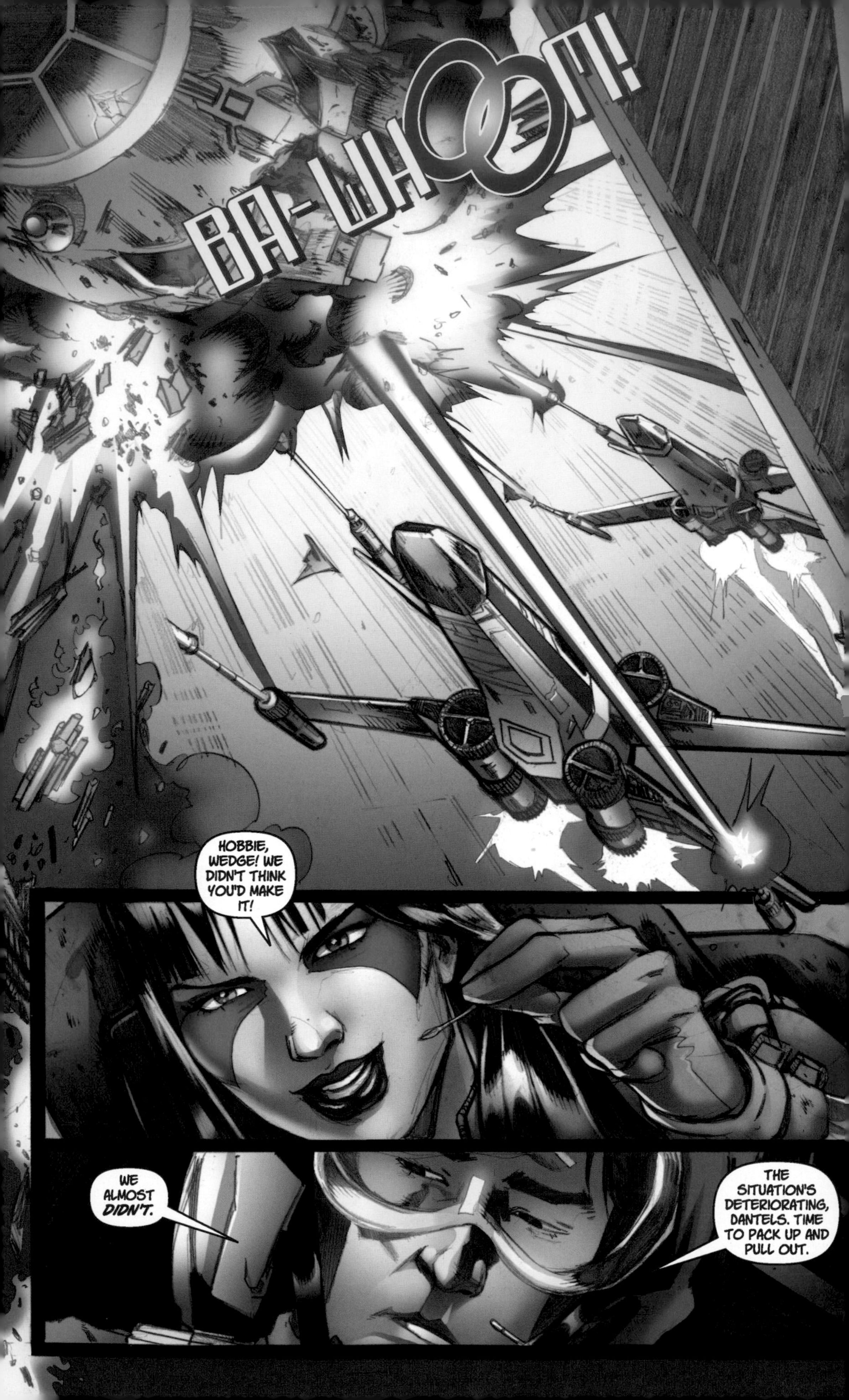
BA-WHOOM!
HOBBIE, WEDGE! WE DIDN'T THINK YOU'D MAKE IT!
WE ALMOST *DIDN'T*.
THE SITUATION'S DETERIORATING, DANTELS. TIME TO PACK UP AND PULL OUT.

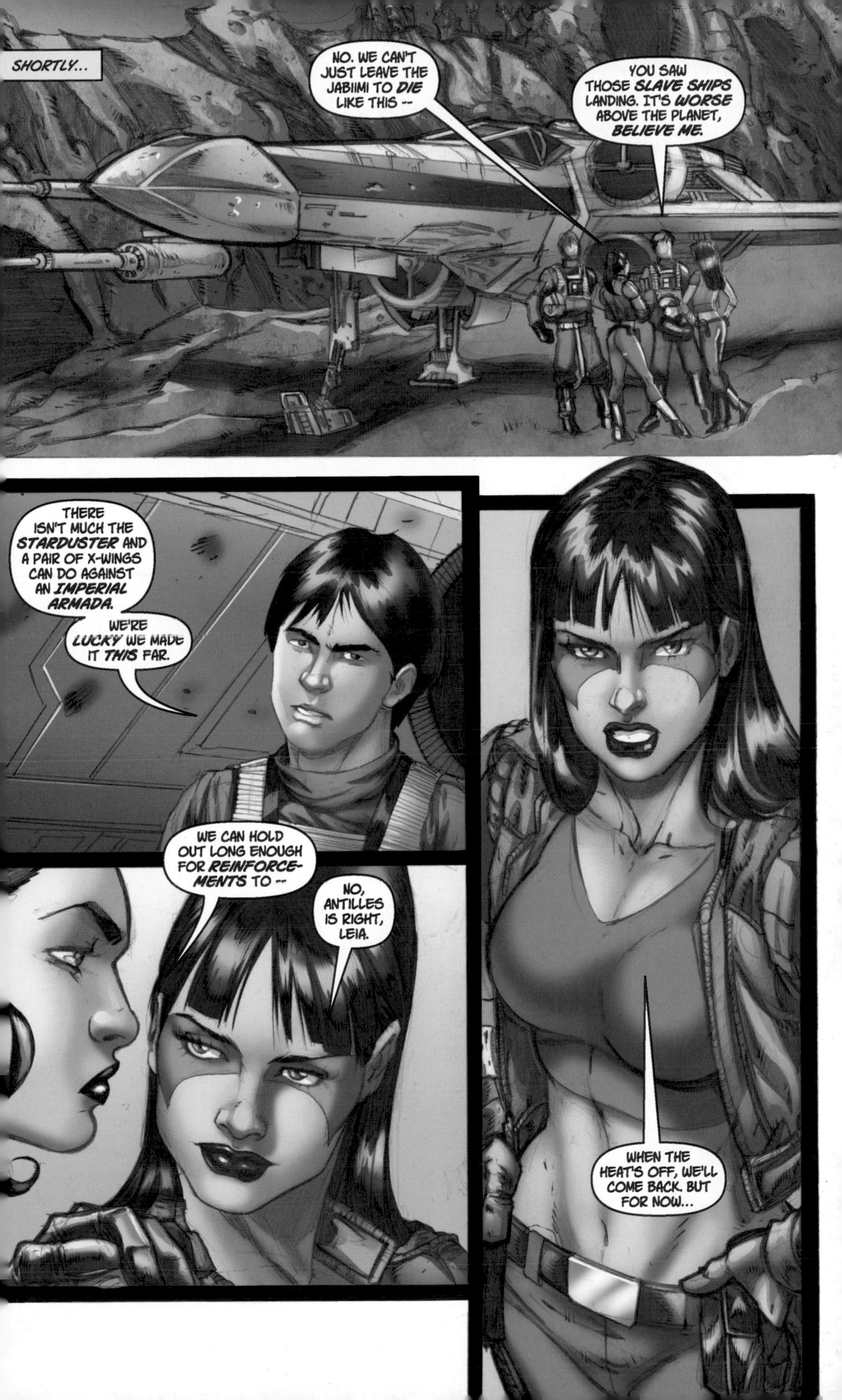
SHORTLY...
NO. WE CAN'T JUST LEAVE THE JABIIMI TO DIE LIKE THIS --
YOU SAW THOSE SLAVE SHIPS LANDING. IT'S WORSE ABOVE THE PLANET, BELIEVE ME.
THERE ISN'T MUCH THE STARDUSTER AND A PAIR OF X-WINGS CAN DO AGAINST AN IMPERIAL ARMADA.
WE'RE LUCKY WE MADE IT THIS FAR.
WE CAN HOLD OUT LONG ENOUGH FOR REINFORCE-MENTS TO --
NO, ANTILLES IS RIGHT, LEIA.
WHEN THE HEAT'S OFF, WE'LL COME BACK. BUT FOR NOW...

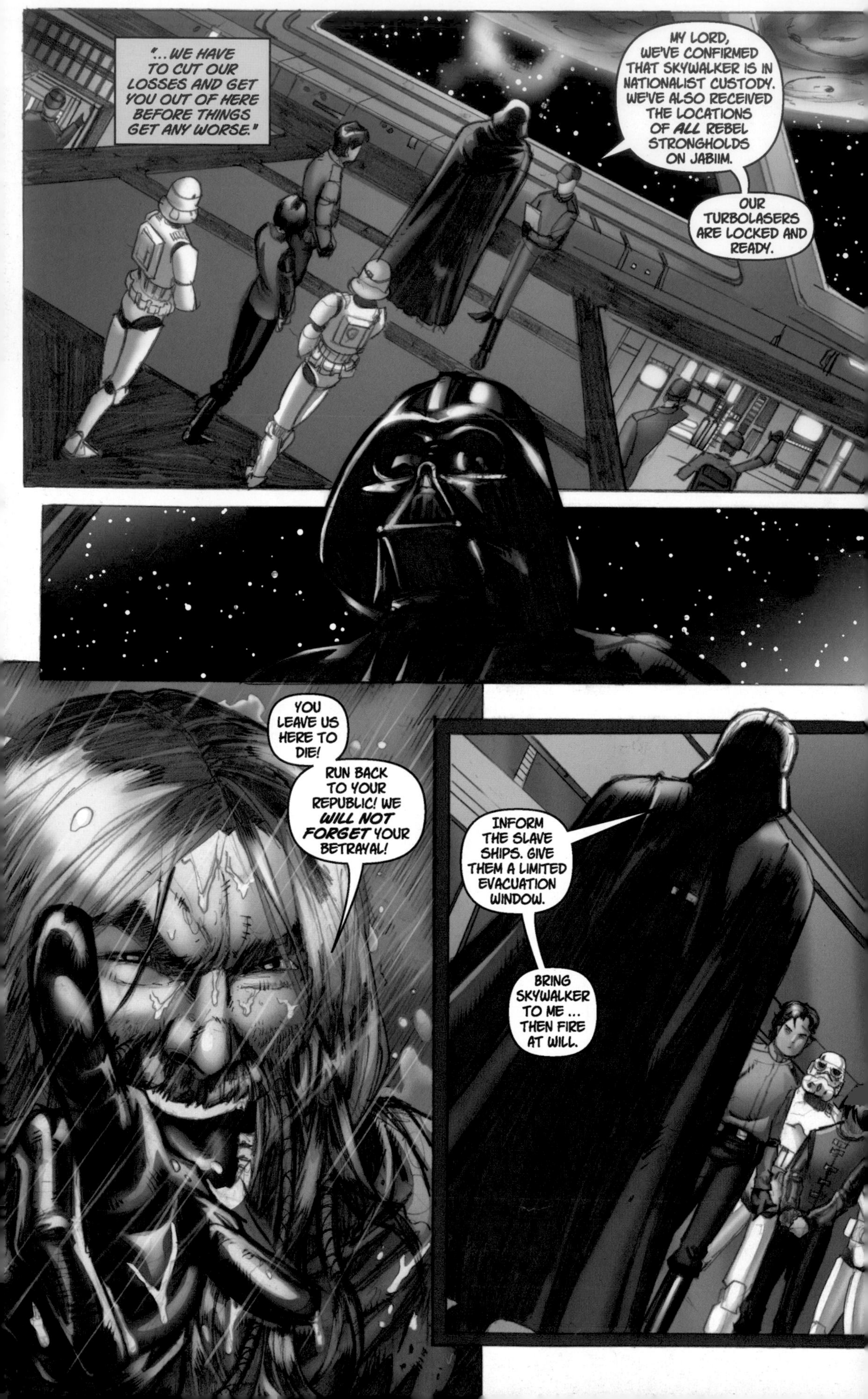
"...WE HAVE TO CUT OUR LOSSES AND GET YOU OUT OF HERE BEFORE THINGS GET ANY WORSE."
MY LORD, WE'VE CONFIRMED THAT SKYWALKER IS IN NATIONALIST CUSTODY. WE'VE ALSO RECEIVED THE LOCATIONS OF ALL REBEL STRONGHOLDS ON JABIIM.
OUR TURBOLASERS ARE LOCKED AND READY.
YOU LEAVE US HERE TO DIE!
RUN BACK TO YOUR REPUBLIC! WE WILL NOT FORGET YOUR BETRAYAL!
INFORM THE SLAVE SHIPS. GIVE THEM A LIMITED EVACUATION WINDOW.
BRING SKYWALKER TO ME ... THEN FIRE AT WILL.

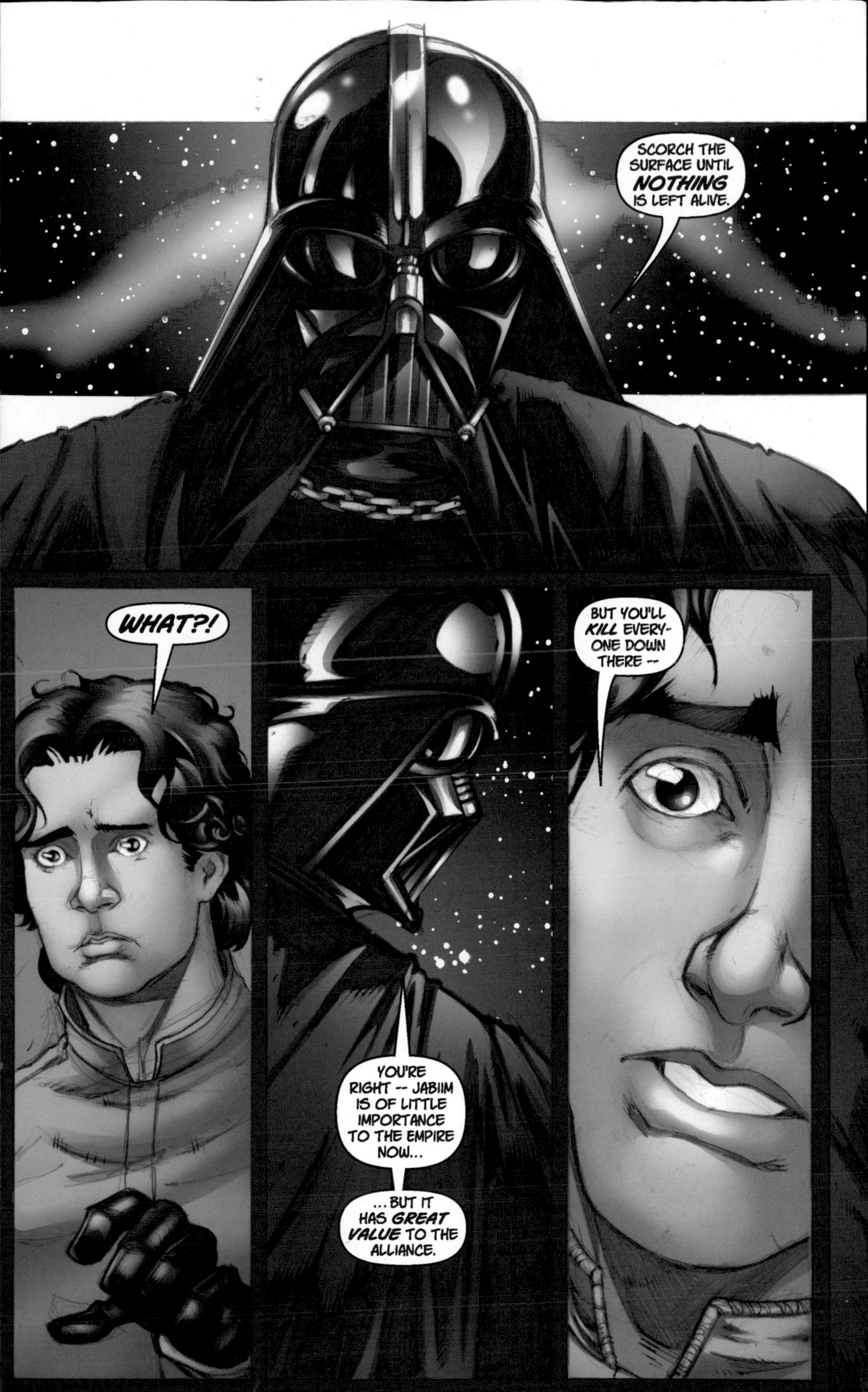
SCORCH THE SURFACE UNTIL NOTHING IS LEFT ALIVE.
WHAT?!
BUT YOU'LL KILL EVERY-ONE DOWN THERE --
YOU'RE RIGHT -- JABIIM IS OF LITTLE IMPORTANCE TO THE EMPIRE NOW...
...BUT IT HAS GREAT VALUE TO THE ALLIANCE.

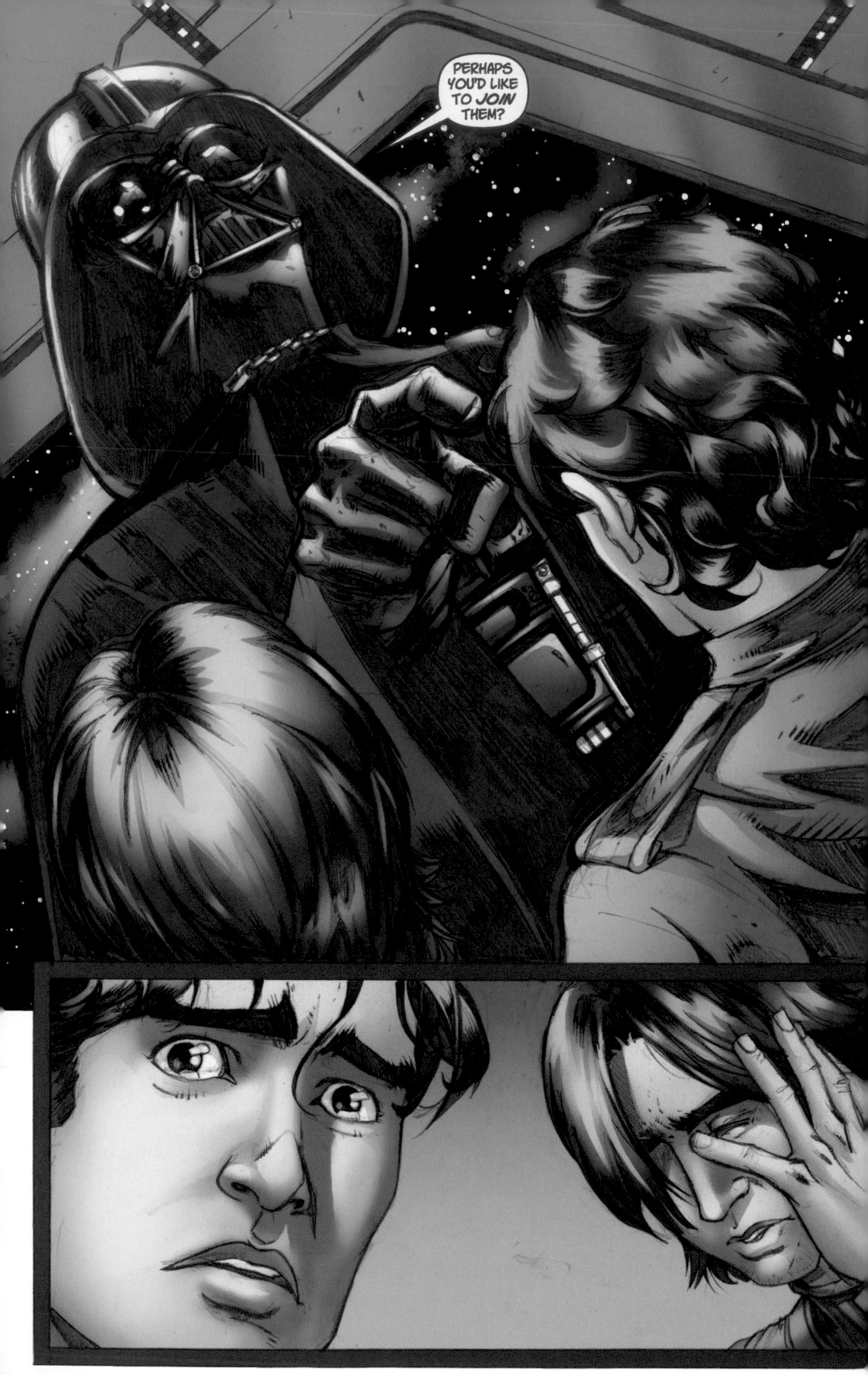
PERHAPS YOU'D LIKE TO JOIN THEM?

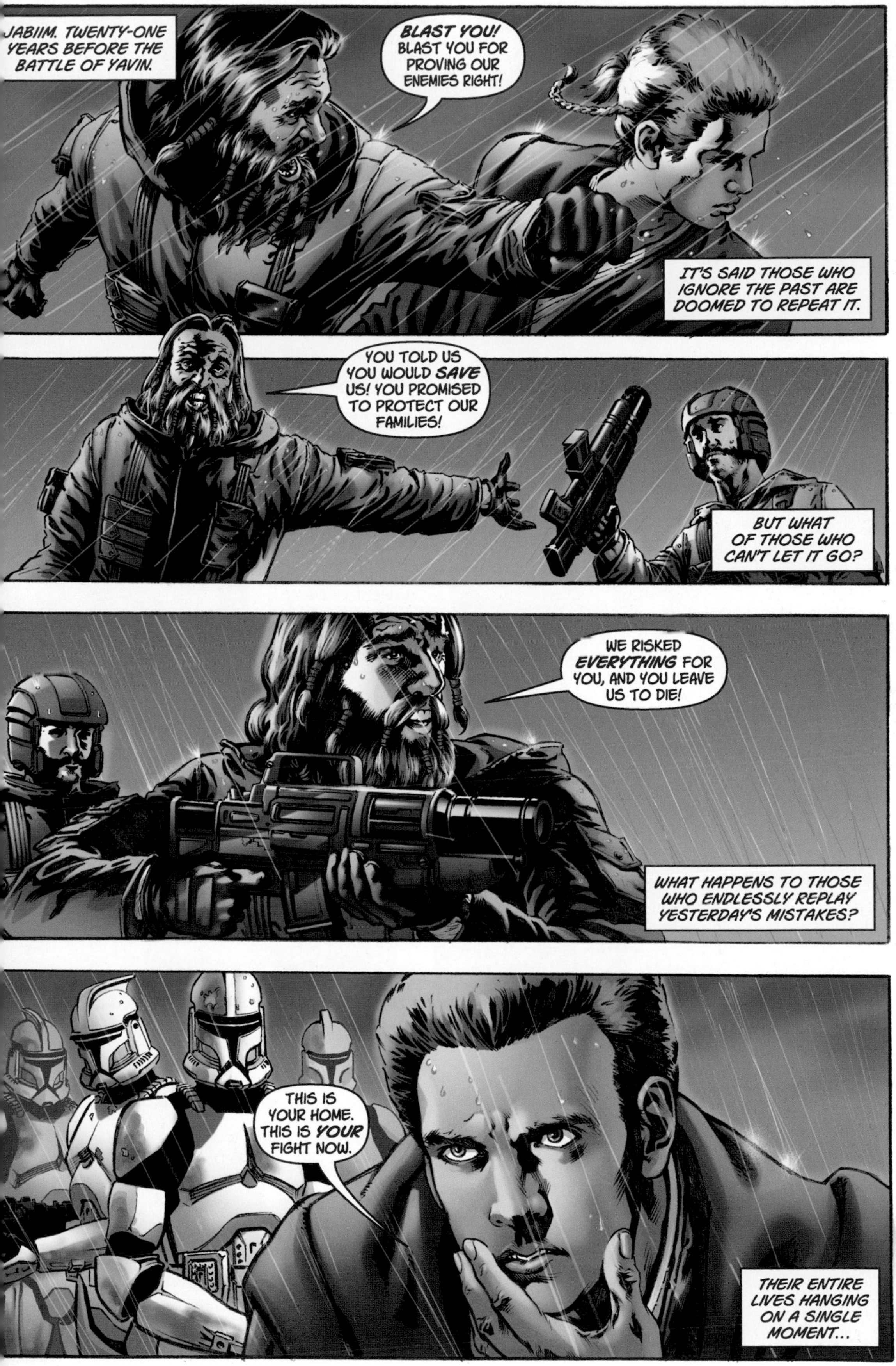

JABIIM. TWENTY-ONE YEARS BEFORE THE BATTLE OF YAVIN.
BLAST YOU! BLAST YOU FOR PROVING OUR ENEMIES RIGHT!
IT'S SAID THOSE WHO IGNORE THE PAST ARE DOOMED TO REPEAT IT.
YOU TOLD US YOU WOULD SAVE US! YOU PROMISED TO PROTECT OUR FAMILIES!
BUT WHAT OF THOSE WHO CAN'T LET IT GO?
WE RISKED EVERYTHING FOR YOU, AND YOU LEAVE US TO DIE!
WHAT HAPPENS TO THOSE WHO ENDLESSLY REPLAY YESTERDAY'S MISTAKES?
THIS IS YOUR HOME. THIS IS YOUR FIGHT NOW.
THEIR ENTIRE LIVES HANGING ON A SINGLE MOMENT...

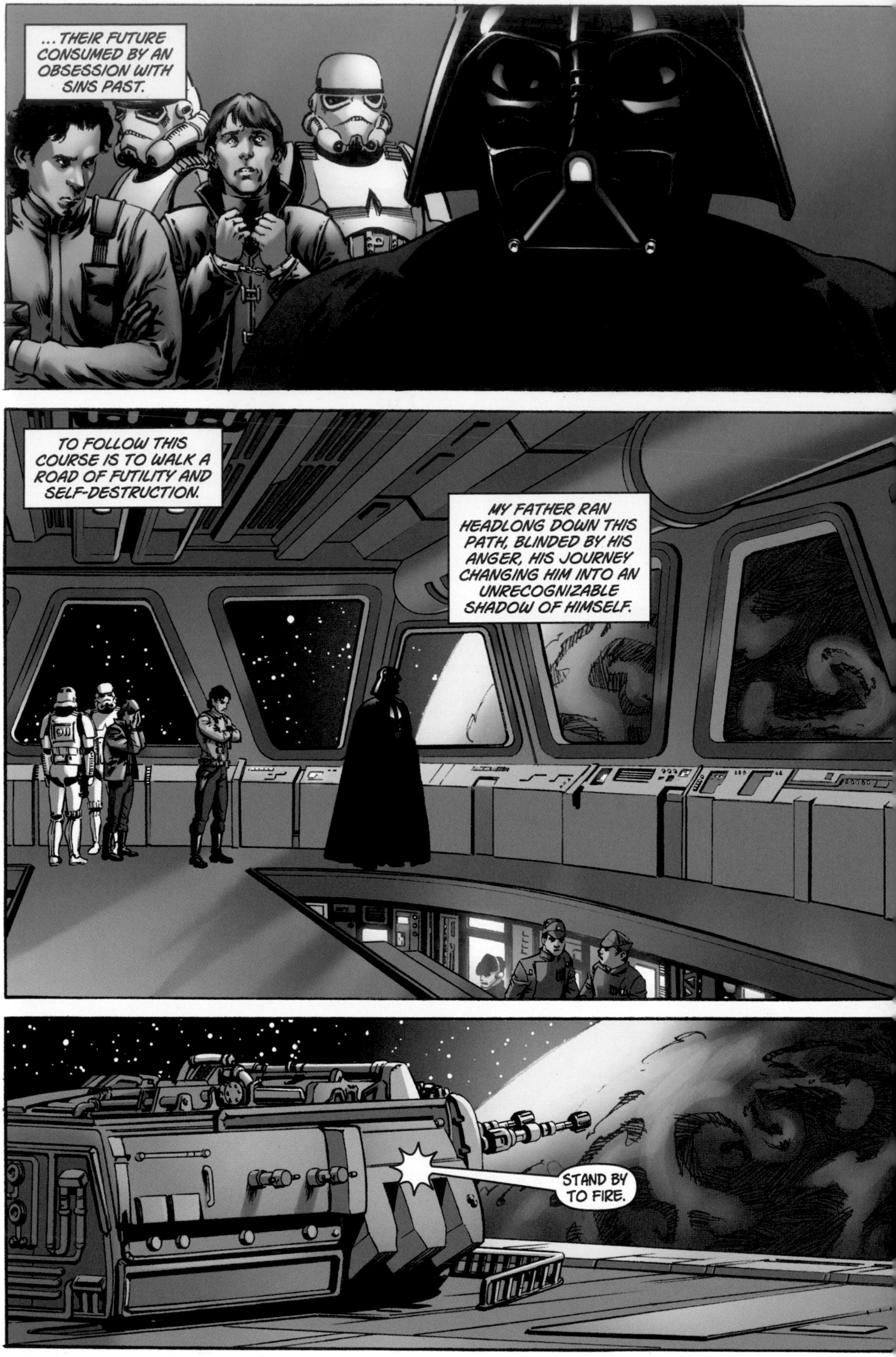
...THEIR FUTURE CONSUMED BY AN OBSESSION WITH SINS PAST.
TO FOLLOW THIS COURSE IS TO WALK A ROAD OF FUTILITY AND SELF-DESTRUCTION.
MY FATHER RAN HEADLONG DOWN THIS PATH, BLINDED BY HIS ANGER, HIS JOURNEY CHANGING HIM INTO AN UNRECOGNIZABLE SHADOW OF HIMSELF.
STAND BY TO FIRE.

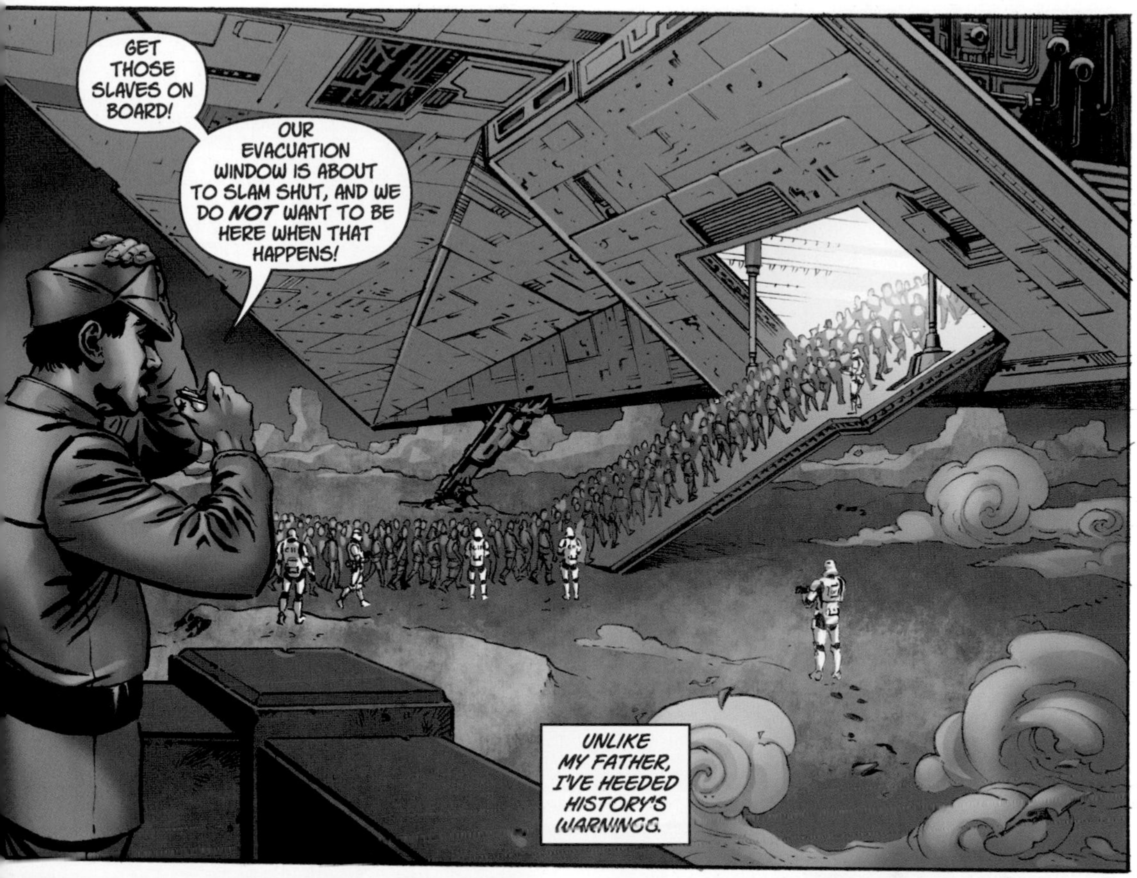
GET THOSE SLAVES ON BOARD!
OUR EVACUATION WINDOW IS ABOUT TO SLAM SHUT, AND WE DO NOT WANT TO BE HERE WHEN THAT HAPPENS!
UNLIKE MY FATHER, I'VE HEEDED HISTORY'S WARNINGS.

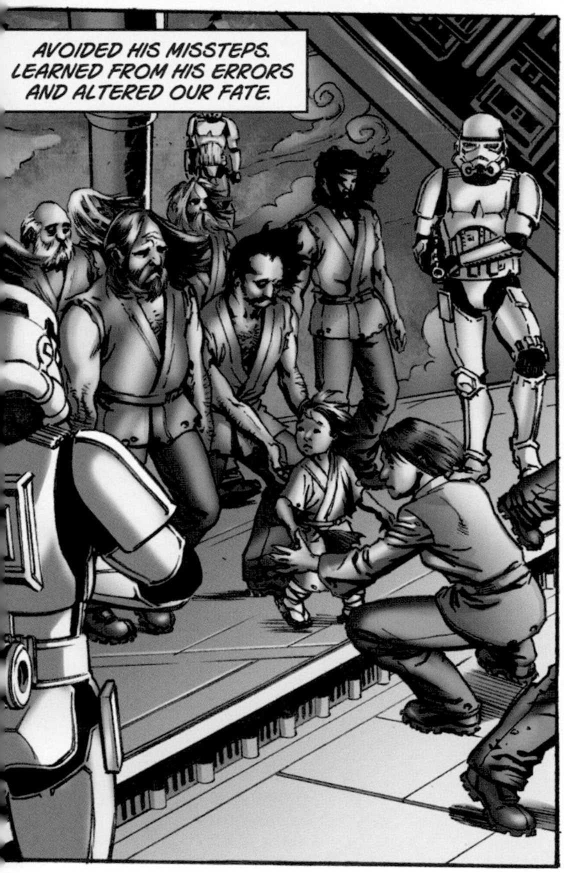
AVOIDED HIS MISSTEPS. LEARNED FROM HIS ERRORS AND ALTERED OUR FATE.

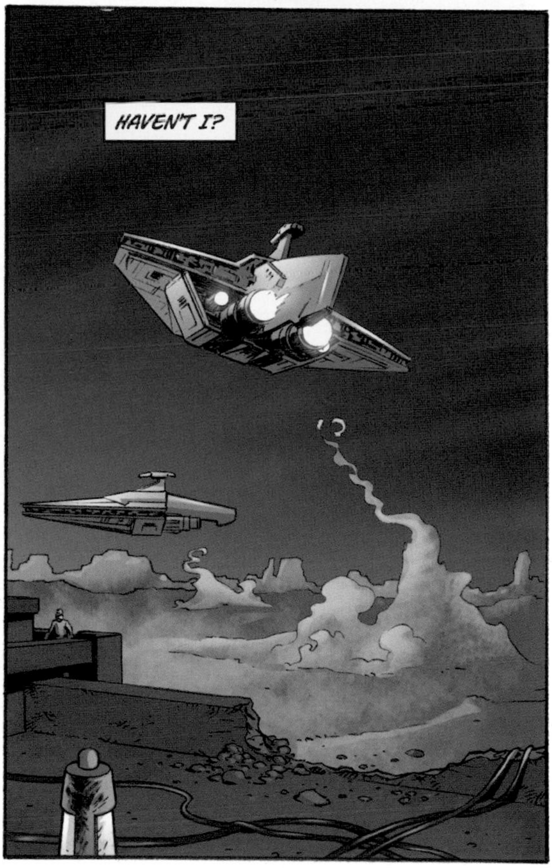
HAVEN'T I?

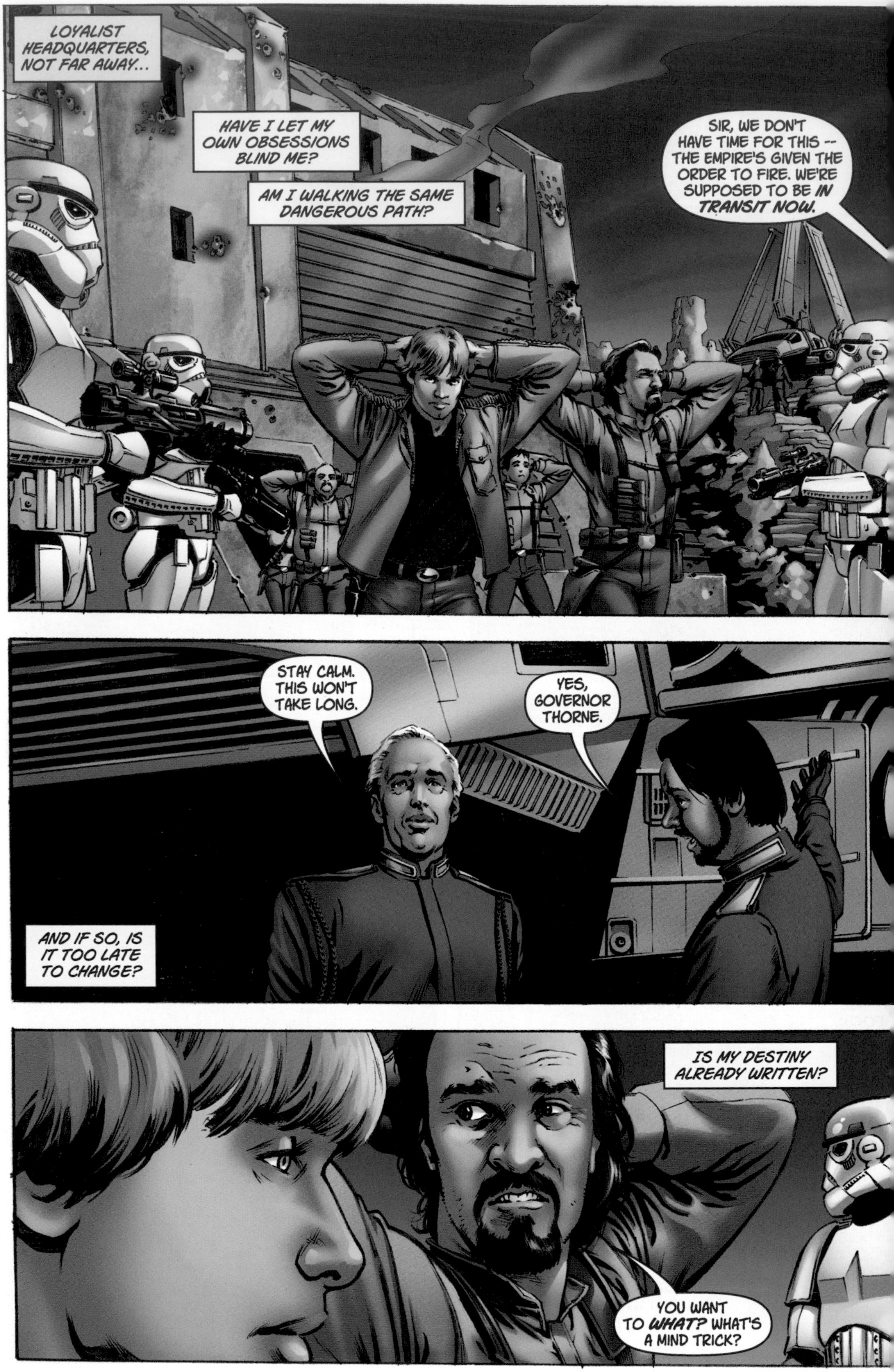
LOYALIST HEADQUARTERS, NOT FAR AWAY...
HAVE I LET MY OWN OBSESSIONS BLIND ME?
AM I WALKING THE SAME DANGEROUS PATH?
SIR, WE DON'T HAVE TIME FOR THIS -- THE EMPIRE'S GIVEN THE ORDER TO FIRE. WE'RE SUPPOSED TO BE IN TRANSIT NOW.
STAY CALM. THIS WON'T TAKE LONG.
YES, GOVERNOR THORNE.
AND IF SO, IS IT TOO LATE TO CHANGE?
IS MY DESTINY ALREADY WRITTEN?
YOU WANT TO WHAT? WHAT'S A MIND TRICK?

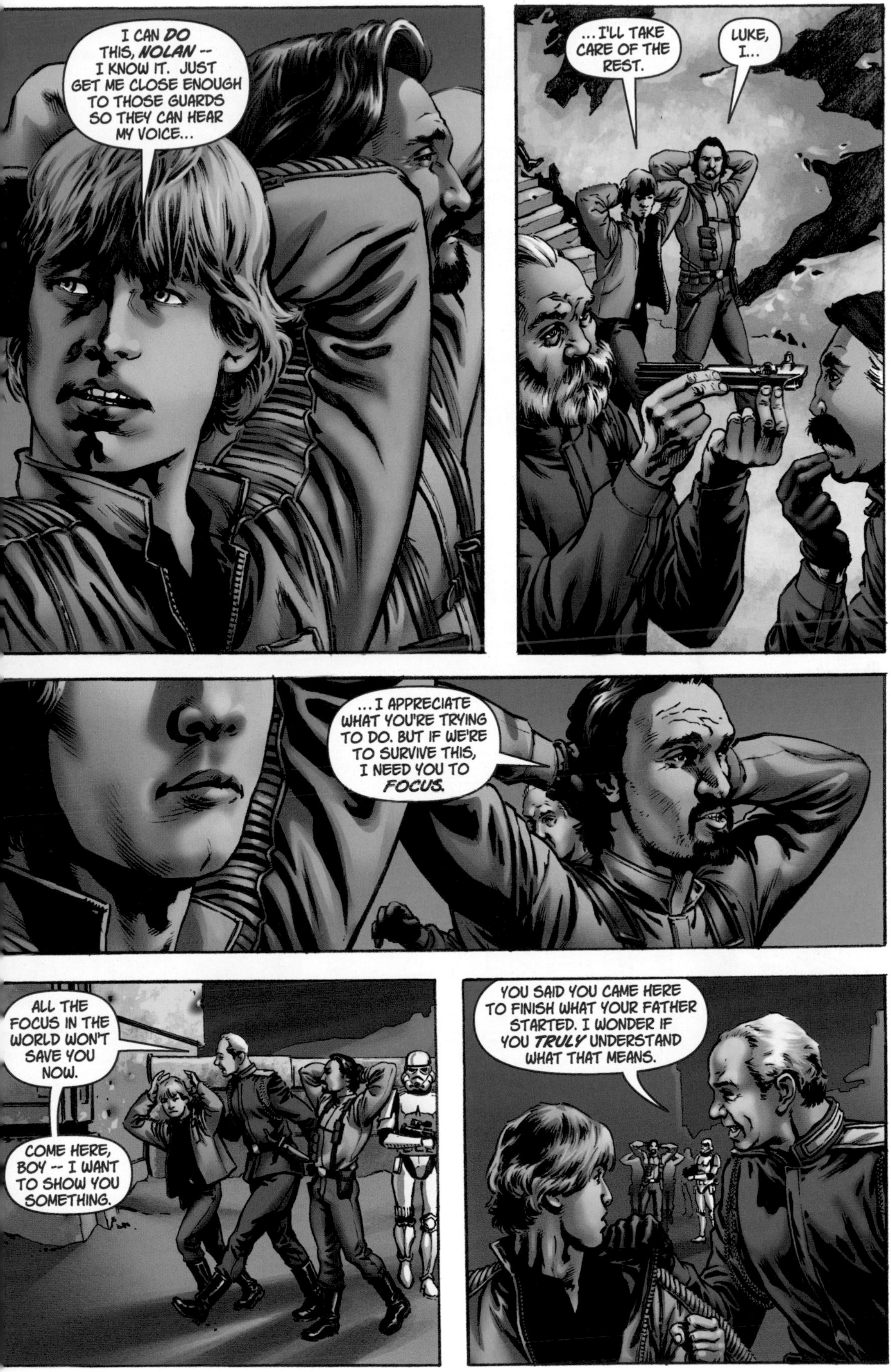
I CAN DO THIS, NOLAN -- I KNOW IT. JUST GET ME CLOSE ENOUGH TO THOSE GUARDS SO THEY CAN HEAR MY VOICE...
...I'LL TAKE CARE OF THE REST.
LUKE, I...
...I APPRECIATE WHAT YOU'RE TRYING TO DO. BUT IF WE'RE TO SURVIVE THIS, I NEED YOU TO FOCUS.
ALL THE FOCUS IN THE WORLD WON'T SAVE YOU NOW.
COME HERE, BOY -- I WANT TO SHOW YOU SOMETHING.
YOU SAID YOU CAME HERE TO FINISH WHAT YOUR FATHER STARTED. I WONDER IF YOU TRULY UNDERSTAND WHAT THAT MEANS.

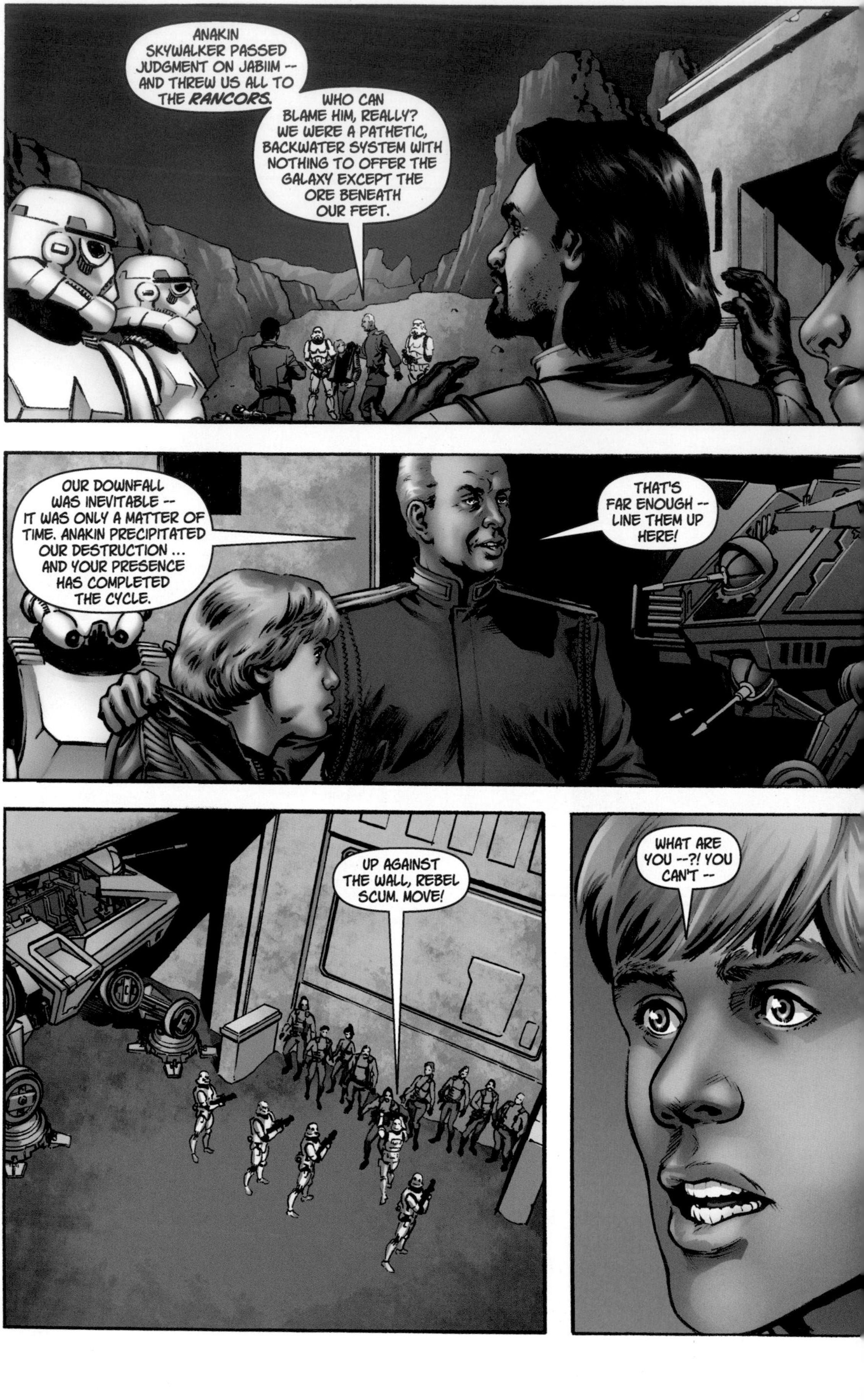
ANAKIN SKYWALKER PASSED JUDGMENT ON JABIIM -- AND THREW US ALL TO THE *RANCORS*.
WHO CAN BLAME HIM, REALLY? WE WERE A PATHETIC, BACKWATER SYSTEM WITH NOTHING TO OFFER THE GALAXY EXCEPT THE ORE BENEATH OUR FEET.
OUR DOWNFALL WAS INEVITABLE -- IT WAS ONLY A MATTER OF TIME. ANAKIN PRECIPITATED OUR DESTRUCTION ... AND YOUR PRESENCE HAS COMPLETED THE CYCLE.
THAT'S FAR ENOUGH -- LINE THEM UP HERE!
UP AGAINST THE WALL, REBEL SCUM. MOVE!
WHAT ARE YOU --?! YOU CAN'T --

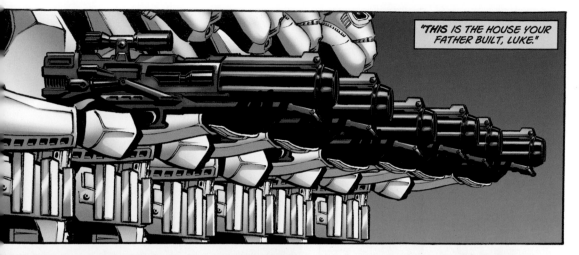

"*THIS IS THE HOUSE YOUR FATHER BUILT, LUKE.*"

THIS IS THE LEGACY YOU'VE BEEN LEFT. YOUR FATHER WOULD BE *PROUD* OF WHAT YOU'VE ACCOMPLISHED HERE.

I'D INSIST THAT YOU STAY AND WITNESS JABIIM'S FINAL, DYING GASPS ... BUT *LORD VADER* HAS OTHER PLANS FOR YOU.

FIRE WHEN READY. KILL THEM ALL.

SIR...?

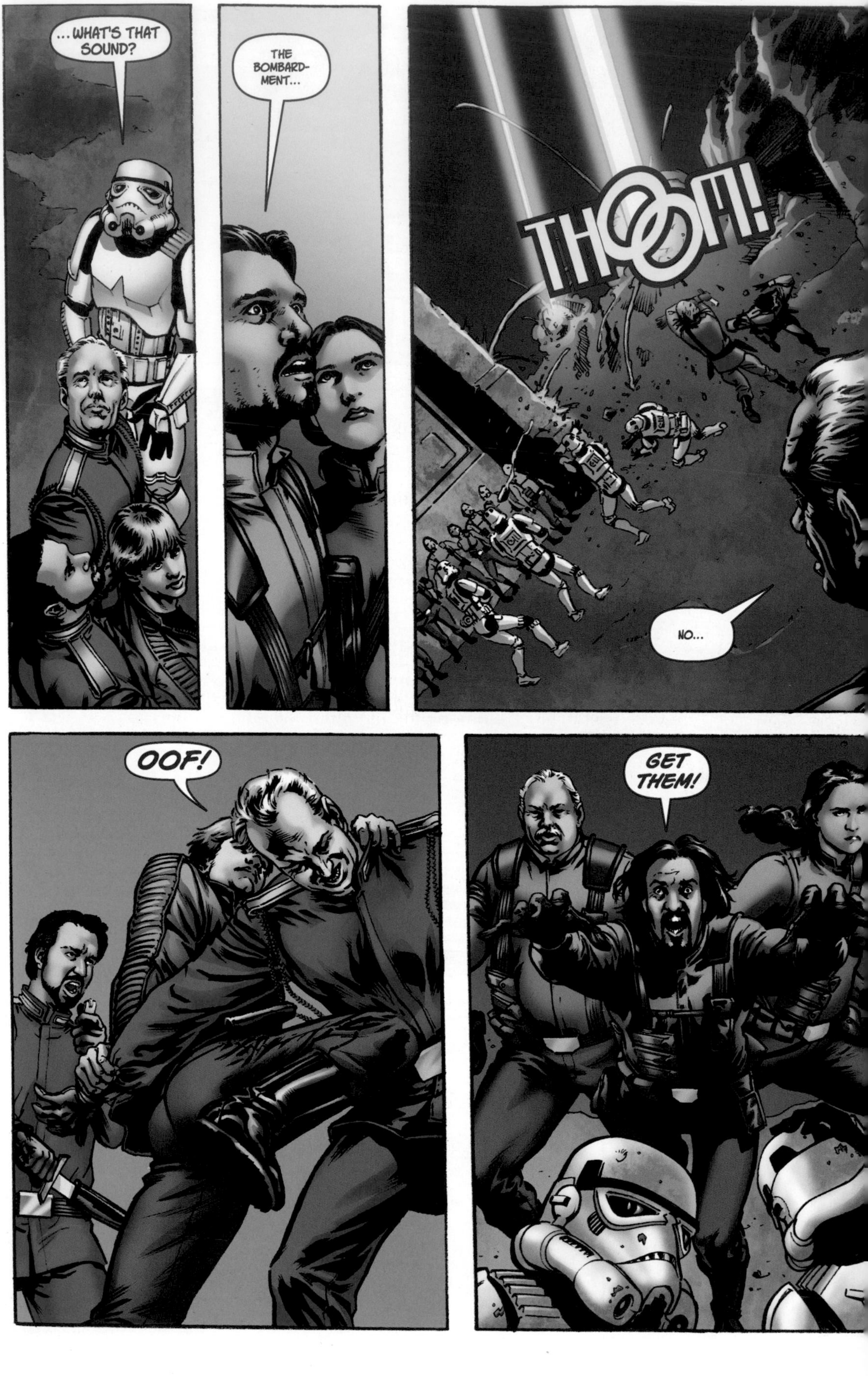
...WHAT'S THAT SOUND?
THE BOMBARD-MENT...
THOOM!
NO...
OOF!
GET THEM!

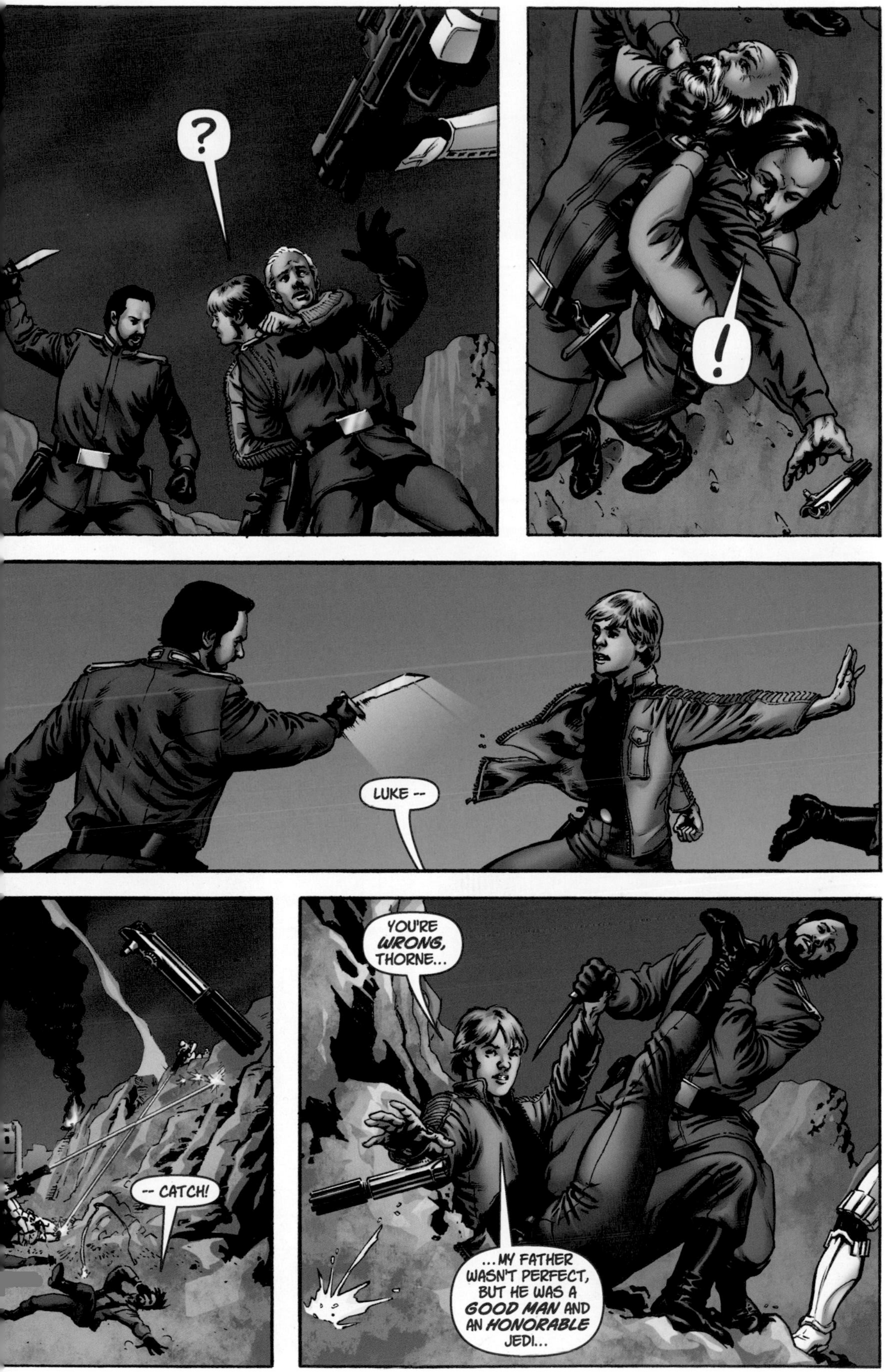
?
!
LUKE --
-- CATCH!
YOU'RE *WRONG*, THORNE...
...MY FATHER WASN'T PERFECT, BUT HE WAS A *GOOD MAN* AND AN *HONORABLE* JEDI...

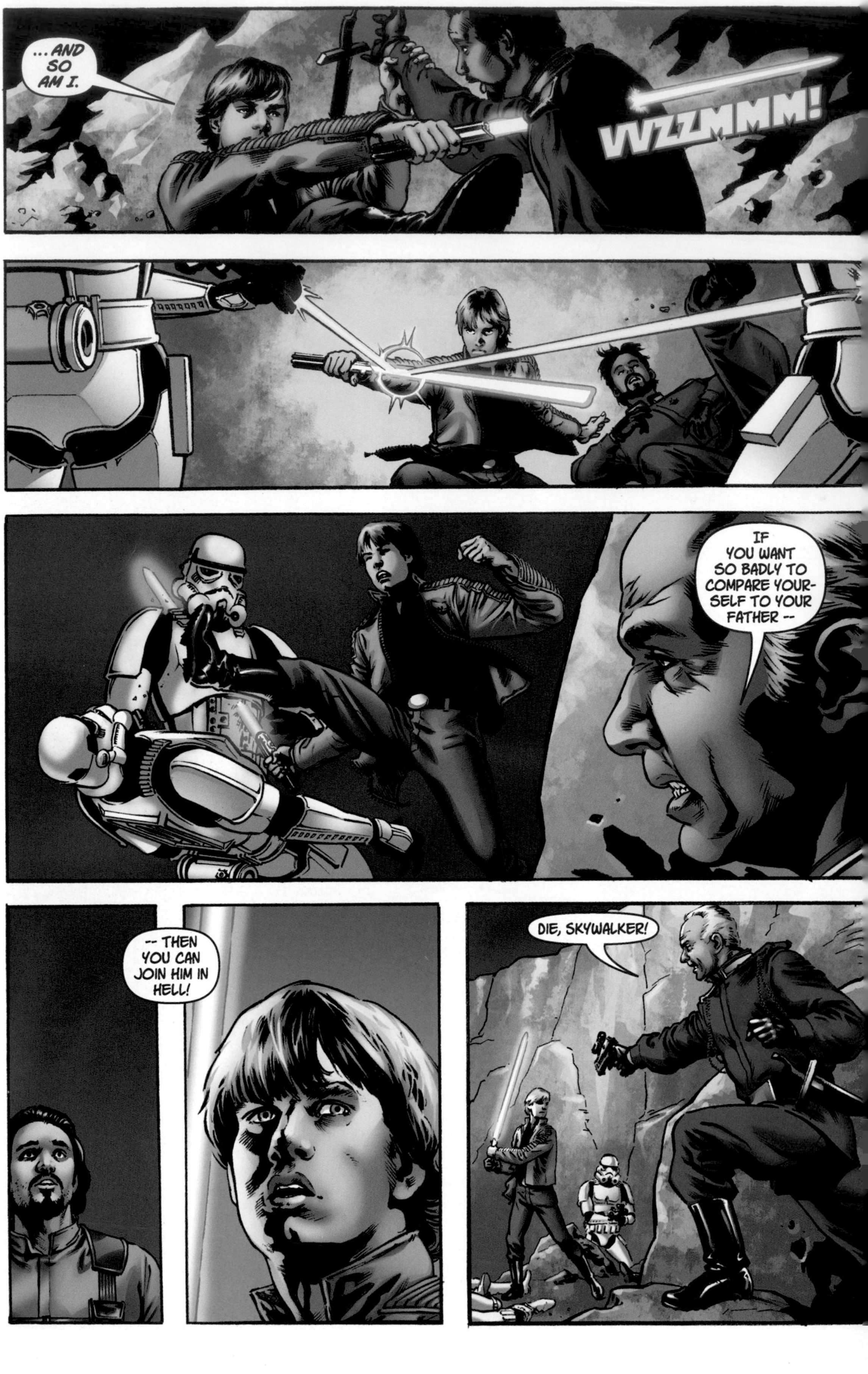
...AND SO AM I.
VVZZMMM!
IF YOU WANT SO BADLY TO COMPARE YOUR-SELF TO YOUR FATHER --
-- THEN YOU CAN JOIN HIM IN HELL!
DIE, SKYWALKER!

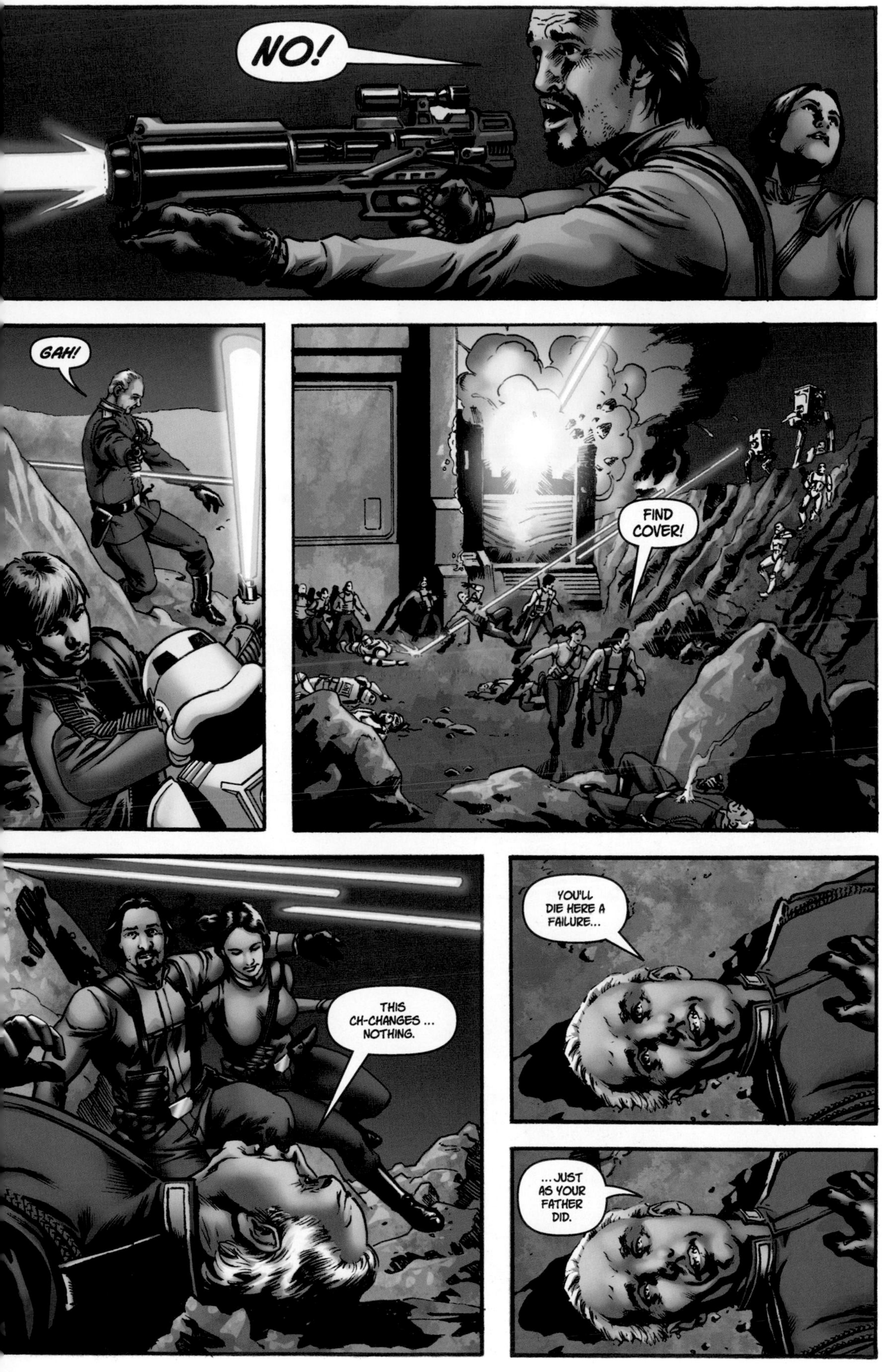
NO!
GAH!
FIND COVER!
THIS CH-CHANGES ... NOTHING.
YOU'LL DIE HERE A FAILURE...
...JUST AS YOUR FATHER DID.

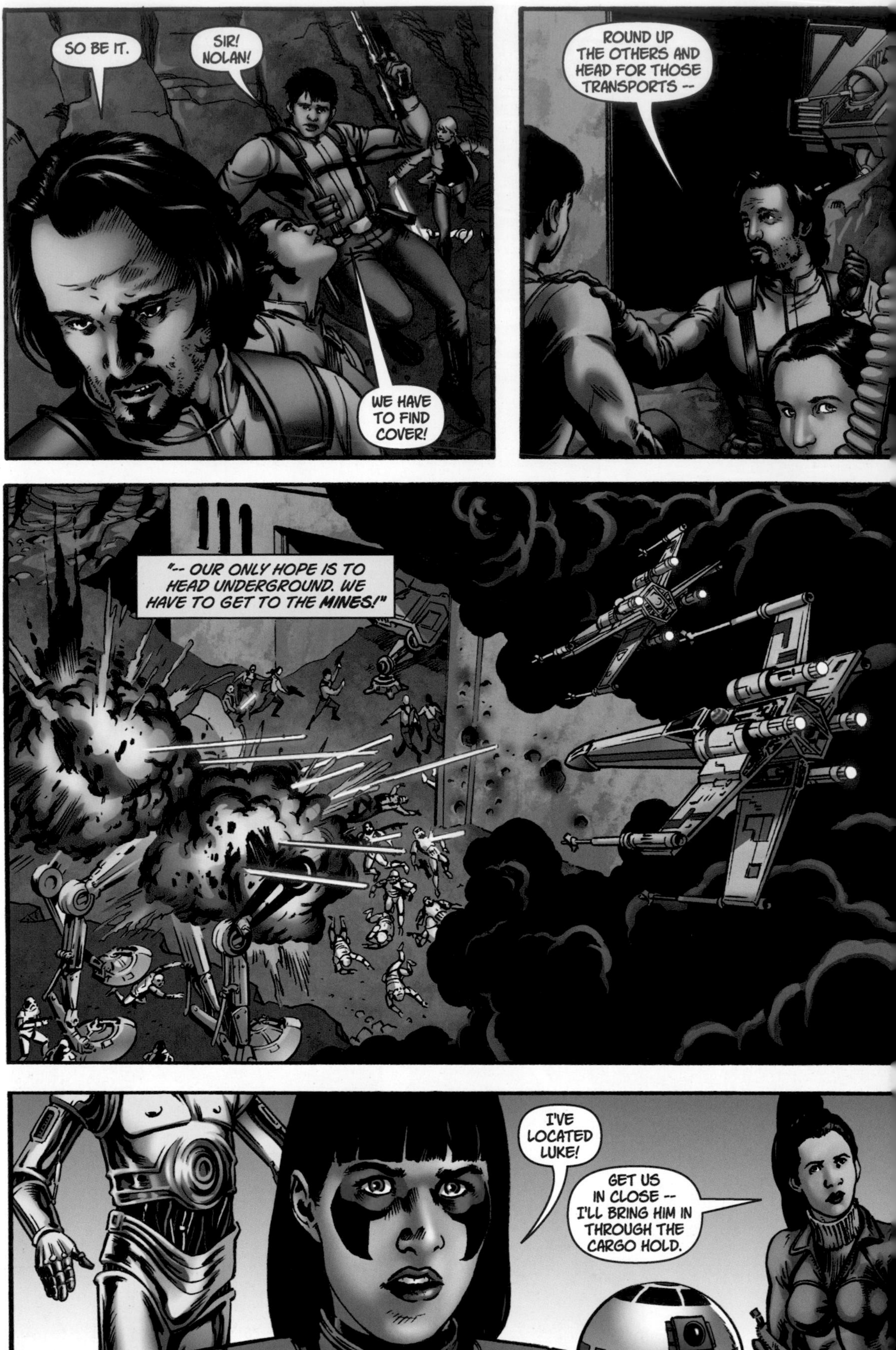
SO BE IT.
SIR! NOLAN!
WE HAVE TO FIND COVER!
ROUND UP THE OTHERS AND HEAD FOR THOSE TRANSPORTS --
"-- OUR ONLY HOPE IS TO HEAD UNDERGROUND. WE HAVE TO GET TO THE MINES!"
I'VE LOCATED LUKE!
GET US IN CLOSE -- I'LL BRING HIM IN THROUGH THE CARGO HOLD.

IT'S WEDGE AND HOBBIE!

LUKE!

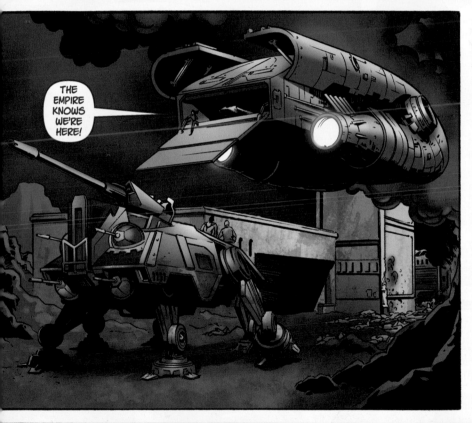

THE EMPIRE KNOWS WE'RE HERE!

LUKE -- COME ON!

I KNOW. LEIA, YOU HAVE TO GET OUT OF HERE -- YOU HAVE TO GET BACK TO THE FLEET AND TELL THEM WHAT'S HAPPENING HERE!

I'M STAYING!

WHAT?

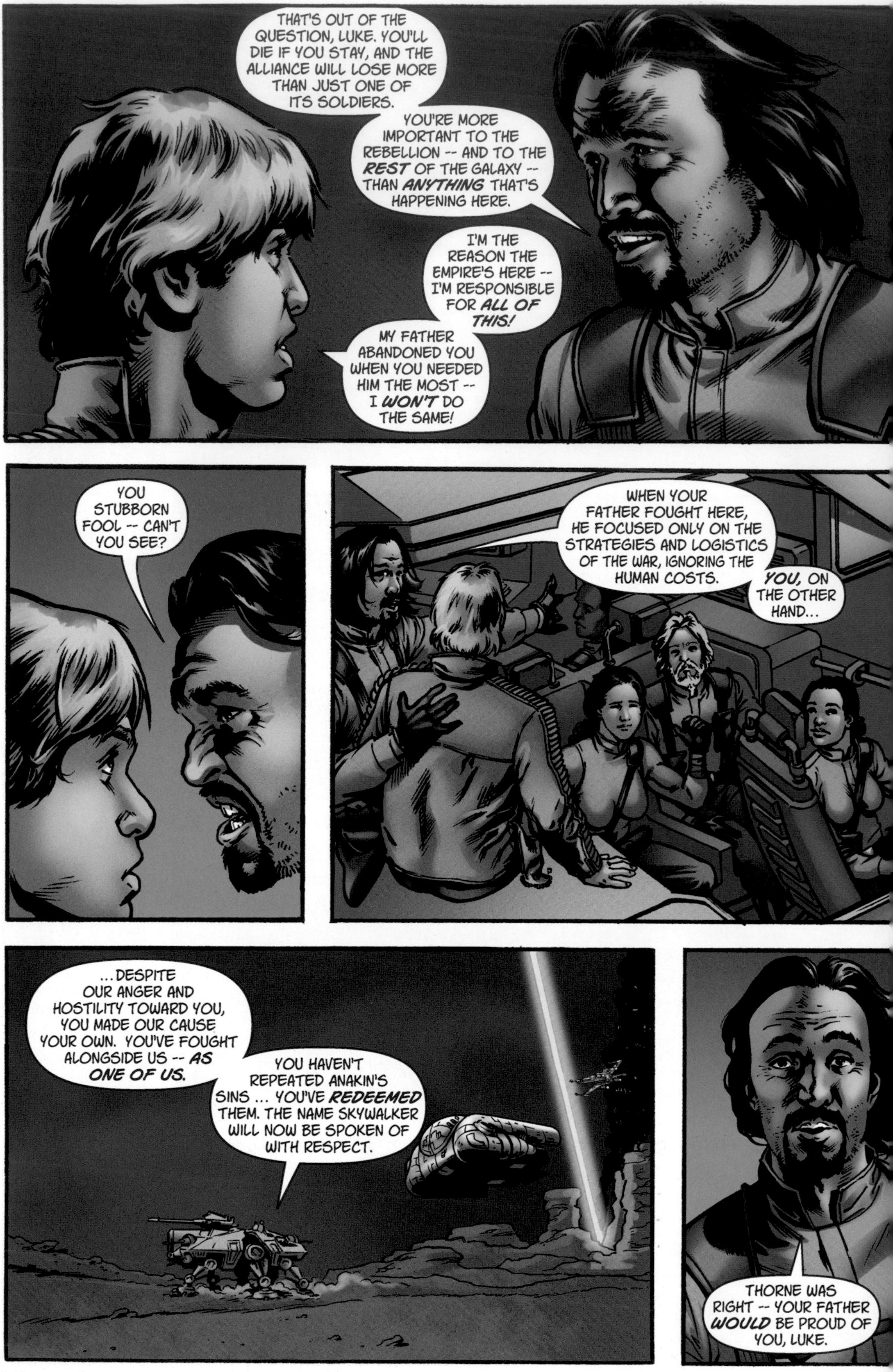
THAT'S OUT OF THE QUESTION, LUKE. YOU'LL DIE IF YOU STAY, AND THE ALLIANCE WILL LOSE MORE THAN JUST ONE OF ITS SOLDIERS.
YOU'RE MORE IMPORTANT TO THE REBELLION -- AND TO THE REST OF THE GALAXY -- THAN ANYTHING THAT'S HAPPENING HERE.
I'M THE REASON THE EMPIRE'S HERE -- I'M RESPONSIBLE FOR ALL OF THIS!
MY FATHER ABANDONED YOU WHEN YOU NEEDED HIM THE MOST -- I WON'T DO THE SAME!
YOU STUBBORN FOOL -- CAN'T YOU SEE?
WHEN YOUR FATHER FOUGHT HERE, HE FOCUSED ONLY ON THE STRATEGIES AND LOGISTICS OF THE WAR, IGNORING THE HUMAN COSTS.
YOU, ON THE OTHER HAND...
...DESPITE OUR ANGER AND HOSTILITY TOWARD YOU, YOU MADE OUR CAUSE YOUR OWN. YOU'VE FOUGHT ALONGSIDE US -- AS ONE OF US.
YOU HAVEN'T REPEATED ANAKIN'S SINS ... YOU'VE REDEEMED THEM. THE NAME SKYWALKER WILL NOW BE SPOKEN OF WITH RESPECT.
THORNE WAS RIGHT -- YOUR FATHER WOULD BE PROUD OF YOU, LUKE.

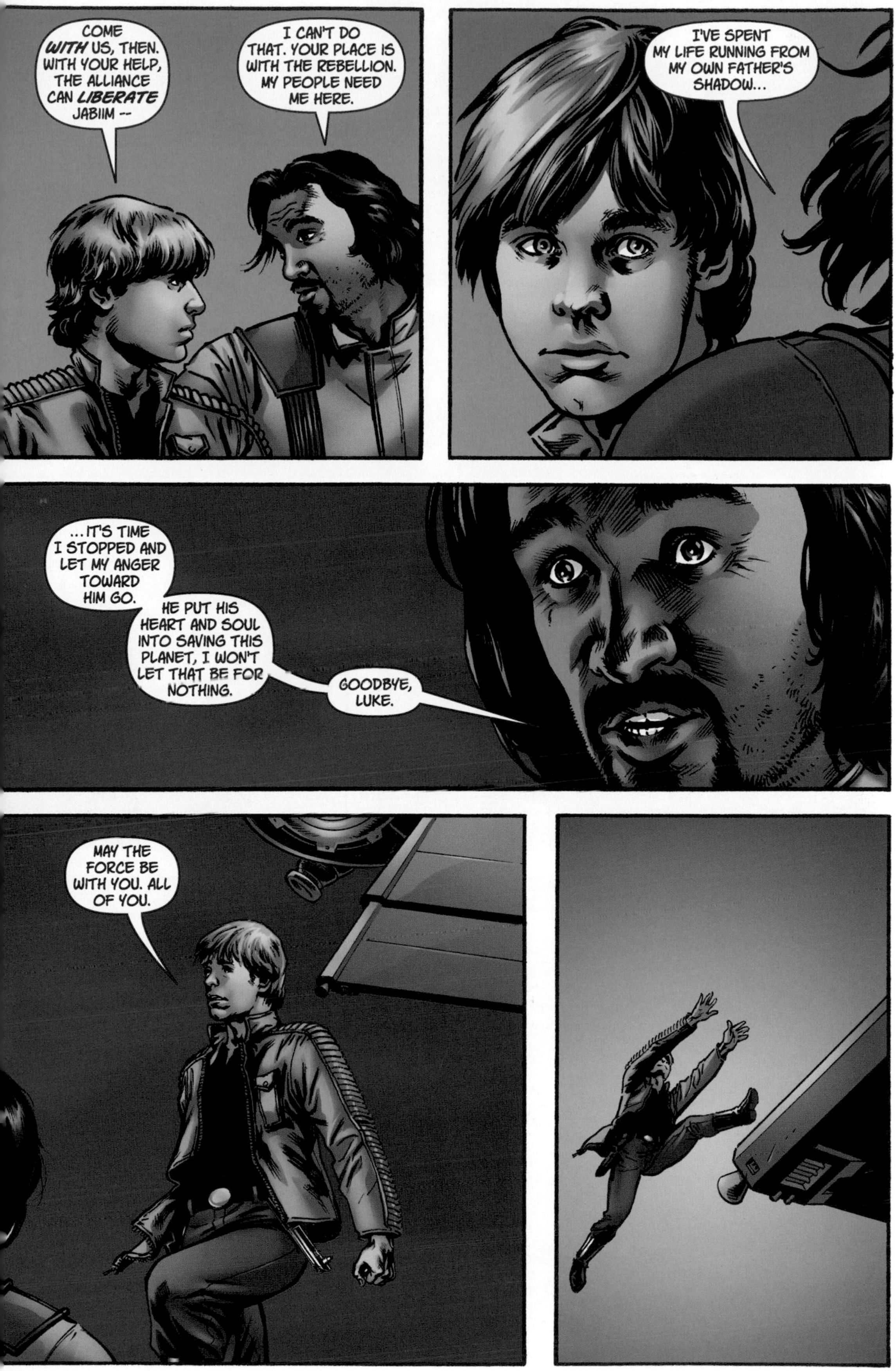
COME WITH US, THEN. WITH YOUR HELP, THE ALLIANCE CAN LIBERATE JABIIM --
I CAN'T DO THAT. YOUR PLACE IS WITH THE REBELLION. MY PEOPLE NEED ME HERE.
I'VE SPENT MY LIFE RUNNING FROM MY OWN FATHER'S SHADOW...
...IT'S TIME I STOPPED AND LET MY ANGER TOWARD HIM GO.
HE PUT HIS HEART AND SOUL INTO SAVING THIS PLANET, I WON'T LET THAT BE FOR NOTHING.
GOODBYE, LUKE.
MAY THE FORCE BE WITH YOU. ALL OF YOU.

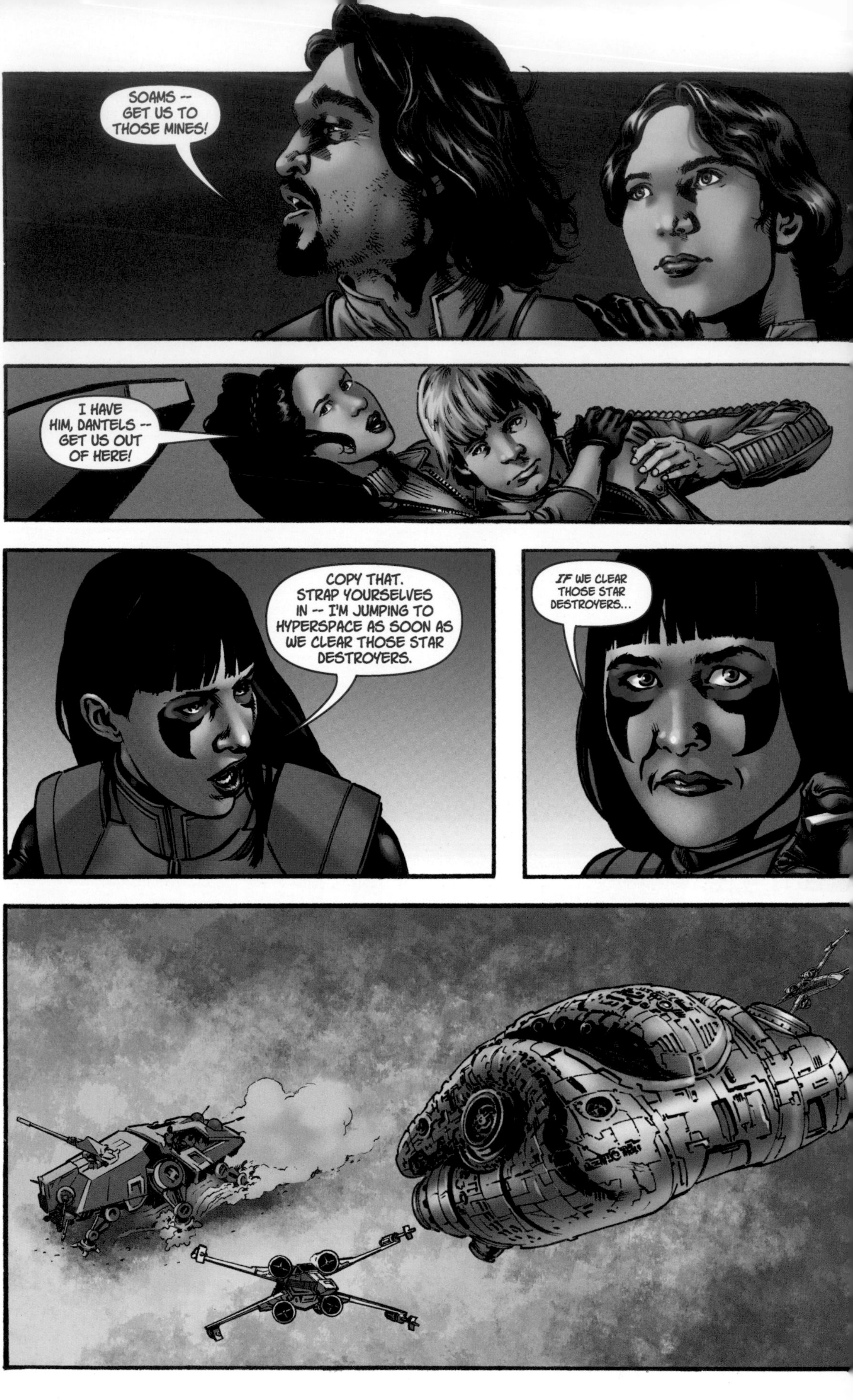
SOAMS -- GET US TO THOSE MINES!
I HAVE HIM, DANTELS -- GET US OUT OF HERE!
COPY THAT. STRAP YOURSELVES IN -- I'M JUMPING TO HYPERSPACE AS SOON AS WE CLEAR THOSE STAR DESTROYERS.
IF WE CLEAR THOSE STAR DESTROYERS...

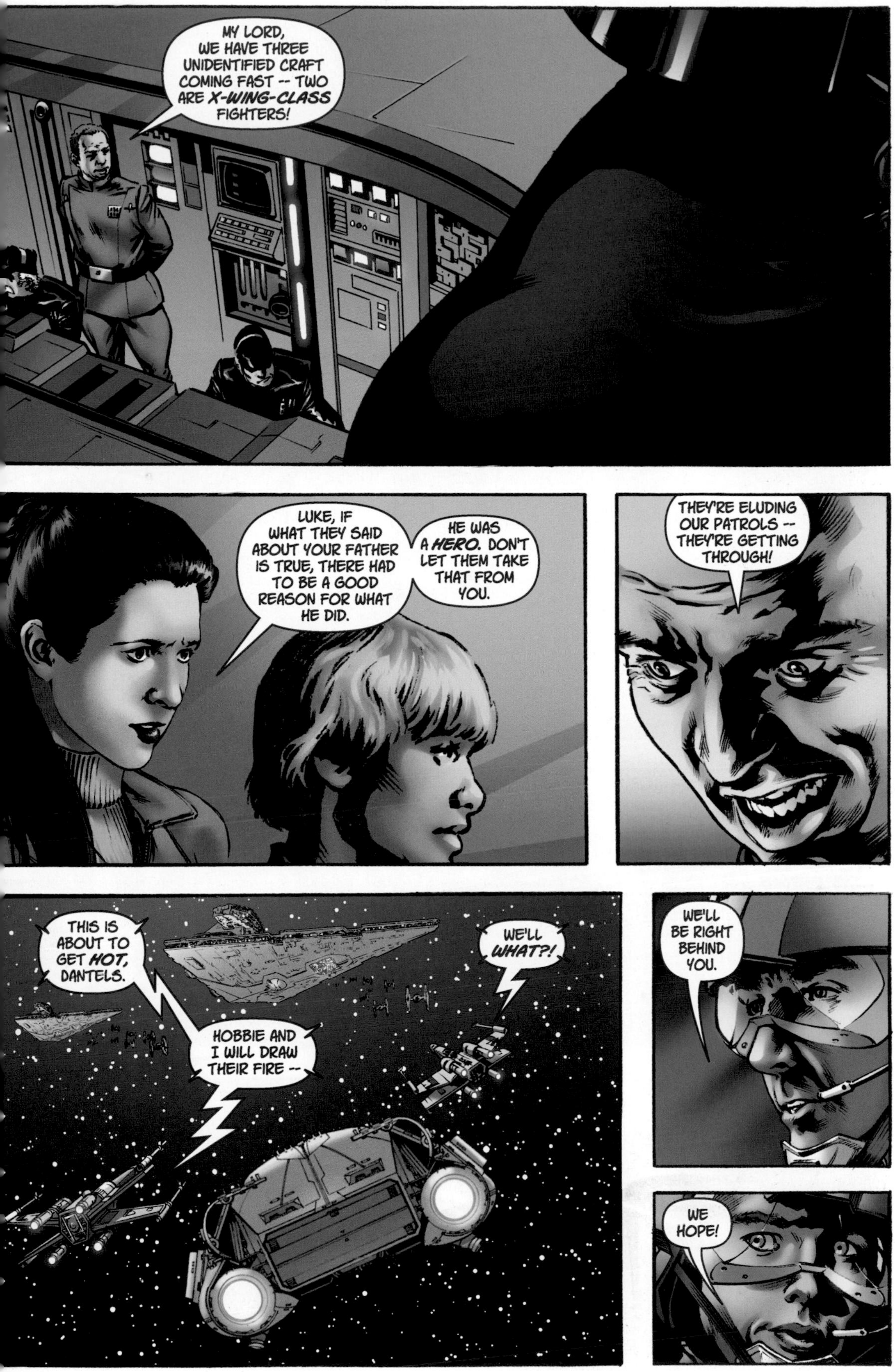
MY LORD, WE HAVE THREE UNIDENTIFIED CRAFT COMING FAST -- TWO ARE *X-WING-CLASS* FIGHTERS!
LUKE, IF WHAT THEY SAID ABOUT YOUR FATHER IS TRUE, THERE HAD TO BE A GOOD REASON FOR WHAT HE DID.
HE WAS A *HERO.* DON'T LET THEM TAKE THAT FROM YOU.
THEY'RE ELUDING OUR PATROLS -- THEY'RE GETTING THROUGH!
THIS IS ABOUT TO GET *HOT,* DANTELS.
HOBBIE AND I WILL DRAW THEIR FIRE --
WE'LL *WHAT?!*
WE'LL BE RIGHT BEHIND YOU.
WE HOPE!

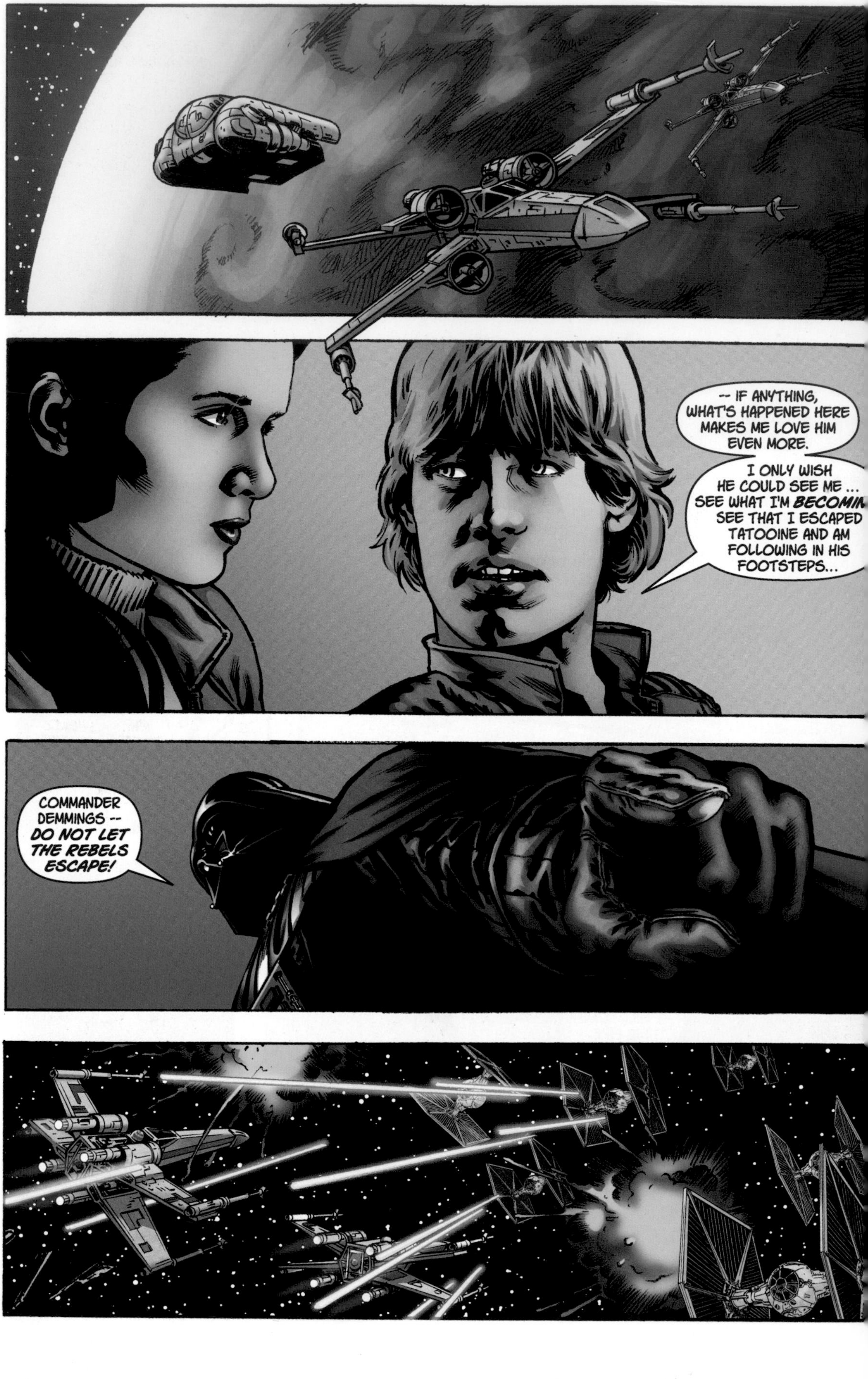
-- IF ANYTHING, WHAT'S HAPPENED HERE MAKES ME LOVE HIM EVEN MORE.
I ONLY WISH HE COULD SEE ME ... SEE WHAT I'M BECOMIN SEE THAT I ESCAPED TATOOINE AND AM FOLLOWING IN HIS FOOTSTEPS...
COMMANDER DEMMINGS -- DO NOT LET THE REBELS ESCAPE!

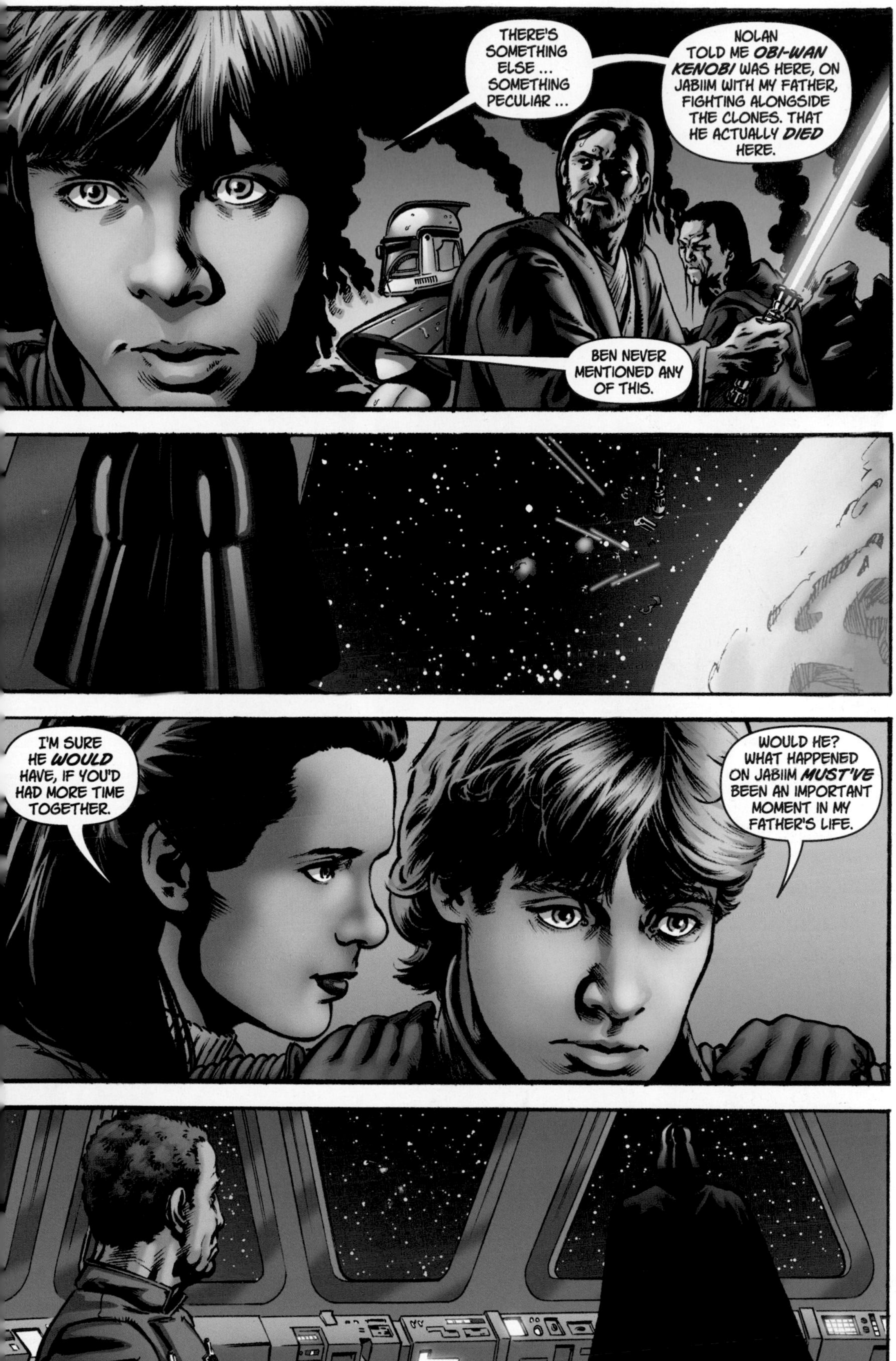

THERE'S SOMETHING ELSE ... SOMETHING PECULIAR ...
NOLAN TOLD ME ***OBI-WAN KENOBI*** WAS HERE, ON JABIIM WITH MY FATHER, FIGHTING ALONGSIDE THE CLONES. THAT HE ACTUALLY ***DIED*** HERE.
BEN NEVER MENTIONED ANY OF THIS.
I'M SURE HE ***WOULD*** HAVE, IF YOU'D HAD MORE TIME TOGETHER.
WOULD HE? WHAT HAPPENED ON JABIIM ***MUST'VE*** BEEN AN IMPORTANT MOMENT IN MY FATHER'S LIFE.

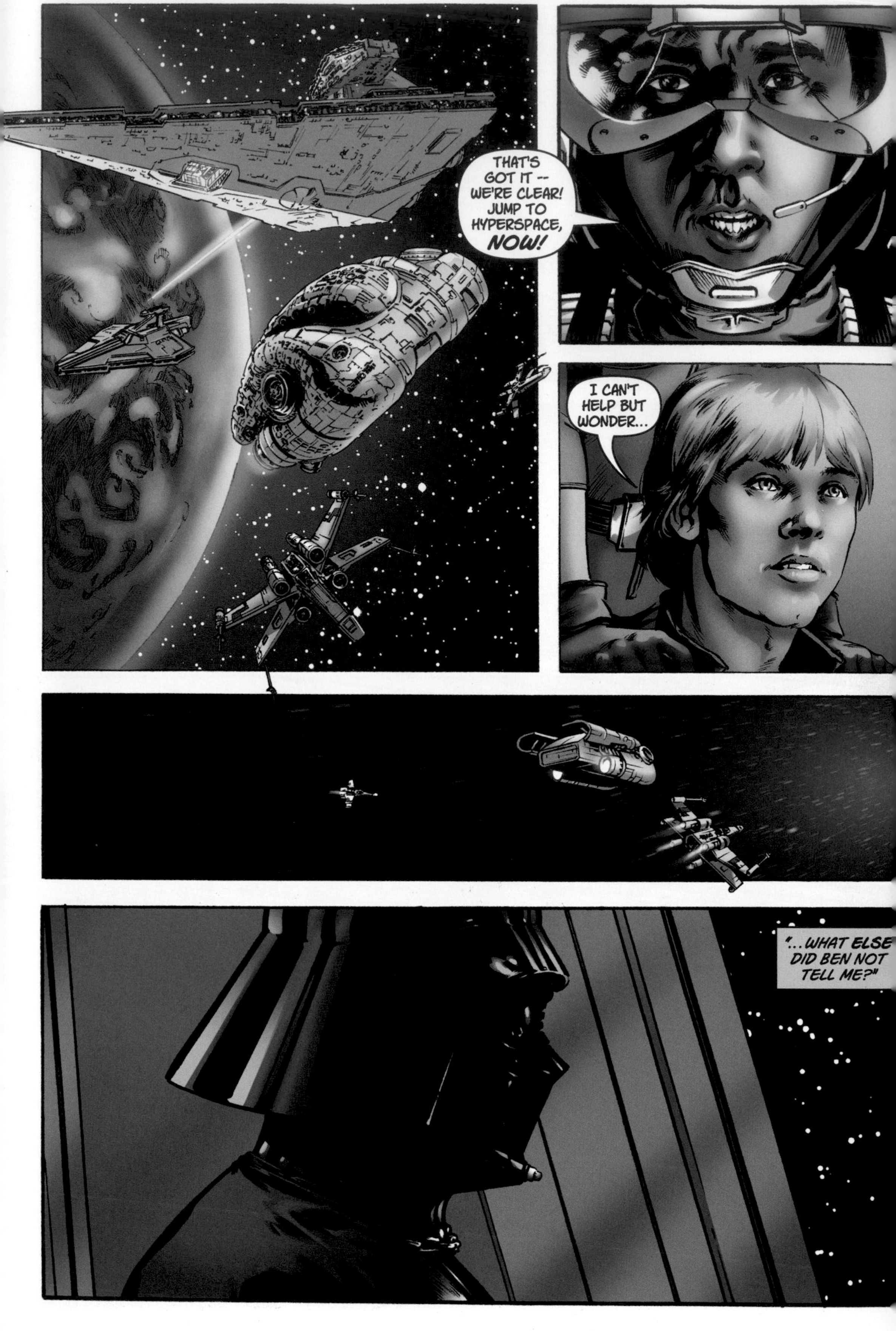
THAT'S GOT IT -- WE'RE CLEAR! JUMP TO HYPERSPACE, NOW!
I CAN'T HELP BUT WONDER...
"...WHAT ELSE DID BEN NOT TELL ME?"

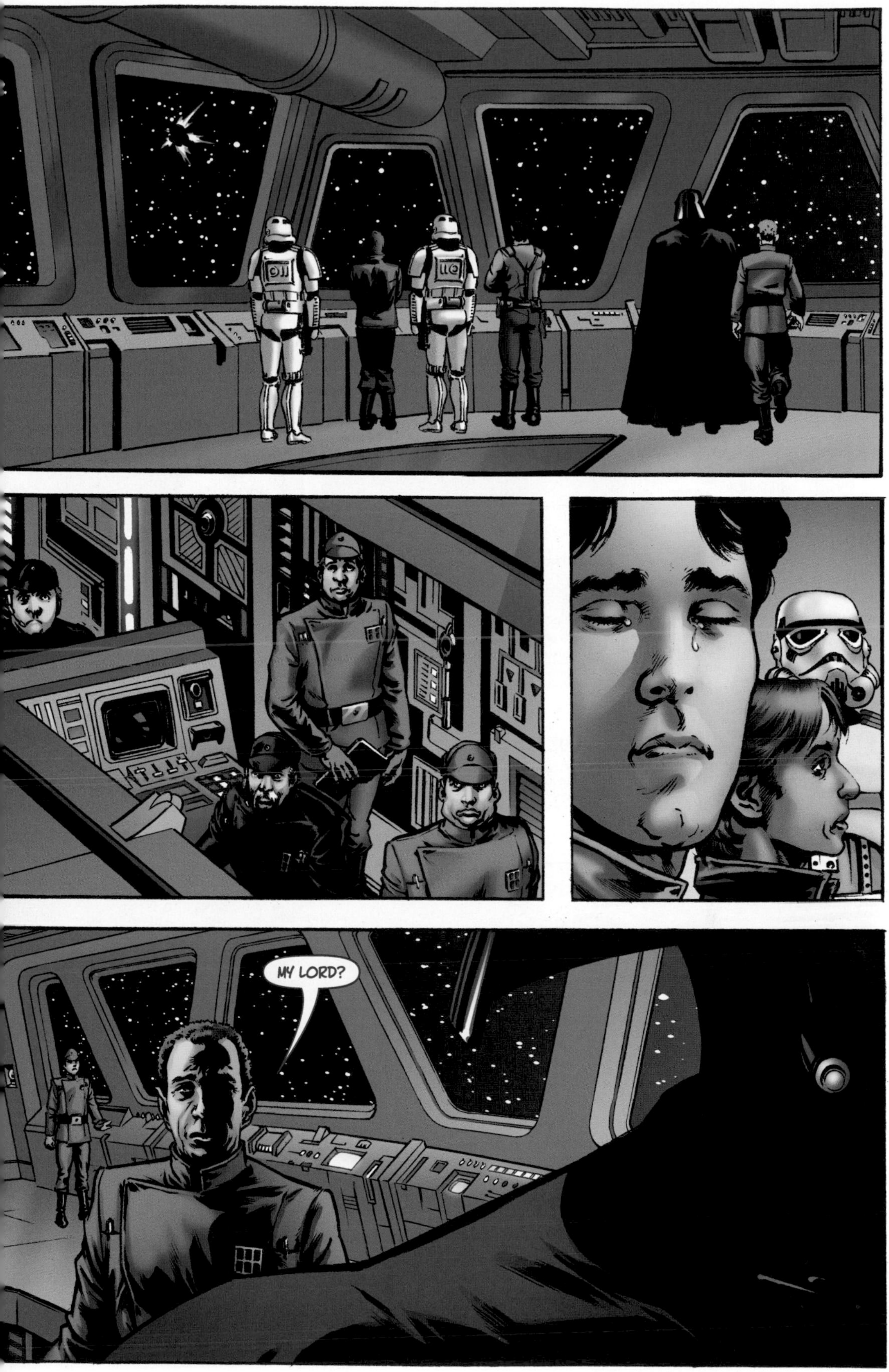
MY LORD?

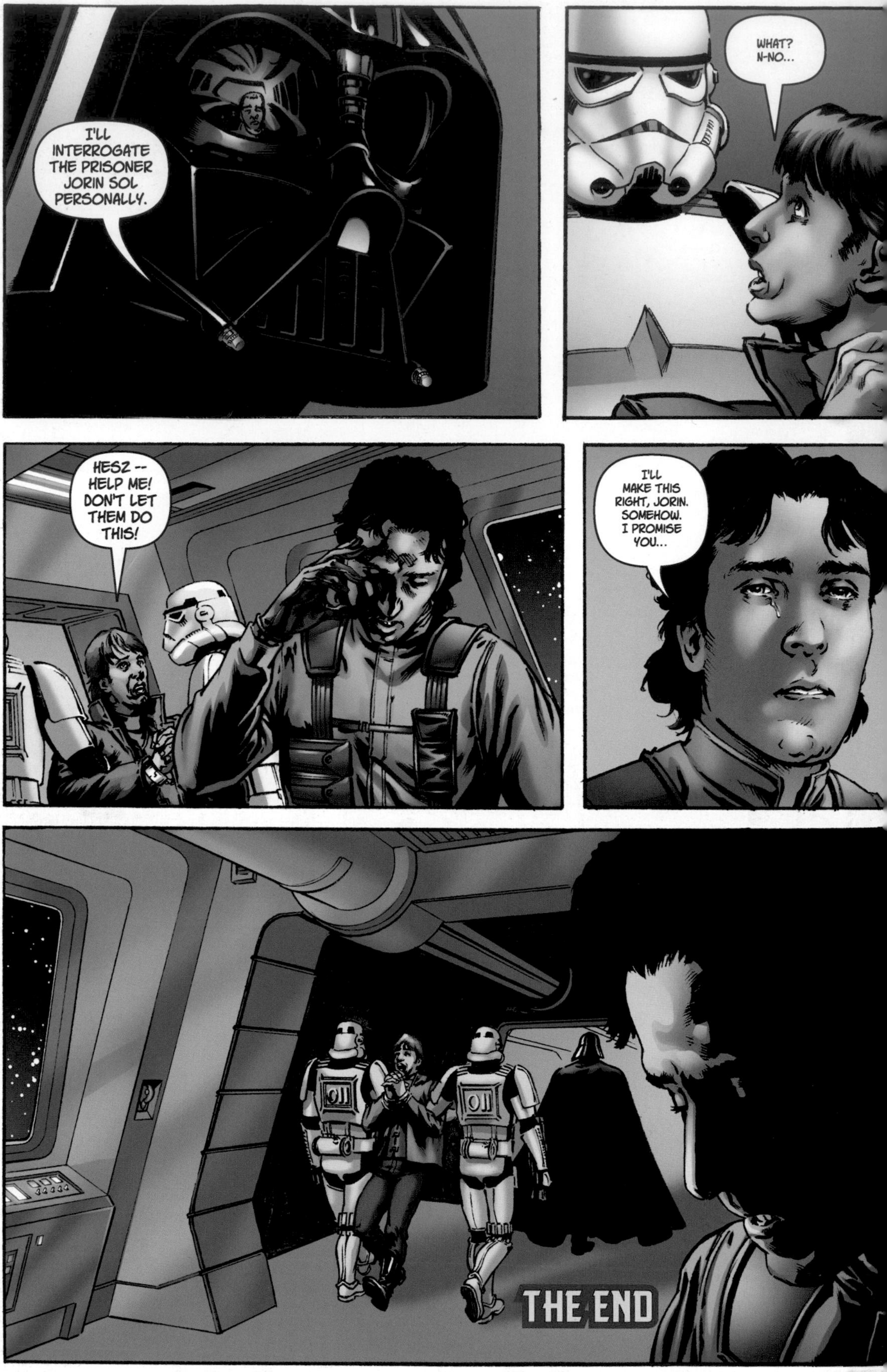
I'LL INTERROGATE THE PRISONER JORIN SOL PERSONALLY.
WHAT? N-NO...
HESZ -- HELP ME! DON'T LET THEM DO THIS!
I'LL MAKE THIS RIGHT, JORIN. SOMEHOW. I PROMISE YOU...
THE END

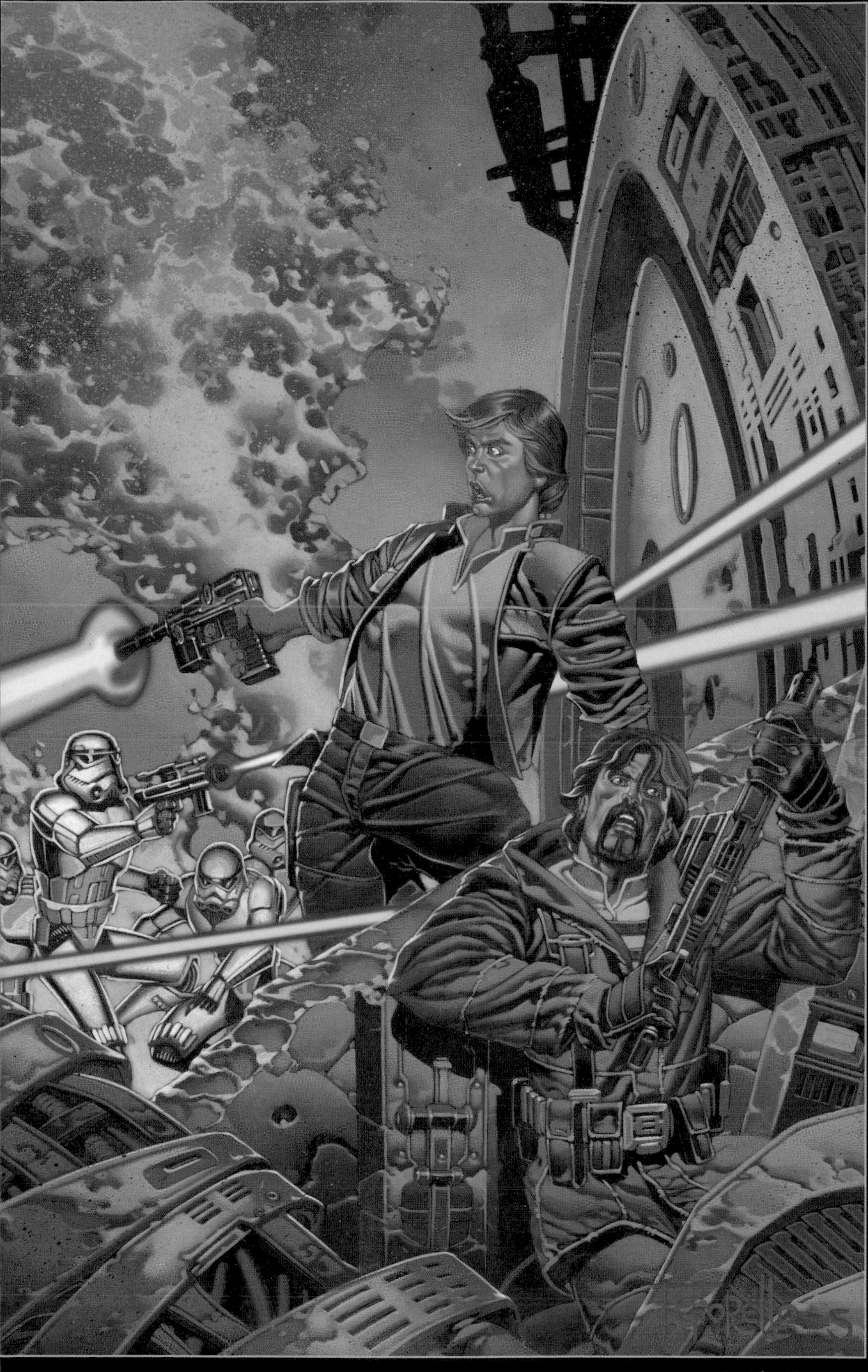

ART: TOMÁS GIORELLO

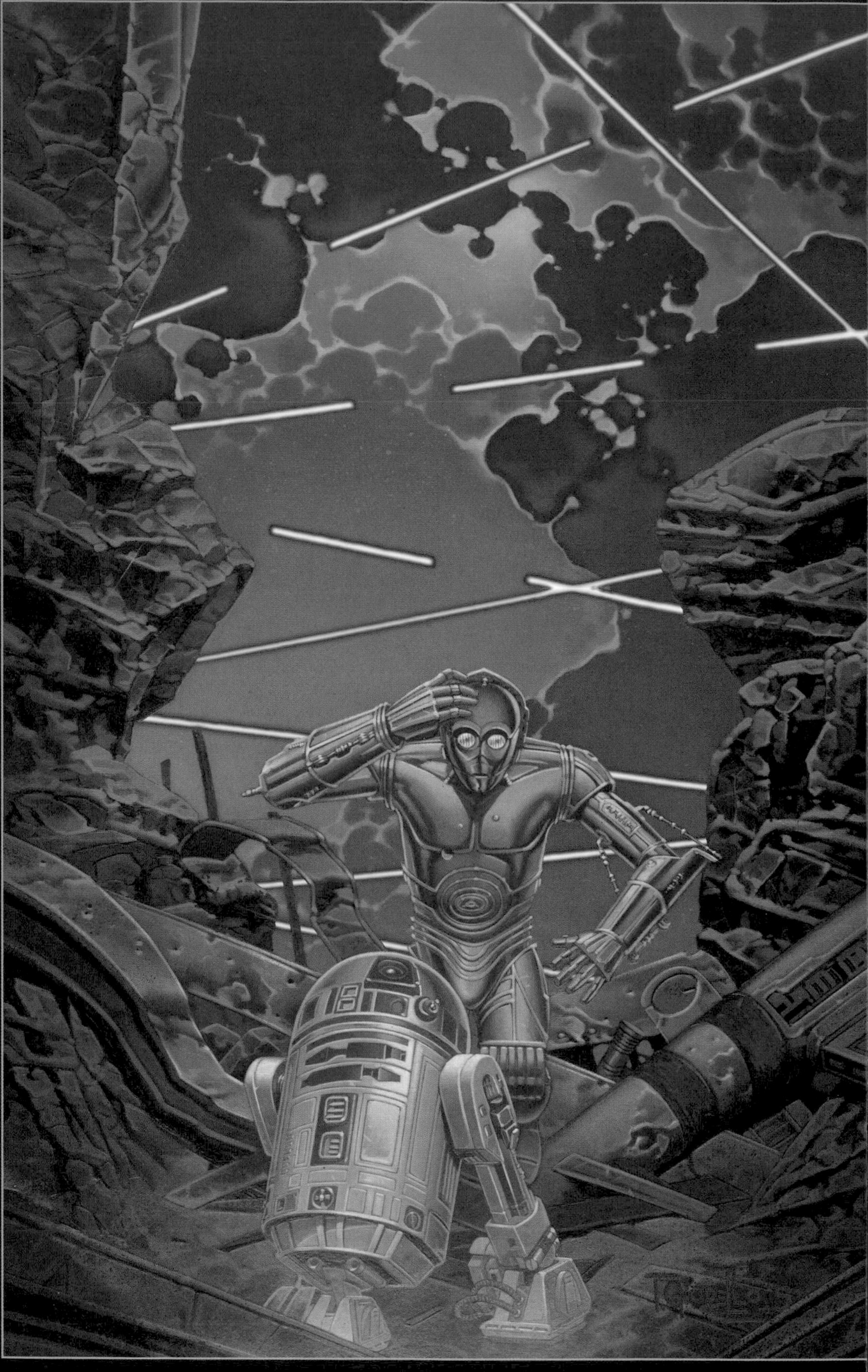

ART: TOMÁS GIORELLO

STAR WARS®

TIMELINE OF GRAPHIC NOVELS FROM DARK HORSE!

LD REPUBLIC ERA:
5,000—1000 YEARS BEFORE
TAR WARS: A NEW HOPE

les of the Jedi—
e Golden Age of the Sith
BN: 1-56971-229-8 $16.95

les of the Jedi—
e Fall of the Sith Empire
BN: 1-56971-320-0 $14.95

les of the Jedi—
nights of the Old Republic
BN: 1-56971-020-1 $14.95

les of the Jedi—
e Freedon Nadd Uprising
BN: 1-56971-307-3 $5.95

les of the Jedi—
ark Lords of the Sith
BN: 1-56971-095-3 $17.95

les of the Jedi—The Sith War
BN: 1-56971-173-9 $17.95

les of the Jedi—Redemption
BN: 1-56971-535-1 $14.95

di vs. Sith
BN: 1-56971-649-8 $17.95

SE OF THE EMPIRE ERA:
000-0 YEARS BEFORE
TAR WARS: A NEW HOPE

e Stark Hyperspace War
BN: 1-56971-985-3 $12.95

di Council—Acts of War
BN: 1-56971-539-4 $12.95

elude to Rebellion
BN: 1-56971-448-7 $14.95

arth Maul
BN: 1-56971-542-4 $12.95

isode I—The Phantom Menace
BN: 1-56971-359-6 $12.95

isode I—
e Phantom Menace Adventures
BN: 1-56971-443-6 $12.95

ngo Fett
BN: 1-56971-623-4 $5.95

m Wesell
BN: 1-56971-624-2 $5.95

Jango Fett—Open Seasons
ISBN: 1-56971-671-4 $12.95

Outlander
ISBN: 1-56971-514-9 $14.95

Emissaries to Malastare
ISBN: 1-56971-545-9 $15.95

The Bounty Hunters
ISBN: 1-56971-467-3 $12.95

Twilight
ISBN: 1-56971-558-0 $12.95

The Hunt for Aurra Sing
ISBN: 1-56971-651-X $12.95

Darkness
ISBN: 1-56971-659-5 $12.95

Rite of Passage
ISBN: 1-59307-042-X $12.95

Honor and Duty
ISBN: 1-59307-546-4 $12.95

Episode II—Attack of the Clones
ISBN: 1-56971-609-9 $17.95

Clone Wars Volume 1—
The Defense of Kamino
ISBN: 1-56971-962-4 $14.95

Clone Wars Volume 2—
Victories and Sacrifices
ISBN: 1-56971-969-1 $14.95

Clone Wars Volume 3—
Last Stand on Jabiim
ISBN: 1-59307-006-3 $14.95

Clone Wars Volume 4—Light and Dark
ISBN: 1-59307-195-7 $16.95

Clone Wars Volume 5—The Best Blades
ISBN: 1-59307-273-2 $17.95

Clone Wars Volume 6—
On the Fields of Battle
ISBN: 1-59307-352-6 $17.95

Clone Wars Volume 7—
When They Were Brothers
ISBN: 1-59307-396-8 $17.95

Clone Wars Volume 8—
The Last Siege, The Final Truth
ISBN: 1-59307-482-4 $17.95

Clone Wars Volume 9—Endgame
ISBN: 1-59307-553-7 $17.95

Clone Wars Adventures Volume 1
ISBN: 1-59307-243-0 $6.95

Clone Wars Adventures Volume 2
ISBN: 1-59307-271-6 $6.95

Clone Wars Adventures Volume 3
ISBN: 1-59307-307-0 $6.95

Clone Wars Adventures Volume 4
ISBN: 1-59307-402-6 $6.95

Clone Wars Adventures Volume 5
ISBN: 1-59307-483-2 $6.95

Clone Wars Adventures Volume 6
ISBN: 1-59307-567-7 $6.95

Episode III—Revenge of the Sith
ISBN: 1-59307-309-7 $12.95

General Grievous
ISBN: 1-59307-442-5 $12.95

Droids—The Kalarba Adventures
ISBN: 1-56971-064-3 $17.95

Droids—Rebellion
ISBN: 1-56971-224-7 $14.95

Classic Star Wars—
Han Solo at Stars' End
ISBN: 1-56971-254-9 $6.95

Boba Fett—Enemy of the Empire
ISBN: 1-56971-407-X $12.95

Underworld—The Yavin Vassilika
ISBN: 1-56971-618-8 $15.95

Dark Forces—Soldier for the Empire
ISBN: 1-56971-348-0 $14.95

Empire Volume 1—Betrayal
ISBN: 1-56971-964-0 $12.95

Empire Volume 2—Darklighter
ISBN: 1-56971-975-6 $17.95

REBELLION ERA:
0-5 YEARS AFTER
STAR WARS: A NEW HOPE

A New Hope—The Special Edition
ISBN: 1-56971-213-1 $9.95

Empire Volume 3—
The Imperial Perspective
ISBN: 1-59307-128-0 $17.95

Empire Volume 4—
The Heart of the Rebellion
ISBN: 1-59307-308-9 $17.95

Empire Volume 5—Allies and Adversaries
ISBN: 1-59307-466-2 $14.95

A Long Time Ago... Volume 1—
Doomworld
ISBN: 1-56971-754-0 $29.95

A Long Time Ago... Volume 2—
Dark Encounters
ISBN: 1-56971-785-0 $29.95

Classic Star Wars—
The Early Adventures
ISBN: 1-56971-178-X $19.95

Classic Star Wars Volume 1—
In Deadly Pursuit
ISBN: 1-56971-109-7 $16.95

Classic Star Wars Volume 2—
The Rebel Storm
ISBN: 1-56971-106-2 $16.95

Classic Star Wars Volume 3—
Escape to Hoth
ISBN: 1-56971-093-7 $16.95

Jabba the Hutt—The Art of the Deal
ISBN: 1-56971-310-3 $9.95

Vader's Quest
ISBN: 1-56971-415-0 $11.95

Splinter of the Mind's Eye
ISBN: 1-56971-223-9 $14.95

The Empire Strikes Back—
The Special Edition
ISBN: 1-56971-234-4 $9.95

A Long Time Ago... Volume 3—
Resurrection of Evil
ISBN: 1-56971-786-9 $29.95

A Long Time Ago... Volume 4—
Screams in the Void
ISBN: 1-56971-787-7 $29.95

A Long Time Ago... Volume 5—
Fool's Bounty
ISBN: 1-56971-906-3 $29.95

Battle of the Bounty Hunters
Pop-Up Book
ISBN: 1-56971-129-1 $17.95

Shadows of the Empire
ISBN: 1-56971-183-6 $17.95

Return of the Jedi—The Special Edition
ISBN: 1-56971-235-2 $9.95

A Long Time Ago... Volume 6—
Wookiee World
ISBN: 1-56971-907-1 $29.95

A Long Time Ago... Volume 7—
Far, Far Away
ISBN: 1-56971-908-X $29.95

Mara Jade—By the Emperor's Hand
ISBN: 1-56971-401-0 $15.95

Shadows of the Empire: Evolution
ISBN: 1-56971-441-X $14.95

NEW REPUBLIC ERA:
5-25 YEARS AFTER
STAR WARS: A NEW HOPE

Omnibus—X-Wing Rogue Squadron
Volume 1
ISBN: 1-59307-572-3 $24.95

X-Wing Rogue Squadron—
Battleground Tatooine
ISBN: 1-56971-276-X $12.95

X-Wing Rogue Squadron—
The Warrior Princess
ISBN: 1-56971-330-8 $12.95

X-Wing Rogue Squadron—
Requiem for a Rogue
ISBN: 1-56971-331-6 $12.95

X-Wing Rogue Squadron—
In the Empire's Service
ISBN: 1-56971-383-9 $12.95

X-Wing Rogue Squadron—
Blood and Honor
ISBN: 1-56971-387-1 $12.95

X-Wing Rogue Squadron—
Masquerade
ISBN: 1-56971-487-8 $12.95

X-Wing Rogue Squadron—
Mandatory Retirement
ISBN: 1-56971-492-4 $12.95

Dark Forces—Rebel Agent
ISBN: 1-56971-400-2 $14.95

Dark Forces—Jedi Knight
ISBN: 1-56971-433-9 $14.95

Heir to the Empire
ISBN: 1-56971-202-6 $19.95

Dark Force Rising
ISBN: 1-56971-269-7 $17.95

The Last Command
ISBN: 1-56971-378-2 $17.95

Boba Fett—
Death, Lies, and Treachery
ISBN: 1-56971-311-1 $12.95

Dark Empire
ISBN: 1-59307-039-X $16.95

Dark Empire II
ISBN: 1-59307-526-X $19.95

Empire's End
ISBN: 1-56971-306-5 $5.95

Crimson Empire
ISBN: 1-56971-355-3 $17.95

Crimson Empire II: Council of Blood
ISBN: 1-56971-410-X $17.95

Jedi Academy: Leviathan
ISBN: 1-56971-456-8 $11.95

Union
ISBN: 1-56971-464-9 $12.95

NEW JEDI ORDER ERA:
25+ YEARS AFTER
STAR WARS: A NEW HOPE

Chewbacca
ISBN: 1-56971-515-7 $12.95

INFINITIES:
DOES NOT APPLY TO TIMELINE

Infinites: A New Hope
ISBN: 1-56971-648-X $12.95

Infinities: The Empire Strikes Back
ISBN: 1-56971-904-7 $12.95

Infinities: Return of the Jedi
ISBN: 1-59307-206-6 $12.95

Star Wars Tales Volume 1
ISBN: 1-56971-619-6 $19.95

Star Wars Tales Volume 2
ISBN: 1-56971-757-5 $19.95

Star Wars Tales Volume 3
ISBN: 1-56971-836-9 $19.95

Star Wars Tales Volume 4
ISBN: 1-56971-989-6 $19.95

Star Wars Tales Volume 5
ISBN: 1-59307-286-4 $19.95

Star Wars Tales Volume 6
ISBN: 1-59307-447-6 $19.95

FOR MORE INFORMATION ABOUT THESE BOOKS VISIT DARKHORSE.COM!

AVAILABLE AT YOUR LOCAL COMICS SHOP OR BOOKSTORE
To find a comics shop in your area, call 1-888-266-4226. For more information or to order direct, visit darkhorse.com or call 1-800-862-0052 Mon.–Fri. 9 A.M. to 5 P.M. Pacific Time. *Prices and availability subject to change without notice.

STAR WARS ©2006 Lucasfilm Ltd. & ™. (BL8009)